DEEP SEA AND FOREIGN GOING

Also by Rose George from Portobello Books

The Big Necessity: Adventures in the World of Human Waste

Deep Sea and Foreign Going

Inside Shipping, the Invisible Industry
that Brings You 90% of Everything

Rose George

Portobello
BOOKS

Published by Portobello Books 2013

Portobello Books
12 Addison Avenue
London
W11 4QR

Versions of parts of this book were published in *Slate*, 2010.

All images © Rose George 2013 except image on page 226, which was supplied courtesy of Queens College, Special Collections Archives, CUNY.

A CIP catalogue record for this book is available from the British Library

9 8 7 6 5 4 3 2 1

ISBN 978 1 84627 263 9

www.portobellobooks.com

Text designed and typeset in Berkeley Book by
Avon DataSet Ltd, Bidford on Avon, Warwickshire

Printed and bound by CPI Group (UK) Ltd, Croydon, CR0 4YY

For Emma Louise Page

I'm not a great admirer of the sea. There's too much of it from my point of view – Maurice Oliver, lighthouse keeper

Contents

DEEP SEA AND FOREIGN GOING

Embarkation

INTRODUCTION

Sea Blindness

Friday. No sensible sailor goes to sea on the day of the Crucifixion, or the journey will be followed by ill will and malice. So here I am on a Friday in June, looking up at a giant ship that will carry me from this southern English port of Felixstowe to Singapore, for five weeks and 9288 nautical miles through the Pillars of Hercules, pirate waters and weather. I stop at the bottom of the ship's gangway, waiting for an escort and stilled and awed by the immensity of this thing, much of her the colour of a summer-day sky, so blue; her bottom painted dull red, her name – *Maersk Kendal* – written large on her side.

There is such busy-ness around me. Everything in a modern container port is enormous, overwhelming, crushing. *Kendal* of course, but also the thundering trucks, the giant boxes in many colours, the massive gantry cranes that straddle the quay, reaching up ten storeys and over to ships that stretch three football pitches in length. There are hardly any humans to be seen. When the journalist

Henry Mayhew visited London's docks in 1849, he found 'decayed and bankrupt master butchers, master bakers, publicans, grocers, old soldiers, old sailors, Polish refugees, broken-down gentlemen, discharged lawyers' clerks, suspended Government clerks, almsmen, pensioners, servants, thieves'. They have long since gone. This is a Terminator terminal, a place where humans are hidden in crane or truck cabs, where everything is clamorous machines.

It took me three train journeys to reach Felixstowe from my northern English home. On one train, where no seats were to be had, I swayed in the vestibule with two men wearing the uniform of a rail freight company. I'm about to leave on a freighter, I said, but a ship. They looked bewildered. A ship? they said. But why on earth do you want to go to sea?

Why on earth.

I am an islander who has never been maritime. I don't sail or dive. I swim, but not in terrifying oceans. But standing here in the noise and industry, looking up 60 metres – higher than Niagara Falls – to the top of *Kendal*, I feel the giddiness of a Christmas-morning child. Some is the rush of escape, for which I had reasons. Some is the pull of the sea. And some comes from the knowledge that I am about to embark into a place and space that is usually off-limits and hidden. The public is not allowed on this ship, nor even on this dock. There are no ordinary citizens to witness the workings of an industry that is one of the most fundamental to their daily existence. These ships and boxes belong to a business that feeds, clothes, warms and supplies us. They have fuelled if not created globalization. They are the reason behind your cheap T-shirt and reasonably priced television. But who looks beyond a television now and sees the ship that carried it? Who cares about the men who brought your breakfast cereal through winter storms? How ironic, that the more ships have grown in size and consequence, the more their place in our imagination has shrunk.

The Maritime Foundation, a charity that promotes seafarer matters, recently made a video called 'Unreported Ocean'. It asked the residents of Southampton, a port city, how many goods are transported by sea. The answers were varied but uniformly wrong. They all had the interrogative upswing of the unsure.

'Thirty-five per cent?'

'Not a lot?'

The answer is nearly everything. Sometimes on trains I play a numbers game. A woman listening to headphones: Eight. A man reading a book: 15. The child in the pushchair: at least four, including the pushchair. The game is to reckon how many clothes and possessions and how much food have been transported by ship. The beads around the woman's neck; the man's iPhone and Japanese-made headphones. Her Sri Lankan-made skirt and blouse; his printed-in-China book. I can always go wider, deeper and in any direction. The fabric of the seats. The rolling stock. The fuel powering the train. The conductor's uniform; the coffee in my cup; the fruit in my bag. Definitely this fruit, so frequently shipped in refrigerated containers that it has been given its own temperature. Two degrees Celsius is 'chill', but 13 degrees is 'banana'.

Trade carried by sea has grown fourfold since 1970 and is still growing. In 2011, the 360 commercial ports of the United States took in international goods worth $1.73 trillion, or 80 times the value of all US trade in 1960. There are more than 100,000 ships at sea carrying all the solids, liquids and gases that we need to live. Only 6000 are container vessels like *Kendal*, but they make up for this small proportion by their dizzying capacity. The biggest container ship can carry 15,000 boxes. It can hold 746 million bananas, one for every European, on one ship. If the containers of Maersk alone were lined up, they would stretch 11,000 miles, or more than halfway round the planet. If they were stacked instead, they would be 1500 miles high, 7530 Eiffel Towers. If *Kendal* discharged her containers onto trucks, the line of traffic would be 60 miles long.

Trade has always travelled and the world has always traded. Ours, though, is the era of extreme interdependence. Hardly any nation is now self-sufficient. In 2011, the UK shipped in half of its gas. The United States relies on ships to bring two-thirds of its oil supplies. Every day, 38 million metric tons of crude oil sets off by sea somewhere, although you may not notice it. As in Los Angeles, New York and other port cities, London has moved its working docks out of the city, away from residents. Ships are bigger now and need deeper harbours, so they call at Newark or Tilbury or Felixstowe, not Liverpool or South Street. Security concerns have hidden ports further, behind barbed wire and badge-wearing and keeping out. To reach this quayside in Felixstowe, I had to pass through several gatekeepers and passport controllers, and past radiation-detecting gates often alarmed by naturally radioactive cargo such as cat litter and broccoli. It is harder to wander into the world of shipping now, so people don't. The chief of the Royal Navy – who is known as the First Sea Lord, although the Army chief is not a Land Lord – says we suffer from 'sea blindness' now. We travel by cheap flights, not liners. The sea is a distance to be flown over, a downward backdrop between take-off and landing, a blue expanse that soothes on the moving flight map as the plane jerks over it. It is for leisure and beaches and fish and chips, not for use or work. Perhaps we believe that everything travels by air, or that it does so magically and instantaneously like information (which is actually transmitted by cables on the seabed), not by hefty ships that travel more slowly than pensioners drive.

You could trace the flight of the ocean from our consciousness in the pages of great newspapers. Fifty years ago, the shipping news was news. Cargo departures were reported daily. Now the most necessary business on the planet has mostly been shunted into the pages of specialized trade papers such as *Lloyd's List* and the *Journal of Commerce*, fine publications, but out of the reach of most when a subscription to *Lloyd's List* costs £1785 a year. In 1965, shipping was so central to daily life in London that when Winston Churchill's funeral barge left Tower Pier to travel up the Thames, it embarked in front of dock cranes that dipped their jibs, movingly, out of respect. The cranes are gone now or immobile, garden furniture for wharves that house apartments or indifferent restaurants.

Humans have sent goods by water for four thousand years. In the fifteenth century BC, Queen Hatshepsut of Egypt sent a fleet to the Land of Punt and brought back panther skins and ebony, frankincense and dancing pygmies. Perhaps Hatshepsut counts as the first shipping tycoon, before the Romans, Phoenicians and Greeks took over. She was certainly the only Egyptian queen who preferred to be called King. Shipping history is full of such treats and treasures. Cardamom, silk, ginger and gold, ivory and saffron. The Routes of Spice, Tea and Salt, of Amber and Incense. There were trade winds, sailor towns, and sails, chaos and colour. Now there are freight routes, turnarounds and boxes and the cool mechanics of modern industry, but there is still intrigue and fortune. Maersk ships travel regular routes named Boomerang and Yo-Yo around Australia and Yokohama, and the Bossa Nova and Samba around South America. There are wealthy tycoons still, Norse, Greek and Danish, belonging to family companies who maintain a level of privacy that makes a Swiss banker seem verbose. Publicly listed shipping companies are still a minority. Even shipping people admit that their industry is clubby, insular, difficult. In this business, it is considered normal that the official Greek ship-owners' association refuses to say how many members it has, because it can.

Maersk is different. It must be, because it is letting me onto its working ship, where no members of the public are allowed. Even Maersk officers are no longer permitted to take family members to sea, because of concerns about their safety from pirates. But Maersk is known for risks, at least in the places where its name is known at all, which is in shipping and Denmark. I find Maersk fascinating. It is the Coca-Cola of freight with none of the fame. Its parent company, A.P. Møller-Maersk, is Denmark's largest company, its sales equal to 20 per cent of Denmark's gross domestic product (GDP); its ships use more oil than the entire nation. I like the fact that Maersk is not a household name outside the pages of *Lloyd's List*; that it has an online store, selling Maersk-branded T-shirts and cookie tins, called Stargate, after the company symbol of a seven-point star, white on a background of Maersk Blue, a distinct colour that can be created from a Pantone recipe supplied on Maersk's website. The star, goes an employee joke, has seven points because they work seven days a week. I like that Maersk is a first name. It's like a massive global corporation named Derek. For much of recent history the company was run by Arnold Maersk Mc-Kinney Møller, who was the son of the founder, and a pleasingly eccentric patriarch who stayed working until he died in 2012 aged 98. Mr Møller was known for his firm control of his firm; for walking up five flights of stairs to his office – although when he reached 94, he allowed his driver to carry his briefcase up; for being one of only three commoners to receive the Order of the Elephant; and for driving around Copenhagen in a modest car although he was one of the two richest people in Denmark. (The other inherited Lego.)

Reuters, in a profile of Maersk, describes it as 'active primarily in the marine transportation sector'. Behind that 'primarily' are multitudes. Founded in 1904 with one ship named *Svendborg*, Maersk – through its subsidiary Maersk Line – now operates the largest container shipping company in the world, with a fleet of 600 vessels. It also has the vast and dizzying interests of a global corporation. It is active in 130 countries and has 117,000 employees. It is looking for and drilling for oil and gas in Denmark, Angola, Brazil, Greenland, Qatar, Algeria, Norway, Iraq, the United States and Kazakhstan. If you have visited Denmark, you have probably shopped in a Maersk-owned supermarket. You can save in a Maersk-owned bank. The list of its companies and subsidiaries is 12 pages long, double columns. Its revenues in 2011 amounted to $60.2 billion, only slightly less than Microsoft's. Microsoft provides the software that runs computers; Maersk brings us the computers. One is infamous; somehow the other is mostly invisible.

This is remarkable, given the size of its ambition. Maersk is known for its experiments with economies of scale. *Emma Maersk*, its E-class ship (rated according to an internal classification system), was built in 2005, and excited the industry partly because she could carry at least 15,000 containers. Triple-E-class ships, expected in 2014, will carry 18,000, and be able to fit a full-sized American football pitch, an ice-hockey arena and a basketball court in their holds, if they care to. *Emma* was envied by naval architects and engineers, but her arrival in Felixstowe in December 2006 also caught the public imagination. Along with her 150 tons of New Zealand lamb and 138,000 tins of cat food, she carried 12,800 MP3 players, 33,000 cocktail shakers and two million Christmas decorations. She became SS *Santa*, come to call.

SS *Santa* demonstrated more than industrial hubris. Emma Maersk also proved how little an ordinary citizen now understands about shipping. For the following two weeks, Felixstowe continued to receive calls from members of the public, who wanted to know if she was still in port. She had come and gone in 24 hours. I have met well-meaning men – and too few women – in boardrooms across London and New York who complain about widespread ignorance of their industry. They want a better public image for an industry that in the UK alone employs 634,900 people, contributes £8.45 billion in tax and generates two per cent of the national economy, more than restaurants, take-away food and civil engineering combined, and only just behind the construction industry. They despair that shipping only emerges with drama and disaster: a cruise ship sinking, or another oil spill and blackened birds. They would like people to know such names as the *Wec Vermeer*, arrived from Leixões and heading for Rotterdam, or the *Zim Genoa*, due in from Ashdod, not just *Exxon Valdez* and *Titanic*. They provide statistics showing how the dark days of oil spills are over. Between 1972 and 1981, there were 223 spills. Over the last decade, there were 63. Each year, a shipping publicist told me, 'more oil is poured down the drain by car mechanics changing engine oil than is spilled by the world's fleet of oil tankers'.

Yet that invisibility is useful too. There are few industries as defiantly opaque as this one. Even offshore bankers have not developed a system as intricately elusive as the flag of convenience, where ships can fly the flag of a state that has nothing to do with its owner, cargo, crew or route. Look at the backside of boats and you will see they name their home ports as Panama City and Monrovia, not Le Havre or Hamburg, though neither crew nor ship will have ever been to Liberia or Panama. To the International Chamber of Shipping, which thinks 'flags of convenience' too pejorative (it prefers the sanitized term 'open registries'), there is 'nothing inherently wrong' with this system. A former US Coast Guard commander preferred to call it 'managed anarchy'.

Kendal has also 'flagged out' in this way, but to the national registry of the United Kingdom. She flies the Red Ensign, the maritime Union flag. This makes her a rarity. After the Second World War, the great powers in shipping were the UK and the United States. They had ships and supplied men to sail them. In 1961 the UK had 142,462 working seafarers. The United States owned 1268 ships. Now British seafarers number around 24,000 and there are fewer than 100 ocean-going US-flagged ships. Only one per cent of trade at US ports travels on an American-flagged ship, and the US fleet has declined by 82 per cent since 1951. Who in Western Europe or

America now knows a working seafarer? At a nautical seminar held on a tall ship – a proper old sailing vessel – in Glasgow, a tanker captain told the following anecdote, which got laughs, but it was sad: when online forms offer him drop-down options to describe his career, he selects 'shipping', and is then given a choice: DHL or TNT?

Two men have descended from *Kendal* to fetch me. They look Asian and exhausted, so they are typical crew. The benefits of flagging out vary according to registry, but there will always be lower taxes, laxer labour laws, and no requirement to pay expensive American or British crews protected by unions and legislation. Now the citizens of rich countries own ships – Greece has the most, then Japan and Germany – but they are sailed by the cheap labour of Filipinos, Bangladeshis, Chinese, Indonesians. They are the ones who clean your cruise cabin and work in the engine room, who bring your gas, your soybeans, your perfumes and medicine.

Seafaring can be a good life. And it can go wrong with the speed of a wave. On paper the seas are tightly controlled. The Dutch scholar Grotius's 1609 concept of *mare liberum* still mostly holds: a free sea that belongs to no state but in which each state has some rights. The United Nations Convention on the Law of the Sea (UNCLOS) is known as the umbrella convention with reason: its 320 articles, excluding annexes, aim to create 'a legal order for the seas and oceans which will facilitate international communication, and will promote the peaceful uses of the seas and oceans, the equitable and efficient utilization of their resources, the conservation of their living resources, and the study, protection and preservation of the marine environment'. Nations that have ratified the convention (the United States has not, not liking its deep-sea-mining regulations) have a right to a 12-mile boundary from their coastline, and also to a 200-mile 'exclusive economic zone'. Beyond that is the high sea. The International Maritime Organization, a UN agency, has passed dozens of regulations and amendments since the 1940s to regulate ships, crews and safety, more than most UN agencies. The International Labour Organization looks out for seafarers' rights. There is also an International Tribunal on Maritime Law for boundary disputes.

The sea, though, dissolves paper. In practice, the ocean is still the world's wildest place, both because of its fearsome natural danger and because of how easy it is out there to slip out of the boundaries of law and civilization that seem so firm ashore. TV crime dramas now frequently use ports as a visual shorthand for a place of criminal, suspicious activity. I don't know why they don't just go to sea. If something goes wrong in international waters, there is no police force, no union official to assist. Imagine you have a problem on a ship while you are on that ship. Who do you complain to, when you are employed by a Manila manning agency on a ship owned by an American, flagged by Panama, and managed by a Cypriot, in international waters?

Or imagine you are a 19-year-old South African woman named Akhona Geveza, fresh out of maritime college, the first in your family to reach higher education, the household earner and hope. In January 2010, you go to sea as a deck cadet – an apprentice navigator – on a good ship, *Safmarine Kariba*, run by a good company, Safmarine. On 23 June, your shipmate reports to your captain that you have been raped by the Ukrainian first officer. He summons you and the officer to his cabin the next day at 11 a.m., as if an alleged rape is a regular human resources matter. But you don't turn up, because you are already dead in the sea.

The Croatian police, whose jurisdiction covered the sea Akhona was found in, concluded she had committed suicide. She had been in a relationship that was 'consensual but rough'. An internal inquiry by Safmarine also concluded suicide, and found no evidence of harassment or abuse. And that, according to sea law, was all that could be demanded.

Reporters from South Africa's *Sunday Times* then interviewed other cadets from the same maritime school. They found that two had been made pregnant by senior officers; that two male cadets had been raped; and that there was a widespread atmosphere of intimidation. A female cadet said embarking on a ship was like being dropped in the middle of a game park. 'When we arrived,' another said, 'we were told that the captain is our god; he can marry you, baptize you and even bury you without anybody's permission. We were told that the sea is no-man's land and that what happens at sea, stays at sea.'

Other workers and migrants have hard lives. But they have phone lines and internet access, unlike seafarers. They have union representatives, a police force, firefighters, all the safety nets of society. Even in space, astronauts are always connected to mission control. Only 12 per cent of a ship's crew have freely available internet access at sea. Two-thirds have no access at all. Cell phones don't work either. Lawyers who work for seafarers' rights describe their clients as moving targets who work in no-man's lands. They describe an industry that is global but also uniquely mobile, and difficult to govern, police or rule. They are careful to say that most owners are scrupulous, but for the unscrupulous ones, there is no better place to be than here. For the International Transport Workers' Federation (ITF), a global union representing four million transport workers, the maritime and fishing industries 'continue to allow astonishing abuses of human rights of those working in the sector... Seafarers and fishers are routinely made to work in conditions that would not be acceptable in civilized society.' If that sounds like typically combative union rhetoric, ITF will point to, for a start, the £20 million they recovered in 2010 of wages unpaid to seafarers who had earned the money, and the year before was the same. The blankness of that blue sea on our maps of the earth applies to the people who work on it too: buy your Fairtrade coffee beans by all means, but don't assume that Fairtrade governs the conditions of the people who fetch it to you. You would be mistaken.

The great Norwegian-American seafarer unionist Andrew Furuseth – known as Lincoln of the Sea for his cheekbones and achievements – was once threatened with prison for violating an injunction during a 1904 strike. 'You can throw me in jail,' he responded, 'but you can't give me narrower quarters than, as a seaman, I've always lived in; or a coarser food than I've always eaten, or make me lonelier than I've always been.' More than a century on, seafarers still regularly joke that their job is like being in prison with a salary. That is not accurate. When the academic Erol Kahveci surveyed British prison literature while researching conditions at sea, he found that 'the provision of leisure, recreation, religious service and communication facilities are better in UK prisons than… on many ships our respondents worked aboard'.

The International Maritime Organization once published a brochure about shipping, entitled 'A Safe and Friendly Business'. Shipping has certainly become safer, but not always friendlier to humans or the planet. This safe and friendly business has been emitting as many greenhouses gases as aeroplanes, but is only just being regulated, decades after gas became lead-free and short-haul flights an ethical issue. In this safe and friendly business, as I disembark on this Friday in June, 544 seafarers are being held hostage by Somali pirates. I try to translate that into other transport industries: 544 bus drivers, or 544 cab drivers, or nearly two jumbo jets of passengers, mutilated and tortured for years for doing their job. When 33 Chilean miners were trapped underground for 69 days in 2010, there was a media frenzy; 1500 journalists went to Chile, and even now, the BBC news website dedicates a special page to their drama, long after its conclusion. The 24 men on MV *Iceberg* held captive for a thousand days were given no special page and nothing much more than silence and disregard.

*

The men from *Kendal* are ready to go. They advise me to hold the gangway rail tightly: 'One hand for you, miss, and one for the ship.' I have travelled plenty and strangely on land: to Saddam Hussein's birthday party in Tikrit, to Bhutanese football matches blessed by Buddhist monks, down sewers and through vast slums in great cities. I look at this gangway, leading up four storeys of height to thirty-nine days at sea, six ports, two oceans, five seas and the most compellingly foreign environment I'm ever likely to encounter. Lead on, able seamen. I will follow.

Some of *Kendal*'s 6188 Twenty-Foot-Equivalent Units

1.   EMBARKATION

Formalization and Filipinos

Kendal looks enormous, but she is a mid-size ship. Her deck is only three football pitches long, when the biggest ship now stretches for four. I find her beautiful, although sailors of tall ships and trim yachts will scoff at this. A container ship? So ugly and boxy. Those practical lines, that unsubtle stern slumped like a fat diner's backside on a restaurant chair. They feel superior with their wooden masts and sails and windy romance. Cruise-ship fans dote on the flanks – pockmarked with cabins – of their floating holiday camps, and all that gleaming preening white. Give me instead this working ship laden with her multi-coloured box stacks, waiting passively at the dock while industry is done to her. The people who work here think there is nothing exceptional about what is going to happen, which is a transformation. Once the loading is done, the ropes unlashed and the gangway withdrawn, *Kendal* will become an astonishing, remarkable thing: thousands of tons of thousands of types of cargo, floating on miles deep of nothing but water, travelling safely to the other side of the world, just as she does every two months, regular as a yo-yo or boomerang. *Kendal's* day job is to travel to Felixstowe, Bremerhaven and Rotterdam; to call at Le Havre in France then go down the Suez Canal to Salalah, Oman; on to Colombo, Sri Lanka, then into the Straits of Malacca to stop at Port Klang in Malaysia, then Singapore, before the final destination of Laem Chabang, Thailand, where she will turn around and come back. The World Shipping Council, attempting to amaze, informs visitors to its website that a container ship travels the equivalent of three-quarters of the way to the moon and back in one year. It doesn't need to quote that fact to impress: an ordinary voyage on an ordinary ship is extraordinary enough.

At the top of the gangway two more escorts await, one Asian and one not; one cheerful and one not. The grump is Igor, second officer, deck, and misery is his default setting because he had been meant to go home weeks earlier so exudes his frustration in his face and like sweat. He has been detailed to show me to my quarters. Some container lines carry passengers: paying guests on working ships can bring revenue, and the experience can be sold as cruising without the crowds. But no commercial ships passing through the Indian Ocean take passengers any more because of piracy risks, so I am here as a supernumerary (dictionary definition: 'not wanted or needed; redundant', or 'not belonging to a regular staff but engaged for work'). I will be the last outsider allowed on Maersk's ships through the Gulf of Aden until further notice.

The people of *Kendal* live and work and play in its accommodation house, a cream superstructure placed towards the rear of the ship, a direction that I should now call 'aft'. The building rises ten storeys up to the bridge, the navigational centre of the ship, which stretches T-like over the breadth of the boxes for superior visibility. I step inside the steel lip of a heavy metal door, into Upper Deck, the lowest level of the accommodation house but so named because of the decks that stretch below it into the engine room and cargo holds. Samuel Johnson wrote that 'being in a ship is being in a jail, with the chance of being drowned', and although Maersk is known for running good ships, the interior décor is the prison side of comfort: plain walls, institutionally dimpled rubber floors, clinical lighting. A ship is both workplace and home, but workplace aesthetics have won.

The decks rise through the alphabet and in height. Senior officers live higher up; non-officers below. My cabin is D-deck, port, in the officer levels but not in the heights of F-deck, where the captain lives, beneath the bridge. Because they usually house visiting officers, the quarters are spacious, with a day room, bedroom and en-suite bathroom. There is a computer, a printer, a DVD player and TV; a hi-fi system, a compact shower room and a biological sewage toilet. The furnishing is business-functional; the colour scheme is beige and dark blue. It is better and bigger than many hotel rooms I have stayed in, and it floats.

Igor departs with a mutter that I will be summoned at some point, so I read a letter left by the Floating Society of Christian Endeavour thanking the cabin's resident for his or her part in bringing cargo to this country, then pass the time before dinner by looking out of the porthole. The view is busy. Every port between Felixstowe and Singapore requires containers – 'boxes' in industry language – to be loaded and others to be discharged. The blankness of the boxes is entrancing, although this is an unpopular, weird opinion among people who work with them, who think they are boring, opaque, blank. Stuff carrying stuff.

At her most laden, *Kendal* carries 6188 boring TEUs, or Twenty-Foot-Equivalent Units. TEU is a mundane name for something that changed the world, but so is 'the internet'. I watch a crane lifting a TEU into the air, its cables dancing it across onto the ship, thudding it into place in front of my porthole, then retracting with serpentine loops. It would be balletic if it weren't for the thuds. My view now is a grey box, its corrugated iron ridges slightly scuffed and rusted, its exterior branded with MAERSK. Other boxes are stamped with Evergreen, Hapag-Lloyd, CMA CGM, Hanjin: household names at sea, in freight yards and in maritime offices but nowhere else. Yet similar boxes and the same brands surround modern life. They lie in stacks in rail freight yards as you pass on a train. Attached to a truck, they slow your passage on a motorway. You buy hair products from London market stalls with those familiar corrugated steel walls, or you sleep in a boutique hotel created from them. I have seen boxes dumped by African roadsides several days' drive from the nearest city, splashes of red among green jungle, displaced deposits of commerce. They are everywhere if you care to look, if you look harder.

The box filling my view is probably empty. Britain is post-industrial and has little to export. 'Waste and hot air,' one laconic port official said, when I asked him what our exports consist of. He could have included weapons too, and scrap metal, exported to Turks who have invested in recycling plants to process it, unlike the British, who call it waste, wastefully. But that would be it. The geographic boundary of the Suez Canal is also a boundary of plenty: beyond it, *Kendal* will begin to collect what the East has made for the West, gathering up goods all the way to Thailand before turning around and fetching the bounty home. This is the usual pendulum of the supply chain, and when it swings it dispenses its own curious logic. Shipping is so cheap that it makes more financial sense for Scottish cod to be sent 10,000 miles to China to be filleted and then sent back to Scottish shops and restaurants, than to pay Scottish filleters. A Scottish newspaper called this practice 'madness', but actually it's just shipping.

Dinner is at 6 p.m. on B-deck. There are two eating rooms, one for crew and the other for officers, who are also part of the crew, but who are not known as crew. This never makes much sense, along with why there are three words meaning some form of backwards (astern, making sternway, aft). Ship life is a foreign country and I must learn the language. The crew mess is homelier, with a large cauldron of rice that is always full, and a microwave with two settings: Instant Ramen for 1 and Instant Ramen for 2.

My seat is in the officers' saloon. Next door the crew eat off Formica, but here the tables have blue cloths and paper doilies, already well used and grubby. I am directed to a seat next to the porthole, underneath a portrait of the Queen. Apparently she is standard decoration on British-flagged ships, although discomfiting to anyone who has travelled to countries – Iraq, for example – where the number of official portraits reflects the level of fear required in the population. But there she is, and I am too unsure of my place to argue about my place. Men drift in and take food from the buffet on the sideboard. No-one speaks. My neighbour is a silent man who eats by holding his bowl close to his mouth in a zone that is improper for westerners and not for easterners. Later I learn that his name is Chan, that he is the third engineer and is from Burma, and that ashore Burmese may be rare and exotic, but they are common in shipping. They make up one of the modern labour pools, in the language of economists, as if rich ship-owners take their rods and fish for able seamen, oilmen, bo'suns among the men of Bangladesh, the Philippines, Eastern Europe. Opposite me is the third officer, a lanky young blond man, then Igor, still grumpy. The silence is intimidating but I try to make conversation with the third officer, out of nerves.

What's your name?

(I think he says 'Maris'.)

Oh. Like the sea? What a good name.

No. Not like the sea. Marius.

He looks at me with fatigued disdain and returns to fuelling, fast and silently.

With further effort I learn that he is Romanian. Igor is Moldavian, not to be confused with Moldovan. The captain is South African. The chief engineer is a Briton called Derek, from Plymouth or nearby, with the rounded vowels of Devon. Mike, another Romanian, is the second engineer, a languid Indian named Vinton is chief officer, and the man whose seat I have taken is Li, fourth engineer, Chinese. Eight places, five nationalities. A normal ship. On the table behind are two British cadets, apprentice engineers. Maersk takes on cadets to qualify for lower tax from the British government, so here are lads from Newcastle and the Western Isles of Scotland, traditional maritime places that still send their young to sea. The cadets don't talk much either. At the end of this sad, silent meal I wonder what I've done, signing up for weeks of this gloom with a big ocean outside to jump into.

I sleep through our departure. For someone used to land, the movement of the ship turns it into a giant crib, though one with engine noise. I wake in German Bight, something that sounds like a tree disease but is a parcel of sea past Dover. For most people it is a place that exists only in the BBC's Shipping Forecast, a nightly broadcast of weather and worse in South Utsire, Dogger, Rockall, Hebrides, of storms rising and boats falling, dispensed in tones so soothing you feel lulled by other people's danger, and a sharp guilty delight at being safe abed.

No ship can protect itself against the sea. When the cruise ship *Costa Concordia* was holed in 2012 by a rock off the coast of Italy and toppled, a headline read 'Big ships still sink', as if this was news. *Kendal*, despite the dimensions of her hull and engine – a Doosan-Wartsila the size of a house – is still a chunk of metal floating on an element that can withdraw its support at any time, that can list us, wind us or hole us, swamp and sink us. So we are as prepared as possible, with life-saving equipment for 34 persons, and safety certificates from the American Bureau of Shipping, one of the leading classification societies, as the setters of ship safety standards are known. The number of interests concerned in this ship and its safety is comforting: line them up and they would stretch from *Kendal*'s smoothly curving bow to her squat backside. An incomplete list includes shipbuilders, owners, financiers, charterers, classification societies, regulators national and international, insurers for its hull, for its cargo and against war risks, and so on. Even with all that interest and oversight, every minute without incident at sea is simply a minute in which danger has been avoided. Every minute trouble is expected, from other ships, from unseen obstacles, from something that sailors call 'weather' but that is a more malign, more elemental version than the weather we have ashore.

The English Channel, for example. A domestic sea, a stretch of water so unthreatening that swimming across it has become commonplace. In this domestic sea in 2010, the yacht *Ouzo* disappeared, probably swamped by a passing P&O ferry named *Pride of Bilbao*, and its crew of three young men were found in the sea, correctly dressed in lifejackets but dead. This was called the sea of sore heads and sore hearts by sailors who knew they should fear it, who were not fooled by its small size or its proximity to two reassuringly safe, civilized countries. The Narrow Sea, as the Channel used to be known, is one of the world's busiest shipping lanes. It contains small boats, fishing trawlers, yachts, container vessels, bulk cargo freighters carrying grain, coal, anything. There are slow-moving tankers and ferries that cross fast and furiously as if with God-given right to take priority. Those are the surface perils. The charts reveal sea places called Garden City, Fairy Bank, the Black Deeps; Foulness, Kentish Knock, Gunfleet Sand. They reveal marked firing ranges, wrecks. They show the Sunk Traffic Separation Scheme, which is not a thoroughfare of disaster but a policing of a sea highway near a place called Sunk. Not being a sailor, I didn't know the sea had highways. My land maps show the smallest lane, but the sea is blank blue, only serving as a contrast to land. Nothing to see, fly over it, move along.

Somewhere in German Bight, I go for morning coffee with the crew in their Ramen room. There is no chance of missing them: eating and drinking times on *Kendal* are strictly kept. Breakfast at 7, morning break 10–10:30, lunch at 12, dinner at 6. Meals are usually well attended: eating punctuates boredom. Some sailors still call the morning break the 'smoke-o', although there is no smoking inside the accommodation house, and hopefully nowhere near any containers containing flammable liquids.

There are only 20 men and one woman – Pinky the cook – employed on *Kendal*, a fact that would baffle anyone working on a military ship, where thousands can live. I'm surprised to find a woman on board when only two per cent of seafarers are female, but I'm glad to see her too. The officers' nationalities are mixed, but the crew – non-officers – are all Filipino. This is to be expected: Filipinos make up more than a third of all crews worldwide. A quarter of a million of them are at sea. They are popular, a Filipino seafarer once told me, because 'we are cheap and speak good English'. They are the new Malays, who were the new lascars – Asian seafarers widely employed up until the Second World War – and they will probably be replaced by the next wave of cheaper English-speaking crews. Introductions: the bo'sun is Elvis. A marine factory foreman, he rules the realm of manual labour in which all the crew work. Beneath him is Julius Jefferson, a muscled able seaman (AB) named after the US President, Ordinary Seaman Dilbert, an electrician named Pedro, and Denis the painter, whose job is to chip rust, then paint, chip rust, then paint. There is Pinky in her chef's whites, and her galley helpmeet and steward, Francis. There are Joselito and Axel, ordinary seamen or ratings, who do the grunt work. Finally, a stocky AB who introduces himself as Archie. Actually, it's Archimedes. 'Archimedes for long; Archie for short.'

They look tired. The officers drive and navigate the ship, but these men care for it, with labour that is manual and exhausting: constantly climbing the stacks to check on six thousand boxes, hosing salt and oil off the decks, fixing, repairing, tending, welding, heaving. Even their work clothes look knackered because the crew leave their boiler suits hanging at the accommodation house entrance, with boots attached. The suits are so heavy they keep their shape, and they look like evacuated people hanging there, faces turned despondently to the wall.

Still, the crew are as friendly now as dinner last night was frosty. They have a ready humour that you'd expect from nationals of the Philippines, where the country's two long occupations by Spain and the United States are often described as '400 years in the convent and 50 in Hollywood'. Besides, a new face is something different. Some have been at sea for months and hardly ashore, but that is how they want it. Unlike the senior officers, they belong not to the ship but to a one-off contract. Pedro and Archimedes could be on *Kendal* for six months, moving boxes, then hauling cornmeal from Iowa or chemicals to Hamburg. More months at sea puts off the uncertainty involved in getting a new contract. (Not just uncertainty: some Manila manning agencies require job-hunters to work unpaid for months before deigning to give them a contract.)

Francis was once on a ship for ten months. Pinky has been on board for six months now. Once, she got home to the Philippines after six months and after three and a half weeks they called her back. She had to go, although she has a small son. Needs must. All the crew have children, even boyish Francis. One says, 'The first time I was home for my son's birthday was when he was seven.' Missing births is as common as missing birthdays. It is the price you pay for the money you earn. Both Pedro and his wife work overseas, like 10 million other Filipinos. He is everywhere and she is in Hong Kong, a domestic servant. Their children are with grandparents, and they have missed all their growing up so far. A special government body, the Commission on Filipinos Overseas, looks out for migrant workers like Pedro, and prepares an annual stock estimate of the size of its diaspora, treating its workers as grain or nails. The human stock is divided by country, and at the bottom of the list, below Vanuatu, are the stateless: sea-based workers. The rush to seafaring began in the Philippines in 1974, when President Ferdinand Marcos created an Overseas Development Board alongside a National Seaman's Board. By now, there are 90 maritime academies pushing out 40,000 seafarers a year. In 2011 they sent home £4.3 billion in remittances.

Pinky's boy lives with her parents, and it is for his sake that she is living with 20 men for months on end, cooking to the best of her ability, having gained her skills, which are variable, on a short cooking course in European food. On the windowsill in the galley she keeps the insides of peppers. 'They are for my big garden. If I plant enough peppers, I won't have to go to sea.' They are all here for the money. They say this with no embarrassment or preamble. A senior government bureaucrat in Manila can earn £200 a month; the minimum seafarer wage required by the International Labour Organization is $555 (£354). If these men worked instead in British or American hospitals, they would be paid British rates. At sea, they work under British law but on Filipino rates. Even so, a lowly ranked AB on *Kendal* gets $1000 a month excluding overtime. Also, ashore, you have to buy jobs, and the bribes can be $5000. These seafarers have calculated carefully: so many years buys so big a house. Fifteen usually, or ten if you are lucky. More buys a shop; more puts all your children through decent schools, colleges and universities. They call their job 'dollar for homesick'. The calculations are not always accurate: Julius has been at sea for 17 years now and is still here. 'But the years go so fast,' he says. 'Every time I come on board

I think, I will stop. But then I can't escape.' He grew up by the sea and has a BSc in Marine Transportation from one of the Philippines' many maritime colleges. His cousin worked on ships and it sounded like a good life. He prefers container ships to bulk carriers because containers at least provide some shade. Bulk cargo – coal, oil, metal ore or grain are the four most common types – means working on an open deck in 35-degree heat. He knows that now, but he was sold on the romance of the sea at first. 'I thought it was nice, you can see the rest of the world, China, Japan. Every kind of people.' Now he wouldn't recommend life at sea to anyone. 'Because I know what it's like.'

A seafarer joke: 'I travel the world but it all looks like my engine room (or bridge, or gangway).' When ships carried general cargo – a cornucopia of everything, in bales and barrels and piles – and dockers unloaded it all by hand, there was more time ashore. There was rest and recuperation. In *The Box*, a history of the container, the economist Marc Levinson introduces a 1954 voyage on a typical cargo ship, SS *Warrior*. It carried 74,903 cases, 71,726 cartons, 24,036 bags, 10,671 boxes, 2880 bundles, 2877 packages, 2634 pieces, 1538 drums, 888 cans, 815 barrels, 53 wheeled vehicles, 21 crates, 10 transporters, five reels and 1525 'undetermined' items: a total of 194,582 pieces, all of which had to be loaded and unloaded by men by hand. The total weight came to just over five thousand tons of cargo and would have taken weeks to deal with. With *Kendal*, several thousand boxes can be unloaded and loaded in less than 24 hours.

The next day brings formalization, when newcomers are introduced in depth to the ship. Third Officer Marius is in charge. He gathers me and the two cadets, a small brood, and we set off from the ship's office on A-deck, past the noticeboard that indicates who is on or off duty. Ashore options – 'in' or 'out' – don't apply here, where 'out' means overboard. First, the interior attractions: a karaoke machine in the crew's lounge, a dart board and Wii machine in the officers'. A library on D-deck is equipped with cheap DVDs, books and two computers for gaming only. *Kendal* is only four years old, but it has no provision for browsing on the internet and no Skype. Internet access is not freely available: crew members pass their emails to the captain once a day and he sends them and transmits the replies. The last time I had that level of internet freedom was in 1995.

There are outdoor facilities: a basketball hoop on the poop deck near the stern, where the decks seem too slippery to play safely, and the low railings an invitation to lose balls to the ocean. Behind the accommodation house is an empty swimming pool, and a set of dingy chairs next to a barbecue made from an oil drum, lashed to a railing for stability. It is an unlikely setting for merriment, right beneath a huge wall of refrigerated containers – popular with producers of fish, medicine and bananas – that hum insistently, constantly, anti-socially. I ask if the barbecue is ever used. 'Oh God, no, not any more,' says Marius. 'It's even worse than dinner. Everyone standing there with long faces and the sounds of the generators and all you can see are containers. Horrible.'

We move to Upper Deck. Here there is a gym, with rowing and treadmill machines, with weights that the buff Julius looks like he uses, although his heavy manual work is probably exercise enough. There is a well-used laundry with one machine marked Boiler Suits Only, for the men who work among the oil, rust, salt and spray of the deck. Up on A-deck is the noticeboard where all electrical items must be declared for customs purposes, and the bond store, the ship's tuck shop. For sale are soft drinks, water and chocolate, and useful sundries like toothpaste and shaving cream. Alcohol is banned now on Maersk ships: its employees are forbidden to drink at sea or ashore and can be breathalysed. There are sensible reasons behind the prohibition: driving a ship requires as much sobriety as driving a car, and alcohol has been linked to accidents ranging from sailors drowning off gangways in port, to smashing a ship into Southend Pier. But it is an unpopular rule, thought to be babying, insulting. It has deadened life on the ship. People used to wind down with a beer after a watch. Now they retreat to their cabins with a DVD and a laptop. The familiar modern lament about the anti-social nature of these machines applies here, but in the intimate, incessant environment of a ship, the effects are magnified.

Now the safety features: large orange lifeboats, in modern times hard and enclosed, and immersion suits for ditching in open waters or in an open life raft. I am allotted to the starboard lifeboat, equipped with water bottles and emergency rations branded 'Seven Seas, Compact for Life, 2500 calories a packet'. The interior looks like a military cargo plane, with harnesses and numbered places on the hard benches. It carries flares, a sea anchor and oars to be used at sea or when beaching so that the surf doesn't crush you or turn you over. There is no toilet, only two red buckets and a hatch that opens. The boat looks both safe and terrifying: if needed, it would either swing its way down to the water suspended on cables, a descent described to me as 'sickening', or drop inadvertently from a height that would break teeth.

Throughout the formalization, the talkative Scottish cadet keeps up a running commentary of gags and opinions. I wonder at his career choice: all the noise and colour of his personality, trapped in an engine room. He has an opinion on that too. 'I won't stay on containers. Boring. I want to go on rig supply ships.' The ships that shuttle supplies to offshore oil rigs are known to have better food, better pay, all in all a better life. Their crews have home time. This boy doesn't understand why I have chosen to come to sea. 'Because shipping is so fundamental and crucial and no-one knows about it.'

'But it's boring.'

• EMBARKATION

I look at the two cadets and wonder how long they will last. They have been at sea for only a few months. There are decades to go. When I ask Marius how long he has been at sea on this contract, he knows to the hour.

Things need to happen in Rotterdam. This is where we take on stores for the whole trip, so Pinky is looking through her books with a slightly frantic air. She is a good bookkeeper, although once misplaced a decimal point so that *Kendal* wasn't carrying 1000 eggs in its stores but 10,000. Pinky of the 10,000 eggs. A fitness instructor is also coming aboard for four days to educate the crew about fitness and nutrition, because of the obvious logic that healthier crews are better crews. Shit, says Marius, who is thin as a beanstalk, I'd better figure out where the gym is. A new third officer will also arrive, and Marius will be promoted although Igor still hasn't managed to leave. His contract has now been expired for several weeks. I hear complaints about shore staff who understand nothing of their life, who don't realize that an extra week after six months at sea feels like a month, and so on. They don't understand that time moves differently here. We make our own, for a start. Already the thick Romanian accent of Marius has come over the PA announcing a 'retardation of the clocks' by an hour. Laminated warnings in the lift reinforce the change. The alerts are required because sometimes this shifting of time is commanded by the captain, not by Greenwich. It confuses humans and computer clocks, but it is done from kindness. Executed properly, this time manipulation causes no crude jetlag, no brutal loss or gain of hours by a bewildered body, just a gentle push from a voice on the tannoy.

The port of Rotterdam is 40 miles long. It is the largest port in Europe, partly because it is used for trans-shipment, whereby big ships decant goods into smaller ones that can then cross the Channel and don't need deep-water ports, which are few and expensive.

There seems nothing but graft about Rotterdam, but you can berth your great ship at Mississippi, Amazon or Yangtze wharves (or at Petrol or Chemical). Shipping can be poetic despite itself. There is the singing of its winds, for one: the katabatics that roll down off Scottish glens to knock over unsuspecting boats in the lochs, or the chocolate gale, a north-west wind of the West Indies and Spanish Main. On mechanized, inhuman docks, people in hard hats look at a ship, estimate how many boxes will be put on it and say, 'A thousand moves.' They talk of containers left in yards building up 'dwell time' (and they charge for it). In maritime offices in London, Hong Kong and New York, they talk of 'wet law', applying to grounding and casualties and such, and its 'dry tail', the follow-up negotiations with charterers and insurers. They discuss the jungle-sounding bareboat charter (the leasing of a ship without paying for its maintenance or administration) or the gaiety of a charter party (a leasing arrangement). There is the elegance of seafarer certificates, shortened to 'tickets', so that a captain has a deep-sea ticket not coastal, and he is foreign-going, not domestic. At Rotterdam, there is also an area I think is called Bootleg, which is charming, except it is Botlek, known by the crew for its duty-free store. This is only five miles from the ship and spares them the €100 it would cost for a taxi ride into town, because the store will provide transport if you promise to spend enough. That won't be difficult: the prices are far higher than their dutied equivalents. I am puzzled that the Filipino crew buy Nintendos here when they are cheaper in Asia. But they do, and with glee. 'For my son.' 'For my daughter: I missed her birthday.' They plug the absence with electrical items.

At dinner, there is a surprise. A new captain. The South African has left. His chilliness makes sense now: he was four days from the end of a two-month tour at sea, and guests were not a priority. Hindsight makes me feel more kindly towards him, to his attempts at warmth, such as when I asked about shipboard rules for supernumeraries: 'Don't fiddle with the anchor.' Now he is gone and here is his 'back-to-back', his partner-captain of *Kendal*, who has been two months at home and will now be two months in command while the other is ashore. He comes to the door of the dining room while I struggle with another indifferent Pinky salad, and introduces himself. Call me Glenn. He is a skinny, friendly man from a northern English town known for coal mines, seafarers and poverty. He is clean-shaven, grey-haired and ascetic to look at, but his accent has the warm tones of the north of England, and so does his manner. Don't worry about formalities, he says. Enjoy your dinner. More importantly, enjoy my ship. And I think I will, now.

To sea

2.   ABOARD

Blue Eyes and His Boxes

Two tribes run a ship. You pick one or the other and rarely cross lines. Deck or engine room; navigators or mechanics; oil or water. Once I step onto *Kendal*'s bridge, I know my allegiance is deck. All those windows and all that sea. And a sofa, a kettle, and, if I am lucky, decent cookies, not just the SkyFlakes biscuits that Filipinos tell me are their only food back home in bad weather. Typhoon crackers. The bridge provides a view, always, to port or sea or weather, and there are binoculars to borrow, charts to read and VHF radio crackles to be puzzled over by my unaccustomed ears.

The bridge of a modern ship is a shock on first encounter. Although this place is still known as the wheelhouse, the wheel at the helm is not wooden and impressive, but mundane plastic, the kind that would suit a video arcade game. Nearly all else is automated. A bank of screens contains radar, ECDIS – an electronic chart system – and AIS (Automatic Identification System), that transmits the ship's name, speed and direction and other details to other ships, port authorities and well-equipped pirates. There is VHF radio, a gyrocompass and a magnetic compass, a tachometer and an echo sounder. There are no voice pipes or telegraphs as *Titanic* had and barely any brass, but so many beeps and screens and so much automation that I wonder if ships will soon be able to drive themselves. I picture Pedro or Julius attempting to wash the exterior bridge windows with beeps in a raging storm or trying to hose down the decks with a computer and think not.

Captain Glenn is often to be found on the bridge. He is here for port approaches and departures, but also whenever he can escape paperwork, which is not as often as he would like now that the role of ship's purser has ceased to exist and all administration falls upon the captain and senior officers. He can be on his computer for four to eight hours a day now. Glenn is the most senior captain in Maersk's container fleet. In past times, he would have been known as a commodore and saluted as such by the raising of flags on courteous passing ships. His talk turns often to earlier times, because he has enough hinterland to have plenty, and because in those four decades, life at sea has changed dramatically. His first ship was a tramp steamer, a freelance ship that picked up trade where it could, unlike a liner with a scheduled route like *Kendal*. A taxi, not a bus. It was iron, had derrick cranes on deck to heft cargo about, and was held together by rivets. Rivets! Not like this Korean-made welded ship, only four years old. Still, he is not entirely nostalgic, and always loves whichever ship he commands. He says of this one, 'Isn't she beautiful?' and salutes her every day with a stroke or a tap, a formal and ritual greeting. He is scornful of a modern trend in maritime journalism – notably led by *Lloyd's List* – to call ships 'it'. What nonsense. His ship is a she. Why? She just is.

If Captain Glenn stands on the bridge facing forward to sea, the old life is behind him and the new one in front. Behind are the national flags that a ship raises when she calls at a port belonging to that nation, each kept in wooden cubbyholes on a shelf that stretches halfway across the wheelhouse. You never know when you might need to be nice to Nauru. There is the chart table and its drawers filled with 169 charts drawn up by the UK's Hydrographic Office, a chart-making entity nostalgically known as the Admiralty. Other nations produce charts – Russia and Japan, for example – but the Admiralty's are known to be the best.

In front, there is sea, but mostly there are boxes. Orange, blue, grey, red. If the captain leaves the wheelhouse to stand on the port or starboard wings – the bridge's two terraces – he will see boxes fore and aft. That is, if he sees them at all. For him they are blank, boring. 'I am indifferent to them. They're just boxes. You've got to admit.' He thinks they have destroyed the soul of ships and of shipping. In a way this is an old lament too. In the middle of the shift from sail to steam, Joseph Conrad complained that whereas 'the loading of ships was once a matter of skill, judgment and knowledge', with the modern steamship, cargo was 'dumped into her through six hatchways, with clatter and hurry and racket and heat, in a cloud of steam and a mess of coal-dust'.

After Rotterdam, I begin to spend hours on the bridge, hanging out, though I choose my hours carefully, avoiding one officer and happy to bother others. It is easy to plan ahead: at sea you always wake up to a different sunrise but the watches don't change. So that *Kendal* can operate for 24 hours a day, each of the three officers has two four-hour watches. The captain is not included: his watch is constant. The 4–8 watch is given to the first officer (also known as the chief officer), Vinton, the captain's second-in-command. Vinton's is one of the plates wrapped in cling film that sit on the table during dinner for later consumption. The second officer gets the 12–4 and the third the 8–12, so that the most junior is in charge at times when senior officers are likely to be awake.

The duty officers are always hospitable, because company is

distraction. There are things to be done on duty, but not enough to fully stimulate four hours of time. The tasks include plotting positions and checking both magnetic and gyro compasses, monitoring changes of weather and general running conditions, keeping an eye on vessels in the vicinity. This list is laminated and pinned to the bridge console, but it can be summed up by 'keep a good lookout'. Good watch officers need to master the gadgets, but they must never neglect the human element. They need sea eyes. Often the captain points out lights that I have not seen or ships that, to me, emerge from the blue horizon only when he indicates them, as he hands me binoculars while managing to keep his disbelief at my ineptitude to himself. Darkness vision is also important: this is why F-deck, where the captain and the chief engineer live and work, is lit at night with red lights only, in the manner of a submarine, so that the eyes of senior officers can adjust to the darkness of the bridge more quickly in an emergency. In 2010, after *Ouzo* disappeared in the English Channel, an investigation laid some blame on the ferry watch officer's photochromic lenses, which handicapped his night vision. To prevent light pollution, the chart room, which needs to be illuminated, is blocked and blacked off with heavy curtains at night. Even with this care, anyone coming into the wheelhouse in darkness will have impaired vision for 10–15 minutes, a significant handicap in a crisis. Ships have sunk in less time.

The captain is aware of this danger, and this alertness is what governs the ship. An affable nature does not mean a lack of discipline. Bridge rules are as follows: strict uniform is not required – boiler suits are allowed, as are sandals, but with socks, so that a watch officer dressed thus looks like a seafarer from the ankles up and a priest below them. An officer on watch may sit down but he must never fall asleep. Every 11 minutes, the 'dead man's alarm' sounds and must be switched off, to encourage wakefulness. I come to learn which are the captain's notices and which are company instructions.

Maersk communications don't include phrases such as 'Slovenliness will not be tolerated'. Every Sunday, the captain's cabin inspections are feared, with good reason, for he runs fingers along lintels for dust, and expects military standards of cleanliness on this civilian ship, and clean mouths too (the Scottish cadet soon learns to speak more sweetly after the captain's interventions).

A happy ship is the result of careful balance that the captain has worked hard to construct. He served under unapproachable masters in the 1960s, when they were meant to stay distant and god-like. He is still the master, but he mixes authority with friendliness. 'Some masters work the crew too hard. They might run a tight ship but it's not a happy ship. There's got to be a living side, a human side.' *Kendal* is a floating warehouse, a means of transport, an office, but also a home. In reality, when only the chief engineer is of an almost equivalent rank, his position as master puts him in social isolation. Sometimes he chooses isolation too. When he comes aboard, he shuts himself away for a day or two, just as captains did in Conrad's day, taking 'a long dive into their stateroom, only to emerge a few days later with a more or less serene brow'. He tries the same decompression technique in the other direction when he gets home, although it is not as effective, and even after weeks ashore he can wake at night at home panicked by quiet, convinced the engines have broken down.

I begin to interview the captain daily, at 11 a.m. ship-sharp, for several reasons. He has the best coffee on board, as well as a cafetière in which to brew it properly. His spacious, comfortable quarters – bedroom, day room and office – are high and starboard, and as such the least vibrating on *Kendal*. I have learned that mine are not, and why in my cabin there were bits of paper stuffed behind picture frames and under the television, and plugging hinges. I assumed they were connected with the Smuggling Precautions form I signed, confirming that the cabin had been searched for contraband, and that a previous, more conscientious occupant had filled all possible cavities where stashing could occur. That didn't explain the TV, but the first night did, because everything in my quarters vibrated beyond tolerance and made sleep impossible. After nights of leaping out of bed and stuffing yet more paper into the bathroom door hinge, into parts of the bulkhead, beneath anything with a space under it, the serenity of the captain's day room was a relief. Yes, says Second Engineer Mike, when I complain at breakfast one morning, my bones still juddering. Port-side cabins are the worst. He has one too. Sometimes he can't use his computer because the mouse is dancing. Some engineers mutter about Korean-built superstructures that vibrate more than a good old British-built ship would have done. If the engine is set to 80 rpm (revolutions per minute) – the average speed of a resting human heart – the shaking is inevitable. Cruise ships modify their structures to prevent this happening and disturbing passengers. Working seafarers must live with it.

The biggest draw of the captain was his 42 years in the Merchant Navy. This means he has been at sea probably as long as the Glaswegian officer on his first ship, who once dampened the arrogance of the young jumped-up cadet Glenn by saying, 'Sonny, I've been at sea since Moby Dick was a sardine.' It also means that he decided to join the Merchant Navy just as it began to change beyond recognition. He had grown up as the box and globalization had grown up, and he had watched a world of general cargo, thieving stevedores and hard work – but one properly leavened by leisure and pleasure – become one of paperwork, foreigners and relentless schedules, stress and fatigue.

In 1968, he needed a career. For boys in his town, that meant the mine or the sea. Ships were his mother's idea. 'She said, what a wonderful world it would be to be a captain, to see the world.' She thought it would always be a safe job because we will always need ships. A local man in South Shields, over the river Tyne, had been teaching him the cornet. In this man's house he had models of wooden sailing ships from his time as a merchant seafarer, and he told stories that, to the son of a miner, sounded like freshness and adventure. They were the opposite of imprisonment in the earth. Even so, Glenn applied to South Shields Maritime College to be an engineer, but realized his mistake: everyone knew then what a ship's captain did. Who knew what an engineer did, except an engineer? That has changed too. Now if he tells strangers he is a ship's captain, they have no idea that that means he is in charge of operating the largest man-made moving objects on the planet. Or they are yachters and seek to impress him with their nautical knowledge, and that's just annoying.

The captain was average at college, better at what he loved, inadequate at what he didn't. Astronomy was easy but navigation took him years, until he applied himself, pennies dropped, and he understood it all beautifully, enough to supply three calculations in his exams when only one was asked for. He still loves navigation as much as he loves *Kendal*, and he made the right choice to scorn the engine room. He knows this every time he socializes ashore with more than one engineer at a time. 'All they talk about is engines.' And if he talked about navigation and charts and stars in the same way? 'They'll be saying, "Who does he think he is, Henry the Navigator or something?"' The captain mentions Henry the Navigator frequently. I don't think it is because of a powerful love for a fifteenth-century Portuguese prince who sponsored great voyages of exploration to the Cape of Good Hope and India: he doesn't like to read about the sea when he is at sea, and even less so when he is ashore. It's just a tic he has, along with his often-expressed conviction that the Merchant Navy is treated as the scum of the earth. Captain Glenn the Navigator commands a ship guided by gadgetry, but he still loves to move through the sea using only what it and the sky can tell him. 'I get great satisfaction just steaming on an ocean passage and plotting the position from the heavenly bodies. The biggest kick is when you've never seen land for days on end and you didn't have a satellite navigator, and then right on the money, where you say there should be land or a terrestrial feature, there it is. Henry the Navigator.'

He is an odd mixture of end-of-career weariness and a fierce attachment to tradition. The rules of watch-keeping: pay attention to the gadgets, but use your eyes most. If you see a target on the radar, turn to your binoculars. You would be surprised how many don't bother looking out of the window. He can quote shipping's rules of the road – anti-collision regulations known as ColRegs – by memory, along with the principle of the sextant. He knows his knots. As a cadet, he took constant compass bearings on a ramshackle general cargo ship owned by the long-gone Scottish shipping firm Ben Line, which named some of its ships after mountains and others after whisky. On an online forum, I find postings from past cadets who write fondly of 'Ol' Blue Eyes', who was kind to them and who taught them well. They reminisce there about his attachment to the sextant, and his attachment to their understanding it. He is the same now, despairing that his officers can't use *Kendal*'s sextant, Chinese-made now, but still kept in a box on the bridge, just in case. If all technology breaks, there will always be the sun or moon or stars and the horizon from which to calculate position. 'It's a lovely bit of knowledge,' he says, and explains with delight about mirrors and reflected light and why it is possible to measure 120 degrees on a curve that shows only 60. It is a long and intricate lesson, and by the end of it I hope that if we sink, I'm in the captain's lifeboat and he has his sextant.

Sometime towards the end of the 1960s, when he was a young cadet, the captain saw his first boxes. They were being carried by an American ship that was departing Hong Kong while his ship was arriving. 'I was out on the poop deck and some of the crew said,

"Look! That's a container. That's a thing of the future.'" He didn't pay much attention because cadets didn't pay much attention to things like the creation of globalization. 'You were too busy blinking learning stuff.' But he listened to the crew, who kept talking about these strange metal things. They said, 'That'll never take off.' They said, 'How are they going to get a truck in that? How will they get steel and timber in it?'

They did and it did. There are 20 million containers crossing the world now, quiet blank boxes, thanks to a US businessman named Malcom [sic] McLean who thought people who moved freight would find it easier if they could shift everything in a box, rather than having the confusion of break-bulk cargo, of barrels and boxes and piles, of each company having its own system. Standardization was not a new concept: ancient Romans tried it when they shipped liquids in amphorae. In the nineteenth century coal was transported in wooden boxes on canal barges. McLean's spark was to call on an engineer, Keith Tantlinger, to create a new design that could be seamlessly stacked and locked, using twist-locks. This new box could fit trains, trucks, cranes and ships alike. This 'intermodality' made perfect commercial sense, and labour unions hated it. Dockers in particular were furious. McLean claimed his box system reduced labour by two-thirds, reducing dockworkers' workload, salary and power. This labour force could be powerfully obstructive when it chose, often instigating strikes that became national. In a 1950 survey assessing the popularity of 30 professions among the British public, dockers came 29th.

For a while they held up the march of the box, as did geography and physics. Ships that carried many boxes would have to be bigger, with deeper draughts. New ports had to be built: New York's maritime wharfs – too shallow, too narrow – became useless, and the massive Greater Port of New York–New Jersey was constructed instead. The rewards of containerization were too great for the dockers to defeat change. Before containers, transport costs ate up to 25 per cent of the value of whatever was being shipped. With the extreme efficiencies that intermodality brought, costs were reduced to a pittance. A sweater can now travel 3000 miles for 2.5 cents; it costs a cent to send a can of beer. In hard economic times, when there is more supply than demand, shipping a container can cost nothing.

By his junior officer days, the captain was in favour of boxes. They looked like a simpler life. 'No more general cargo, all the work involved, no more gear, cranes, derricks, nothing. I thought, this has got to be easier.' On his first cellular container ship – one specially built for boxes rather than fitting them in and among derricks and holds – they carried only ten containers. Then more, and still more, and he learned that the boxes gave the gift of speed, but they sucked away his time. You wouldn't get any sleep when port hours were so rushed and hurried. Before boxes, he would wonder if he had time to go ashore for dinner. Now he wonders if he has time to get a newspaper.

He doesn't wonder about the boxes. They are things full of things, to be moved according to schedule. He doesn't know what's inside them and he doesn't care. I know he drives a Harley-Davidson at home, so I needle him. What if there were a box full of Harleys? 'Then there's one full of Harleys. I'm used to the fact that there's no way to get to see them anyway.' It would take him days to read the full manifest of all the cargo on *Kendal*, and anyway there isn't one on board. A modern container ship is crewed by people who have no idea what they are carrying.

Kendal's crew only know the contents of the refrigerated boxes and the flammable or toxic goods, so that they can put out fires if necessary. We are carrying paint, lacquer, enamel, stain, shellac solutions, varnish and polish. Somewhere there is liquid flavouring which is highly flammable and may cause vapours that explode when they meet air. Elsewhere there is some octahydro-tetramethyl-naphthalenyl-ethanone, a chemical that can be used in air fresheners or to reduce odour in permed hair. There are 1828 kilograms of carbamate pesticide, a substance highly toxic to humans, and 180,000 kilograms of metal powder, self-heating. 'This,' I read, 'may react violently with water.' On a ship at sea, in containers that are weather-proof, not waterproof. Marius can guess at other contents. He sees the listing for 'BMW airbags, batteries wet, filled with acid' and says that means we are carrying cars to the markets of the East. He knows that Thailand makes airbags but no-one sends them the other way, and Asia likes German cars. Not that he cares much either. 'When the Navy call us in the Gulf of Aden and ask us what type of ship we are, we say, "Container." "What's in the containers?" "No idea."'

One of the crew tells me he can defeat the blankness of boxes. That's not how he phrases it. He can break a container seal and re-seal it convincingly, although I suspect his intent would be for monetary, not intellectual, gain. This skill is more common than it should be. The US Government Accountability Office (GAO) reported on a US Customs & Border Patrol study that showed 'that existing container seals provided inadequate security against physical intrusion'. Criminals who didn't know how to re-seal a seal could do an adequate workaround by taking the door off.

Much of modern security rests on theatre and assumption. That applies to airport lines, questionable laws about liquids, and the supposed safety of 18 million containers containing who knows what. Who does know what? Only 13 per cent of containers in Europe are physically inspected. Worldwide, the rate is thought to be between 2 and 10 per cent. US ports receive 17 million containers a year and physically inspect 5 per cent of them. Container manifests rely on the legal term 'said to contain'. Security people will assure you that intelligence and clever analysis can fill in the rest of the percentages, that they can spot smuggled goods, people or weapons. I wonder. When MSC *Napoli* grounded off a Devon beach in January 2007, its burst boxes of motorbikes, shampoo and nappies attracted looters and treasure-hunters. It was also a rare opportunity to compare what was declared on container manifests with the actual contents. In 20 per cent of the containers, the contents and weights were wrong. The difference was sometimes as much as three tons. When a ship must be carefully stabilized with weight and ballast, if there are enough of those differences, it could overturn.

All sorts of criminals like ships. Counterfeiters: they ship £125 billion worth of fake goods, or more than the GDP of 150 countries. People traffickers regularly send their desperate clients off in boxes. In 2006, Seattle police arrested 40 traffickers for procuring foreign women to work in brothels. Some had paid £30,000 to travel in shipping containers. Drug barons love boxes. In an earlier report, the GAO was blunt: 'US initiatives relating to cargo container security have been limited and generally ineffective for the international counter narcotics effort.' In 2012 the Stockholm International Peace Research Institute (SIPRI) published data from its Vessel Maritime Incident Database which showed that container ships were six times more likely to be involved in destabilizing military and narcotics-related transfers than their share of the world market fleet would suggest.

In 1939, Albert Einstein wrote a letter to President Roosevelt about the feasibility of setting off a uranium chain reaction. He thought of dropping his new bomb not by air but by ship. 'A single bomb of this type, carried by boat and exploded in a port, might very well destroy the whole port together with some of the sur-rounding territory.' Einstein was wrong and Enola Gay was right, but the 'bomb in a box' theory still concerns plenty of US security analysts. The fashionable threat is not cocaine but Al-Qaeda, and has been ever since Osama Bin Laden said that 'if [the US] economy is finished, they will become too busy to enslave oppressed people. It is very important to concentrate on hitting the US economy with every available means.' Bin Laden was not a Bin Laden – a powerful, business-minded family that uses shipping in its construction empire – for nothing. In 2004, Al-Qaeda reportedly recruited a maritime expert. In 2010, US security sources revealed that the organization had been working out how best to blow up oil tankers. Though, as the urban planning academic Stephen Cohen writes, why bother with intercontinental missiles or explosives when you can just ship everything you need in parts, and assemble it at the required destination? 'Containers… are the poor man's missiles: you no longer have to be a big powerful government to create catastrophe.' This is not hypothetical. In 2003, ABC News shipped depleted uranium from Jakarta to Los Angeles in an attempt to expose the weaknesses in port barriers. It didn't go down well at the Department for Homeland Security, whose declared mission is to 'stop dangerous things and dangerous people from entering the country', even if those things are sent by dangerous people from a national news channel. 'Can a reporter rob a bank to prove that bank security is weak?' said a spokesman, complaining that as he understood things, you don't break laws to break news. In fact, shipping uranium is legal, as long as you declare it. ABC didn't, and no-one checked the shipment.

Connecting the sea to terrorism has become popular in security studies. Al-Qaeda certainly understands ships: not only because it rammed USS *Cole* with a boat, but because it is also thought to own or charter a small fleet. North Korea has its own flag, a fleet of 242 vessels and the ability to make maritime mischief. *Lloyd's List* revealed in 2012 that 120 vessels had reported GPS malfunctions in seas near North Korea, in an article entitled 'Pyongyang Death Jam' that pointed to the work of a North Korean signals jammer. I wouldn't bother with shipping a dirty bomb: a GPS jammer can be bought in the UK for £60 (though they are banned in the United States) and can cause mayhem. When the UK's General Lighthouse Authorities experimented in 2010 with what happens to ships whose signals are jammed, its experiment vessel showed that it was travelling to Belfast, overland. Captain Glenn would be pleased that *Lloyd's List* recommended reliance on traditional navigational equipment. The anti-terrorist sextant.

A senior US government official was asked in 2002 about the threat of maritime terrorism. 'This industry is a shadowy underworld,' he said. 'After 9/11 we suddenly realized how little we understood about commercial shipping. You can't swing a dead cat in the shipping business without hitting somebody with phony papers.' But phony papers aren't always the problem. In 2010, Nigerian security forces discovered 240 tons of rockets, mortar shells and small arms ammunition in 13 containers that had been shipped on the German-owned, French-operated, Marshall Islands-flagged *Everest* from Bandar Abbas in Iran despite UN sanctions that prohibit Iran from selling arms. The contraband was hidden behind marble slabs and glass wool. The manifest showed that the recipient was 'to order'. In short, as Hugh Griffiths wrote in SIPRI's report, 'the ship's owners, operators and officers had no knowledge or reason for suspicion regarding the container'. Ship operator CMA-CGM's defence was telling: the containers had been loaded and sealed by an Iranian company that was not on any list of prohibited traders. They had done nothing wrong.

In response to such uncertainty, the Customs and Border Protection Agency is charged with implementing a 'layered security strategy' to prevent terrorism from reaching the United States by water. It wants to lower a portcullis around its borders and turn the whole ocean into a manageable moat. With various initiatives like the Safe Port Act, Secure Freight Initiative and Container Security Initiative (CSI), suspect containers are supposed to be identified via intelligence and screening. Nations buy the screening equipment in return for their containers getting faster entry into the United States, whose customs officers are deployed to foreign ports to oversee the process.

Under this layered security scheme, the perfect US-bound container behaves like this: first, it is packed in a foreign factory that belongs to the Customs-Trade Partnership Against Terrorism (C-TPAT), and has been previously vetted. A safe pair of packing hands. Importers and carriers then provide information to US Customs, which uses an automated tracking system to identify high-risk containers. The box is then shipped to a foreign port that has signed up to the CSI, where foreign officials working harmoniously with US Customs identify and scan containers using 'non-intrusive inspection equipment and radiation portal monitors', in the words of the GAO. While the box is sailing safely onwards, updates on its progress are electronically transmitted to the United States. If further doubt remains about the level of risk it poses, upon arrival the container is screened with more non-intrusive inspection equipment and detained or set free to furnish an American home or fuel an American car.

It is a beautiful vision of a safer global supply chain. For now, it is still only a vision. According to the Implementing Recommendations of the 9/11 Commission Act, enforced in 2007, a system to scan 100 per cent of all US-bound cargo had to be in place by July 2012. Six foreign ports signed up to the 100 per cent requirement, and by February 2012, five had dropped out. It was too expensive and too difficult, said Salalah, Southampton, Busan, Hong Kong and Puerto Cortés, leaving only Qasim, a port in Pakistan. In reality, scanning every single US-bound container is an outlandish idea: customs officials attempting to scan 100 per cent of US-bound containers leaving one Hong Kong terminal managed only five per cent. It is more outlandish than a proposal by a company named Inscentinel to use sniffer bees to detect drugs and explosives. The authors of a study commissioned by the European Union (EU) thought the 100 per cent target akin to a trade barrier, and undiplomatically said so. Many customs and security experts think it unworkable. The technology to do the scanning isn't yet good enough; the blockages would choke ports. The new scanning and radiation equipment required, the report's authors wrote, would cost the EU alone €10 billion, and could cost world trade €17 billion. Trade is movement. Trade is sacred. In 2012, the US Department of Homeland Security quietly pushed the 100-per-cent deadline to 2014, and counting.

There is a message from the office. The office is in Europe but the message is written in the lovely phrases of sub-continental English. It begs the captain to get 'earlier gangs for your good vessel', and instructs *Kendal* to be at the pilot station – the pick-up point for the port pilot – at 16.30, earlier than planned. Schedules can slip in shipping when ports are clogged and berthing space is precious and expensive. The speed is adjusted accordingly, and we are on time to pick up the pilot for Le Havre. Le Havre is a harbour whose name means Harbour. It is on one of shipping's superhighways, because all Europe's stuff arrives across these waters, and all its empty boxes are sent Asia-wards for more. If these shipping channels were roads they would be potholed. Instead they have shallows and quirks. For this reason, a local pilot is required, on the assumption that even the officers on a regular loop like this one can't learn the intricacies of all the foreign ports they call at. Once, while looking at charts, I asked Marius what some funny-coloured patches of blue were. A different blue. He didn't know that they were lagoons. He shrugged. 'If I don't have to sail through it, I'm not interested in it.'

Some captains resent pilots. Failed seafarers, they say, who couldn't hack it at sea. Or seafarers who escaped, more likely, and who delighted in talking of their better pay and hours to these men trapped on a ship for months, and of how they can go home every day. Perhaps this pilot-officer rivalry is required, just as ship life needs tribes or hierarchies to provide boundaries in limited space and endless time. So there is oil and water still, though the rivalry is not vicious as it was in the days of black gangs, when the coal-stokers called sailors kulaks or drones, and the sailors called them moles or bats. 'Bad weather,' writes Theodora Fitzgibbon in *A Taste of the Sea*, 'was "those kulaks are at it again", for whenever the ship rolled it was the fault of the bridge.' One day the Scottish cadet invites me to do an engineering shift and visit the bow thruster, 'going down as far as you can go and it's dark and spooky'. I decline, as anyone who has watched *The Poseidon Adventure* would, and he says, 'You deck people do nothing! Nothing!'

There are officers, then crew. There are Europeans against Asians and Russians against Ukrainians. There are probably Filipinos from one island against Filipinos from another. There are seafarers, and then there is everyone else. Anthropologists put seafarers into a 'high-contrast folk group', along with firefighters, loggers and miners, where the group binding is shared danger ill understood by others. The Scythian philosopher Anacharsis was once asked whether there were more people alive or dead. Anacharsis said he couldn't answer, because he didn't know where to place seamen. 'Seamen,' concluded the seventeenth-century clergyman John Flavel, who quotes the philosopher's remark, 'are, as it were, a third sort of persons, to be numbered neither with the living nor the dead; their lives hanging continually in suspense before them.'

This was true in the seventeenth century when Flavel wrote his book. It has not yet become untrue. Seafarer fatalities are still ten times those of land-based occupations. Men fall off gangways or are crushed between the ship and the quay. They are thrown by swells against steel machinery. They suffocate. In 2007, the crew of the emergency response vessel *Viking Islay*, 25 miles off the northern

English coast in the Amethyst gas field, heard clanking from the anchor. Some cabins abutted the anchor locker, where the chain was stored, and one night it disturbed their sleep. The following morning, Robert Ebertowski, a 40-year-old Polish AB, and Bob O'Brien, a 59-year old Scot, went to see what was happening. His crewmates heard Ebertowski say on the radio, 'I'm going to put a clip on this,' then silence. Findlay MacFadyean followed, wearing protective gear as he should, but he was a big man and couldn't get into the anchor locker wearing it, so he took it off. In the few seconds it took the cook to go and fetch some torches nearby, there were three dead men on a ship of 12. The chamber had rusted and the oxygen had been sucked from the air. They had all suffocated immediately, or in the time it takes to say eight words.

Worldwide, four times more people die in ferry accidents than in aeroplanes, in mundane commuting ferries like *Doña Paz*, a Filipino passenger vessel that collided with a tanker in 1987. In that disaster 4375 people died. It still counts as the worst peacetime disaster in Filipino history. In the same year, the *Herald of Free Enterprise*, a cross-Channel ferry, sank just outside Zeebrugge, drowning 193 people. The bow doors on the *Herald of Free Enterprise* were supposed to be closed by an assistant bo'sun, who was asleep on his bunk when Harbour Stations were called and all things were to be readied for departure, things like making sure the sea was on the outside of the ship. For years afterwards, 'he left the bow doors open' was a metaphor for general or colossal incompetence. But still I disembark cross-Channel ferries realizing that I didn't listen to the safety announcements, and I didn't know where the lifejackets were or which muster station to go to, and that if the ship had gone under or tipped, and the darkness had made a mockery of its layout, so that the bar was over my head and the doors didn't work upside down, I would have had nothing to protect me but my assumption that I would survive. But I wouldn't have, probably, and if I had it would have been through luck and upper-arm strength: the majority of survivors on the *Herald of Free Enterprise* were the younger and fitter passengers, who could haul themselves through windows.

The sea drowns the solid outlines and protection of modern technology and society. To go peaceably to sea, you need pretence. You are buoyant on assumption and water, even though the water is two miles deep, downwards, but you can't see it like you can from a plane, so it is not there. (When the Dutch cargo ship *Soekaboemi* was sunk in 1942, a young British radio officer sitting in one of its lifeboats asked a Dutch crewman how far nearest land was. 'Two miles away,' said the crewman. 'Straight down.')

Such dark thoughts surround the apparently mundane activity of getting a ship safely into harbour. It is not mundane. I like to listen to port approaches, because the practice of getting this enormous ship into a safe harbour is acted out aurally: Starboard 10 please, Captain. Starboard 10, Pilot. Thank you, Captain. Thank you, Pilot. Everything is repeated for certainty. They are safety echoes. And as has happened thousands of times before, *Kendal* is nudged into her berth by two tugs with their noses pushed into her side, their enormous horsepower engines a match for ours, their azimuth propellers engineered to turn on a tuppence, marine donkeys, gritty and underappreciated. I once travelled on a tug up the Thames, escorting HMS *St Albans* into Canary Wharf, and watched with amusement as spectators gathered to gaze at the glamour of the grey warship and her white-uniformed sailors, and ignored the astonishing nimble mass of horsepower behind her that was the tug.

Slowly, noisily, but safely, the good vessel slows, slides and stops. We have found safe haven in a port named for it.

Marius at rest, briefly

3.   HARBOUR

Another Day in Paradise

Port hours are busy hours. Cargo must be watched, because the crew must do dockers' jobs now, caring for containers and watching out. Things aren't as tricky as they used to be, when cargo was loose and undefended by steel uniformity. The captain remembers all sorts of waywardness in all sorts of ports. There were stevedores who were all kinds of thieves. 'And we were little cadets: how were we supposed to stop them? These huge, grown men? We just said, "No, no, no."' But the stevedores – dockers who work in ship holds – still deliberately dropped the cases of whisky they were carrying, punched holes in the cases and poured the whisky directly into tin mugs they had brought for the purpose. In the Far East, they didn't bother with tin mugs: there, they just took the bottles. London dockers demanded an 'embarrassment tax' for having to unload toilet pans. It was a penny a pan. They got it.

He remembers sweet revenge in Penang, when the cargo being discharged looked like chocolate bars but was laxatives. Of course the stevedores helped themselves, and the crew enjoyed the consequences until they went down in the hold later and had to clean up all the crap. 'The stevedores used to pee and do all sorts down in the cargo hold. Now we've got internal systems, but then you've got no idea.' He describes a thunderbox; a box rigged over the side, simple to use in ports for crew and dockers. In ports, the thunderbox contents could fall directly on the docks, so they used 'shit-boards', chutes rigged from planks that redirected the offending material into the water. It didn't always work, if the shit chute wasn't properly in line. Sometimes it used to land on the quay, and the dockers would go crazy and the crew would have some hilarity. I have seen pictures of on-ship sanitation that was a little better: a toilet in an engine room that was only a toilet with a curtain round it. On ships that the Second World War merchant seaman Frank Laskier sailed on, you expected little and were given less. In his autobiography – in which Laskier barely disguises himself as 'Jack' – he writes of a 'sailors' Gethsemane' that he worked on, where the lavatory was a doorless cubicle in the engine room, and the sanitation itself a simple drain, flushed with a hosepipe if there was water, not flushed if not. 'The smell was terrific and it was the condiment to every meal Jack had on board. The flies were murderous.'

There are no stevedores in *Kendal*'s cargo holds; instead the dockworkers lounge outside smoking cigarettes, standing up every so often to manipulate the twist-locks that pin down the containers in their stacks. Maersk locks are branded with the seven-point star. It is not the dockers' job to safeguard either the cargo or the metal boxes that hold it, so one ship's officer or another is usually running around looking harried, chasing dents and damage, holding a camera for evidentiary purposes. The captain is not to be seen at these times, because port time for him means a stream of visitors to his office: the ship's agent, who looks after the ship's affairs while she is docked; chandlers who supply it; customs people who inspect it; various busybodies who find something to ask, who have some forms to be filled in, who exhaust him with questions. To cheer a captain in port, you just need to arrive without a clipboard. There are few hours for rest for anyone when their ship is alongside.

Telling sea stories is known as swinging the lantern, and the captain's memories of trips ashore swing a wide arc. He supplies every story I expect and hope for: being arrested and shot at in West Africa; throwing soap bars at maidens in the northern Philippines so they would dive down to fetch them under the gaze of dazed lads from North Shields and Plymouth and the Clyde; encountering banana spiders as routine and foot-long millipedes that scared stevedores. He has tales of bar life and sailor towns, probably, but he doesn't share those beyond agreeing that there was wine, women and song, and drink and knives. He would not agree, though, that sailors are the 'Devil in harbour', as they were known by shore people who only ever saw sailors when they were relaxing ashore, mostly alcoholically. The first ever agony aunt, an eighteenth-century bookseller named John Dunton, once advised a woman fearing a lonely spinsterhood to get down to the docks, obviously, and find a sex-starved sailor.

These days, Captain Glenn only goes ashore when strongly persuaded by the chief engineer. The pressure is applied most insistently in Pattaya, the notorious Thai resort near Laem Chabang. The captain sometimes cedes to the persuasion, not because it is Pattaya, but because it is the final port on the loop, and he can relax a little. But the sight of all those old Caucasian men with young Thai girls is disgusting. He doesn't know how the men have the gall to do it, and he doesn't want to be mistaken for one of them, so he only goes ashore every other trip, if that often. The crew may do as they please, though he feels obliged to tell cadets to be careful. I am surprised that he has the chance to do this fatherly stuff with them, when the cadets are usually sprinting down the gangway as soon as we berth. They are 19 years old: wouldn't you? Once, the captain had to report seven of his crew in one day for a freedom bid, when they leapt off the gangway in Hong Kong while the ship was still a metre from the dock, a manoeuvre that looked uncomplicated but risked a nasty squashing death between a ship surging on swells and not yet moored, and the quayside. For that, they were 'logged' in the ship's daily log. That seems a tame discipline, but the powers of a modern captain have become limited, when all manning is controlled by offices in Singapore, Cyprus or Manila. The captain used to be able to fire troublemakers, or anyone who disturbed the harmony of the ship. He had one trip where a sailor got a spike in his arm, and another where a man pulled a colleague out of his bunk with two fingers up his nostrils. If something goes wrong, there is a bo'sun's locker full of wonderful murder weapons: spikes, hammers, clubs. He told the aggressor that his goose was cooked and sacked him. He sounds wistful about this autonomy, long dissolved.

Hardly anyone can manage to get ashore in daylight hours. But Marius has somehow found some time between his morning and evening shifts. He can go ashore.

Marius is a junior officer, but he has been at sea for years and seen hundreds of ports. He has spent two weeks in a Force 11 storm in the Bering Sea, watching his ship roll to a degree that sent all objects flying. He wasn't seasick. That is, he may have been, but the nausea was overpowered by his being unable to sleep. The strongest storm is Force 12, when winds blow at more than 65 nautical miles per hour, the air is filled with spray and visibility seriously affected. On the Beaufort scale, a Force 11 storm is thought to produce seas 37 feet high. This kind of force is what Charles Dickens encountered when he sailed to America. The sailors on his ship called it 'weather':

> And so [the ship] goes on, staggering, heaving, wrestling, leap-
> ing, diving, jumping, pitching, throbbing, rolling, and rocking;

and going through all these movements, sometimes by turns, and sometimes together; until one feels disposed to roar for mercy.

Dickens attracts the attention of a passing steward, who tells him this is but 'rather a heavy sea on, sir, and a headwind'. A headwind? It sounds benign.

> Imagine a human face upon the vessel's prow, with fifteen thousand Sampsons in one bent upon driving her back, and hitting her precisely between the eyes whenever she attempts to advance an inch.

Marius has survived two weeks in an Arctic storm, but he has never been nearer to France than the deck of a ship berthed in one of its ports. He asks shyly if he can come ashore with me, and we head with little foreknowledge to a main square for coffee. This is usual for seafarers: they can't Google for maps or tourist information without the internet, and are reliant on old brochures and word of mouth as guides to all the new places they encounter. When we called at Bremerhaven, the chief engineer went off to find some culture, and at dinner reported that 'it was freezing and everywhere was shut'. Still, he had wandered around for hours, in a cold Sunday town, because it was not the ship, and the people he saw were not his shipmates.

It is not Force 11 nor fifteen thousand Sampsons, but a gale is blowing and tables and chairs are tipping and toppling. Marius looks about him. Is this what France looks like? I look at what he is seeing: a desolate square of concrete, surrounded by brutal concrete buildings, flat and squat. No, Marius. It's what a town obliterated by Second World War bombs looks like. I try to describe Paris, and its narrow shuttered windows and cast-iron balconies; its elegance and softness. I try to describe what France looks like, but it isn't possible in the face of this concrete and gale. Instead we explore. Marius wants to see some Second World War beach defences, so off we walk, a mile along the beach, then up a road, then into some bushes. There is no sign of the defences on the beach. Maybe they are on the other side of the hill. But the bushes are dense, and every so often they produce a lone man, staring out to sea. Marius doesn't ask again if this is what France looks like but I think he is thinking it. Finally I understand where we are when I see a poster for a gay disco. Quick march, Marius. I didn't mean to take a seafarer cruising. Instead, we shop for supplies: coffee and green tea, kilos of fruit; a dozen yogurts. Perishables are likely to run out no matter how good Pinky's calculations. The ship's fruit is already forlorn. Also these will be the last shops for a while, and Pinky hasn't yet understood what 'vegetarian' means. She still offers fish as an option, or bean soup 'with a little meat. Only a little.' It is best to stock up.

We leave Le Havre in evening light. Unusually, the port of Le Havre is attached to its town, so our exit route passes the town beach and windsurfers profiting from the gale, nipping past. See how many we can run down, says someone on the bridge. The windsurfers survive us, and by breakfast we are off Finisterre. The Bay of Biscay defeated Charles Darwin on *Beagle*, and he wondered how on earth he would survive the dreadful seasickness. *Kendal* has passed through with ease.

At the end of breakfast, Mike says, have a good day.

Marius says, another day in paradise.

Mike says, SSDD as the Filipinos say. Same shit, different day.

Actually it is a different day today. There is a new passenger. A pigeon arrived during Igor's watch the night before and now sits, its feathers puffed from cold or nerves, on the starboard window ledge of the wheelhouse. It has a ring on its leg, so it must be a racing pigeon, and I tell Marius about the pigeons of the Second World War who won medals for taking messages to important places. He says, 'I'm going to stick a sticker on it to say it was on the *Maersk Kendal* and it cheated. It didn't fly, it sailed.' The pigeon is an excitement. Really. Even the captain pays the pigeon attention. 'We're 40 miles out so it can't go anywhere. It might get a scent around Lisbon or Gibraltar and try its luck.' He is not hopeful. Already it has a tray of water to drink from and a bowl of bread. Later it will have dried rice, split peas, dried foodstuffs in a variety that means affection. The pigeon also has a name on a leg-tag: 4097430 BELG 2009. In less than 24 hours it has become the ship's mascot, and as such has a long line of antecedents, at least according to *Ships' Cats*, a particular favourite on my shipping bookshelves. Cats suit ships, despite the water. They are self-contained creatures, and find places to hide in. And they eat rats. Every modern ship, still, has rat-guards – plastic collars on the mooring ropes – more to prevent rats climbing off the ship than to stop them climbing on it, a disturbing thought. Cock-roaches also cause bother. They come on board, but there is no food in the walls of the bridge house so they explore until they find some. For this reason Francis is kept busy cleaning crumbs, and food in cabins is discouraged.

Cats also soothe a lonely life: there are plenty of extant pictures of ships' cats snoozing in tiny hammocks fashioned by lonely sailors, even in wartime. Able Seaman Simon, ship's cat on HMS *Amethyst*, still managed to catch five rats a day, even after being wounded in 1949 by shells from Chinese communists on the Yangtze River. He was given the Dickin Medal – awarded to courageous animals – and became a national celebrity. The US Coast Guard preferred dogs. A mongrel puppy adopted in 1938 by the crew of the Coast Guard cutter *Campbell* retired with honours after the war, its rank Chief Petty Officer (K9C), Dog. One wartime cat was named U-Boat.

Cats were banned by the Royal Navy in 1975 for health and hygiene reasons. They ate rats, but they were also dirty. But unexpected animal passengers still give shipping some sought-after positive press. In 2011, the crew of *Skagen Maersk* found that a crab-eating macaque monkey had jumped aboard in Malaysia. A crew member saw the stowaway searching for food near the mess, and the chief engineer paused from running a ship to build a humane trap. Sinbad – of course – now lives in Wales Ape and Monkey Sanctuary along with a Japanese snow monkey called Julie, found wandering the streets of Antwerp. It need not have been a happy ending, a Maersk source tells me. 'The older seafarers said they would just have thrown him overboard. But the younger crew turned him into a pet.' It's sad it takes a pigeon or a monkey for crews to bond. But what else do they have?

Kendal seems like a harmonious ship, but that is due to the captain and happenstance. Nearly two-thirds of ships have more than one nationality on board, but 38 per cent have several. This is not new: ships have always made up numbers from their ports of call. Spanish ships sailed with Greeks, English, Norwegians, Portuguese. Lascars were numerous enough to have their own sailors' homes in foreign ports. Because navies liked to steal crew from merchant ships, merchant crews were re-stocked from passing ports: Portuguese, Greek, Norse, Maltese. That was happenstance globalizing. Today's multinational crews are selected by planners in shore offices in Manila, Mumbai, Singapore. Rumours abound about their choices. They put Ukrainians and Russians together because they will stand each other off, like magnets, and what lies in between will be harmony. Filipinos drink and sometimes fight but they are hard workers. The Chinese are also cheap, and adequate seafarers, but their English is poor. Indians are good officers but are getting to be expensive. Pakistanis cause problems these days in security-sensitive US ports, so that one manning company simply sacked its Pakistani staff. American hostility to seafarers is now regularly cited as a reason why the job has worsened. American ports have been difficult ever since the entry into law of the 2004 International Ship and Port Facility Security Code (ISPS). Although international maritime law specifies that seafarers should be freely allowed some time ashore, the practice is very different. A survey of 230 seafarers' unions and 700,000 seafarers found that more than half had been denied shore leave, particularly in the United States. A survey by the Associated Marine Officers' and Seamen's Union of the Philippines (AMOSUP) found that 70 per cent of its members had been forbidden to go ashore, even though seafarers are far more likely to be victims of crime or terrorism than to perpetrate it.

It is a skill that requires care, this mingling and melding of the world's peoples. For the most part, it works. 'We have found many seafarers who actually prefer mixed nationality crews,' writes the maritime academic Tony Lane. 'After all, a single nationality crew will inevitably be some sort of microcosm of the society from which it is drawn, and might therefore carry within it the conflicts of that society.'

Kendal's officers know what their nationalities mean in the present and the future. The captain says often that he is being used to train his replacements, because British officers are good, but they cost too much. Romanians and Ukrainians are cheaper and also well trained by maritime academies in Odessa and Constanţa. But they are more expensive than Filipinos and Chinese and have already had pay cuts. All the Europeans are gloomy and apprehensive, with reason. In 2009, *Lloyd's List* reported that Maersk had sent a memo headed 'Zero Recruitment in Europe'. The columnist was scathing. 'Famously, there are already more blue whales than there are British seafarers on British ships. The difference is that people are taking conservation measures to save the whale.'

All immigration has waves and changings of guard. There were lascars and now there are Filipinos. But the diminishment of the British and American merchant navies is unprecedented. There is regular fretting about recruitment in the pages of the shipping press. Some British seafarers plan to retire early or move into shore jobs. The captain doesn't want to do that. He can be cold about his job – it is moving giant boxes, and that is that – but the force of his anger about his changed industry conveys something other than coldness. Before the oil crisis in 1973, there were British crews, British labour laws. 'After that they took the companies offshore. They offered us contracts with 30 per cent lower wages, take it or leave it.' The captain won't tell me how much he earns, but it is enough for his house to have grown, for his neighbours to envy him, and for his car to have become a nice Mercedes. Also, British seafarers pay no income tax. On a good ship with a good company, the seafaring life has obvious attractions. The captain of a liquefied natural gas (LNG) tanker controls a multi-million-pound asset and earns accordingly: one told me that he earns $100,000 tax free for six months of sea time.

Kendal's captain's grievances are bigger and deeper. He loves the sea still. Often he comes up to me while I am gazing at the water, just to join in. His complaints are about an industry he once loved and now can't bring himself to. The manning: 20 men to run a ship this size? 'The only thing they can cut down is manpower, wages and victualling.' Fatigue is inevitable. Chris the cadet was up until 2 a.m. the other night doing refuelling, and the next fuel barge arrived at 4 a.m. Marius had three hours' sleep last night, four the night before and three the night before that. Through Suez or Panama, there is no sleep. It is too risky; there is too much to watch out for. The captain can be awake for 36 hours. Staying awake for 24 hours increases the chances of being involved in an accident by seven times. Until 2012, international standards allowed seafarers to work a 98-hour week.

Even then, a study by the Marine Accident and Investigation Branch, looking into the role of fatigue in 1600 accidents, found seafarers actually falsifying papers to show they had only worked 98 hours when actually they had worked more. The new Maritime Labour Convention – known as the Seafarers' Bill of Rights – reduces the maximum work week to 72 hours. That's still twice the maximum recommended in the EU's Working Time Directive. A 2006 study found that half of seafarers worked at least 85 hours a week and one in four had fallen asleep while on watch. That level of fatigue is as dangerous as drinking seven times the legal limit of alcohol. Sixty per cent of shipping accidents are due to human error. When *Exxon Valdez* struck Alaska's Bligh Reef in 1989, spilling 11 million gallons of crude oil, an investigation found that the watch officer had been mostly awake for 18 hours before his shift.

Kendal's captain knows this, but what can he do? He knows, as do maritime academics, that fatigue can be alleviated by a quiet environment and good nutrition, but victualling is a cost that can be more easily cut than fuel or insurance. *Kendal's* officers, confronted by Pinky's offerings on the sideboard buffet, often remember out loud when they had lobster and fresh seafood. Instead, here is a frankfurter stuffed with Cheez Whiz, or a lamb chop speckled with sesame seeds, like mini-maggots. This is nothing, says Marius. 'I've been on ships where you have to stand staring at the food for minutes, wondering what it is.' You can tell how good the food is by how long the crew spend eating it. The average on *Kendal* is six and a half minutes. Pinky is in a thankless position: the ship's cook has been the subject of seafarer humour for centuries. In 1942, a young seaman named Arthur Montaigne was interviewed on a New York radio station. It was the year of the worst losses of ships on the Atlantic, and Montaigne had just returned from there. The interviewer asked him whether he had ever had a chance to be a hero.

Yes, once I saved the whole crew of the *Tuscorora*.
You did? How?
I shot the cook.

Not long ago, Maersk's container fleet was free to fix its own food budget. Captains were trusted to be careful. Now the money per head is $7 and the food goes from adequate to worse. The captain once took photographs of the dishes they were being served – including soup so watery you could see the pattern on the china – and sent them to the office. He sends regular dispatches about it and something is done – for a week or so Pinky doesn't serve chips as the foundation of quite so many meals – but it never lasts.

I think he probably sends dispatches about many things, protected by his position as senior captain and his approaching retirement. Napkins, for example. Flimsy scraps of tissue with solid, powerful significance. Earlier that year, the company had sent out a memo: serviettes were no longer to be used by container ships like *Kendal*, the container line business of Maersk being its least profitable. Until further notice, the officers and crew of the container fleet would be expected to use kitchen roll to dab their lips and mop their crumbs, and this would save the company £30,000 a year. This still sends the captain into a rage. He would never allow kitchen roll at the dinner table at home. 'We're supposed to be officers and gentlemen. We're professionals. And they're treating us like third-class citizens.' Maersk tug crews have serviettes; Maersk shore staff have serviettes: he has checked. Not the Merchant Navy, scum of the earth.

These feelings have nothing to do with the ship. 'When people see my ship, I want to say, what did you think? It's like I want to show off my girlfriend. She's smooth as anything and she looks the business. She's pretty.' He is never this passionate unless he is talking about his Harley-Davidsons or the importance of shaving daily with cut-throat razors, of which he has two on board. Cut-throat razors on a moving ship, and never a nick or cut. That's my captain.

His last ship was a G-class, only 292 metres long to *Kendal's* 300; 32 metres wide to Kendal's 40. She had a sloping stern 'like an old man of war'. He liked the G, but he loves the K-class more. In the corner of his day room is a framed photograph of *Kendal's* godmother. I am flummoxed. Ships have godmothers? What for? 'It's a Danish thing. I'd never heard of it until I came to Maersk. We used to have a woman to break a bottle of champagne but not a godmother.' On the first new ship that he took out from the yard – the privilege of a senior captain – the office emailed a reminder to send the godmother a Christmas card. It is singular, this softness in the middle of a giant company like Maersk, and it is strategic: Tesco is a customer, and *Kendal's* godmother is the Korean wife of a Tesco executive, a Frenchman. Madame takes her duties seriously. There are pictures of her at the naming ceremony in the Korean shipyard that built *Kendal*, and she has given the ship two small effigies of Korean gods for luck. They sit on the corner table between the captain's two sofas, quietly protecting. There are no naming ceremonies now; they cost too much and shipping is suffering. In 2008, shipping entered its worst recession for decades. Recession happens now and then: there was one after the 1973 oil crisis and another in the early 1980s. When times are good, ships are built, then something flattens the market, freight rates drop, and there are too many ships and not enough business. In 2005, time charters – rental rates for tankers – were £47,000 a day. Very Large Crude Carriers (VLCCs) could cost £300,000 per day. Times were excessively good. New shipyards were appearing everywhere, countless new shiny ships. Three years later, day rates had dropped to £4000 or worse: sometimes owners were effectively paying oil companies to shift the oil companies' cargo. Talk to anyone in shipping about this period and they will at some point use the word 'cliff' or 'precipice'. People were going bust. Seafarers were being abandoned on ships that were suddenly cheaper to scrap, and stuck on board for months while they waited for wages that were never paid.

That was one gift of recession. The other was that ships needed to be parked. Before *Kendal*, I visited six Maersk ships tied together in the middle of Loch Striven near Glasgow. Barnes Wallis tested his Dambusters bouncing bombs here. There are still bounced bombs on the bottom of the loch, and in 2009, for nearly a year, there were six blue ships tied up together in its middle. It was a sensible option economically: Maersk had done a deal with Clydeport, which owns the loch, for long-term parking, which was vastly cheaper than £4000 daily berth fees in port. But it was a scientifically risky enterprise. No-one knew then what would happen to ships that were laid up for so long. There is more knowledge now, gained from long-term parking of pirated ships anchored off Somalia. Several have sunk, though whether through failure or for insurance purposes is unclear. Some have steamed into Mombasa or Djibouti followed by sharks attracted to the crustaceans and sea life that had moved to this new, strange artificial reef and liked it enough to stay. On Striven, the engineers had been inventive. All the engine parts were wrapped in cling film, the kind you buy in your local shop and which the engineer had actually bought in the local shop in Rothesay, along with other supplies like fresh water, which boosted local trade and soothed locals who complained of 'rust buckets' coming to spoil their pristine, stunning loch. They were not rust buckets. Five of the six were Maersk B-class, according to the company's internal ship classifying system, and only four years old. They were special, because they had been built for speed, with sleeker lines than other container ships, less cargo space, engine and accommodation decks in the middle of the ship rather than aft, as *Kendal* had. They were fast. Marius once travelled with a B-class through the Straits of Malacca at 32 knots, and other ships were hailing them on the radio saying, 'What is that, a jet engine?' The B-class were intended to do a shuttle route from China to the United States, but as soon as they launched, the price of fuel escalated. They would have cost £22,000 a day to run, and they were the first into lay-up, the fate of new hires. The B-class weren't the first to suffer this indignity. In a way, nothing is ever new in shipping. Pirates come and go; fortunes come and go along with tycoons; and so do grand ideas. Tea clippers were the B-class of their time and were made unemployable by engines. The US shipping company Sea-Land Service, Inc. – now owned by Maersk – had tried the same thing in the 1970s with SL-7 ships. They had a top speed of 33 knots, and their fuel bills wiped out any advantage. They were soon sold to the US Navy, which has more money or braver accountants.

There will be no stops for seven days now. Sea time will cover 5167 nautical miles and will last through the Bay of Biscay, down the edge of Western Europe, around Gibraltar, through the Pillars of Hercules, along the Mediterranean, past Malta, between Libya and Greece, past Egypt and through Suez, through the Red Sea, through pirate waters, into the Gulf of Aden, and round the corner past Yemen to Salalah, a lyrically named port in Oman.

Before I came aboard, people asked me how I would fill my days. They also asked me whether I would be safe. By now, I have stopped locking my cabin door when I leave, and leave it wide open like everyone else. And filling days is easy. They move along, fast. First breakfast and a walk on deck. I am supposed to report to the bridge when I go outside, and to wear a hard hat. But as the days go on my clothing gets less safety conscious. My heavy-toed boots – required for deck activity, according to my leaflet of ship instructions – become trainers or sandals as the weather gets more southern. The hard hat is soon discarded. I have seen jogging corridors on some ships, but there is no running on *Kendal's* deck. The mileage –

four loops to a mile – can be walked only, and the boredom of those loops is leavened by changing directions. One morning forward, the next aft. I wonder at the eccentricities of maritime English. It can't be easy for a non-English speaker to understand 'making sternway' for 'going backwards'. Maritime colleges try to account for this by teaching a dialect known as Maritime English. This dispenses with inessential grammar, so that 'Are there fenders on the berth?' becomes 'Are fenders on berth?' There is also Seaspeak, which requires users to identify what they're going to say before they say it. Hence: 'Question. Are fenders on berth?' Both dialects sounded intriguing, but hardly any seafarer uses them. Broken, pidgin, Filipino: when you're screaming down a radio on a ship rolling 45 degrees each way, any English will do. I wonder about communication when I learn that my unspeaking Burmese table neighbour is the ship's safety officer. His English is poor, but one of his duties is to evacuate a terrifying sinking ship if need be.

There are other miscomprehensions. I tell the captain one morning during sea time that I have been for my morning constitutional. He looks aghast.

'A what?'

'A morning walk.'

'If you say "constitutional" on a ship it means you're going for a crap.'

I often head for the fo'c'sle. It has become my terrace and garden. Unescorted, I am free to lean over the bulbous bow and watch it move water. This doesn't feel like a hazardous activity, but it is. A swell could tip me with ease. Who would know? Francis sailed on a ship where a crew member was killed when he was thrown across the fo'c'sle by a wave. The bridge can't see the fo'c'sle because of containers in its line of sight, and I have no radio. The crew on deck are too busy: there is usually the whining sound of a drill somewhere as one of them chips off the rusted paint to replace it with new. Or they are working in the narrow corridors between containers, or head down splicing ropes. They have no time to look out to sea, and no reason to. A small head in the water would not be seen. Nothing can be heard over the engine and the waves.

The ship needs constant care, an 80,000-ton toddler. It is constantly assaulted by salt, wind and corrosive weather. Shore staff expect the crew to repeatedly blast salt off the metal structure with pressure hoses of fresh water, let it dry, then repaint it. But when can they do that? Only in port or at anchor, and there is never time to let it dry. 'So we paint over the salt,' the captain says, 'and the shore staff say, "You've painted over the salt!" But there is no other way.' Once when they departed freshly painted, the captain had been asked to scatter the ashes of a departed fellow captain, who wanted to be dispersed at sea. The ceremony was done on the poop deck, the ashes were sent out into the wind, and the wind blew them back again onto the fresh paint. They had to chip it all off and scatter the painted ashes. That's not quite as bad as a tale I read in *Flotsametrics*, by the oceanographer Curtis Ebbesmeyer, who flushed the ashes of a deceased oceanographic colleague down the toilet when her friends had got too drunk to sail into the bay and leave her directly in the waters of Puget Sound, as she had asked. 'With heads bowed and hands crossed, we launched Keiko on her journey.' To Seattle's West Point sewage treatment plant.

Off Portugal, on a Sunday. At lunch the usual four remained: Marius, me, Mike and the captain. The talking ones. The conversation turned to entertainment. The captain remembered an organization in his early days that provided the crew with films. 'Back then there were wooden hatches, and the accommodation was amidships. So the officers would project the film out of the officers' saloon onto the canvas that covered the wooden hatches and all the crew would sit on the next hatch and watch the film. That was the monthly entertainment.' On Mike's first ship, he travelled from Constanţa to Victoria, Brazil. Thirty days each way, no stops. They had no kind film-providing association. No TV, no books, only a backgammon set. By the end the winner had over 400 matches on his score.

There are no film screenings now. Why would I watch a film in the saloon, says Marius, genuinely mystified, when I can watch it in my cabin? Instead, they watch DVDs, 'and then we watch them again'. Efforts are still made to fill on-board time with something other than work, but the socializing now is solitary, sad. The captain always travels with two guitars, though I never hear him play them. He reads books, but only fiction and never sea stories. Conrad? No chance. Everyone else retreats to laptops. I unearth the unused backgammon set in the officers' saloon and begin to play Marius daily, with him maintaining throughout a deliberately destabilizing commentary that conveys his level of fatigue better than an academic survey could: not too tired, extremely irritating. Exhausted, he is tolerable.

The Filipinos play computer games and sing. It is common to climb the accommodation house stairs to the faint caterwauling of a Journey song in a Tagalog accent. Perhaps other entertainment happens behind cabin doors too: in a paper entitled 'The Filipino Seafarer: A Life between Sacrifice and Shopping', the Norwegian academic Gunnar Lamvik revealed the alarming practice among Filipino seafarers of slicing open their penis with a razor and implanting ball-bearings or coffee beans. The implants are called *bolitas*, and the logic behind their use is flexible. Either they keep wives from straying by enhancing their sexual pleasure, or they are useful for attracting Brazilian prostitutes. This 'secret weapon of the Filipinos', wrote Lamvik, has something to do with the fact that 'the Filipinos are so small, and the Brazilian women are so big'. Lamvik is told that nearly every Filipino seaman is equipped with *bolitas*. I don't intend to verify that, not even verbally.

Sheep pens on livestock transporter *Danny FII*

4. OPEN SEA

Calves Can Swim

Loss: Propelled merchant ships of not less than 100 gross
tons which have ceased to exist.
—International Maritime Organization

Shipwreck. It seems such an old word that contains old worlds, of
wood and dashing surf; of wreckers who wait with malign patience
on beaches; of things and incidents definitely past. It seems as far
away from *Kendal*, this serene ship, as gaslights and horse carriages.
It is not far away though. Two thousand seafarers die at sea every
year. The International Union of Marine Insurance declared 2006 a
catastrophic year for 'hull claims', for compensation for lost ships.
The following year it was four times worse. Even now, even with all
our efforts and intentions and instruments, more than two ships are
lost a week.

Christmas 2009. The time was late afternoon, the skies were
dark, and *Danny FII*, a livestock carrier arriving from Uruguay, was

a few miles off Lebanon on her way to a port call in Tripoli. She carried 10,224 sheep, 17,932 cows and 83 men. The sheep and cattle were being taken to the Middle East to become meat. *Danny FII* was a modern-day Noah's Ark, going about her business.

Danny FII had not always been a livestock carrier. She began in 1975 as *Don Carlos*, a car transporter. Back then, she was spruce, well kept, the sheer cliff sides of her flanks that are the sign of car carriers – since high sides keep fragile cargo securely enclosed – painted bright green. Her hull was red so that, despite her size, she was almost jaunty. Before she was 20, *Don Carlos* became *Danny FII*, when she was sold to a Singapore company and named after who knows who. In a way it doesn't matter how her new name arose, only that it was changed: name-changing is considered bad luck at sea. A year after that, *Danny FII* was sold to Rachid Fare Enterprises, a livestock transporter. Her paint changed, and so did her flag, once again. In 34 years, she had flown the flags of Sweden, Singapore, Liberia, St. Vincent and the Grenadines. Now she was painted wholly white, and looked grubbier, less tended. The rust was more obvious against the white paint. The air of her had changed.

By 2009, *Danny FII* was operated by Falcon Point International, a Cairo-based company. She flew the flag of Panama, the largest maritime registry in the world, and her crew was mixed: a British captain and electro-technical engineer, an Australian stockman, Uruguayans, Pakistanis, Filipinos and Lebanese. The captain was John Malcolm Milloy, a well-respected and jovial Scot from Campbeltown in Argyll. The electro-technical engineer was another Scot, 50-year-old Alan Atkinson. He was a quiet man, says his identical twin brother Martin, who lives in Prestwick in Ayrshire. Alan had been working at sea for 27 years, and when he came ashore, he liked to build model ships from kits, or play golf. The twins were unmarried and liked to hang out together. Martin was a firefighter, and between them they both thought that Martin had the far more dangerous job.

Alan hadn't really wanted to sail on *Danny FII*. He had started his career on supply vessels, then BP tankers, both of which are known for having the best conditions at sea. The Scottish cadet on *Kendal* talks of working on supply vessels with child-like dreaminess, as if he is a crop sprayer who wants to fly space shuttles. But Alan Atkinson's eyesight had deteriorated, he failed a medical and so was no longer accepted for work on tankers or supply ships. Ferries and livestock transporters had less exacting standards, so he applied to Stena Lines, his first choice, and for *Danny FII*, his second. The offer from *Danny FII* came first and he accepted it. The next day Stena wrote too with an offer but he didn't think it was right to go back on himself. He would go to sea on the livestock carrier, to work in a sector of shipping that he knew nothing about. Possibly he was seduced by the friendly email sent by Falcon Point's head of shipping, Captain Richard Thomas. 'I must say,' wrote Thomas, 'you will find the livestock trade extremely interesting. Best job I ever had at sea and I have been on all sorts of ships in my time.'

On 26 October 2009 Martin Atkinson took his twin to Glasgow airport to catch a flight to Beirut. He presumes that is where Alan was picking up the ship, but he didn't ask and Alan didn't tell. *Danny FII* did a regular run between South America and the Middle East, usually from Montevideo to Beirut, or to Tartous in Syria or Sokhna in Egypt. Six people were listed on the manifest as passengers, including a 35-year-old Uruguayan, Nicolás Achard, but this was a fiction. Nicolás was a veterinarian, and that is the job he had been hired to do. He now thinks that listing him as a passenger, along with two other Uruguayans also working on the ship, meant that they didn't have to go through health and safety training. Some crew couldn't swim, including 19-year-old Guillermo, another Uruguayan. Some were veterans, such as the popular captain, and the head stockman, Gary Baker, an Australian who had been going to sea for years. They were both big, friendly men, serious on the job but fond of a joke. Baker once managed to convince the captain's wife that koalas were fish.

Snapshots from previous trips show on-board life that looked fine, even fun. There were barbecues on the open deck, and European-looking men in shorts and short-sleeved shirts mingling with smaller, wiry, older men in kurta pyjama. That is more group socializing than I ever see on *Kendal*. There are shots of the ship on a glittering, benign blue sea, and another of a wall-map showing *Danny FII*'s route marked with dots of Blu-Tack. A no-frills ship, an ordinary journey, no trouble expected. 'I am sure,' wrote Captain Thomas to Alan Atkinson, 'that you will thoroughly enjoy yourself.'

I wonder. Welfare organizations dislike livestock carriers profoundly, and with reason. (So do Somali pirates: they have captured then released a few livestock carriers without asking for ransom. Too much hassle.) The welfare groups criticize the overcrowded conditions, the lack of food and water, the inadequate bedding for the beasts. They point to countless reports of swine, sheep or cattle being crushed on their journey and think that shipping frozen meat would be more humane. The Australian Royal Society for the Protection of Animals says that every year 40,000 cattle and sheep die while being transported from Australia. It keeps a casualty list: 1683 sheep and 6 cattle died during a 2006 sea voyage on *Al Messilah* because of heat and failure to eat. Six thousand sheep were stranded at sea for three months in 2003 when their Saudi Arabian importer rejected them. When another buyer could not be found, the sheep were bought by the Australian government and given free to Eritrea. In 2002, 6119 sheep died in high temperatures on four ships. One, *Al Shuwaikh*, was then allowed to load more sheep, and 2304 of those died too. Live meat traders, as livestock transporters are known, dismiss such statistics. 'What these loony lefties fail to understand,' wrote a contributor in *Meat Trade News Daily*, 'is the fact that the animals are better off on the vessels running with food and water, than they are in the drought-stricken outback of Australia.'

Alan phoned his parents now and then from the ship's satellite phone, but he never expressed any grave concerns. There was dirty water in the taps. There were cockroaches, but that was to be expected with so many animals. Otherwise he didn't complain. Probably he didn't want to worry them. They were elderly and knew nothing of life at sea beyond what he told them. As children do, Alan edited what he told them, although the conditions must have been hard for a man used to the sleeker environments of tankers and supply ships. Nicolás Achard describes conditions as 'horrible'. He was working mostly with the animals, whose pens were on decks below sea level. Although she had passed the safety inspections required by Panama, the flag state, *Danny FII* by many accounts was rusting, old, decrepit. The decks were in such a bad state that regularly the floor would cave in and the leg of a heifer would appear from the deck above, an inch from Nicolás' head. He was used to working in the open with animals on Uruguayan ranches; he didn't much like this confined, cramped, noisy, smelly ship, but he needed the money.

The journey from Montevideo to Lebanon took three weeks with no land calls. On 16 December, the crew watched *Titanic* together. The following day, they prepared the ship for port. After so many days at sea, the animals had made a colossal amount of mess. Nicolás remembers that they stopped about 13 miles off Tripoli. He isn't sure about the sequence of events, but thinks that a storm came, and that the captain thought it was a good opportunity to clean up. This seems an odd decision from such an experienced captain. Perhaps they were already cleaning and the storm came. The usual cleansing method is to tip the ship slightly and hose the muck into the sea. But all weight on ships, whether ballast water, cargo or animals, must be carefully distributed to maintain stability. Some of the weight on *Danny FII* was animal feed, stored on the lower decks, but after three weeks the volume had depleted. For Nicolás, this meant that the ship was by now unavoidably unstable. When the ship tilted slightly to let the water and dirt off into the sea, the balance was skewed. Not only that, but the animals moved too, destabilizing it further. The cows weighed an average of 350 kilograms each and the sheep 50 kilograms: that makes up a lot of weight to suddenly shift. Perhaps the discharge of the manure, the movement of the animals, and the waves all came together to overcome the ship. On deck 2, working with a couple of colleagues, Nicolás began to hear 'weird sounds'. It was livestock on the decks above falling over. With his crewmates, he headed up to deck 6, above the water line. There, they could see that the ship was tilting far more than it should be. It looked drunk. More crew gathered and looked worried together. Then everything got worse very quickly.

Nicolás went up to deck 13 and found a lifejacket. The boat's list was too much for them to launch the enclosed lifeboats that *Danny FII* carried: one side of the ship was too near the water, the other too high and too tilted. Nicolás looked for life rafts – self-inflating dinghies that can be tossed into the sea by hand – but saw none nearby, and they could all see that the ship was sinking quickly. Ahmad Harb, a Lebanese crew member, remembered that the captain sounded the alarm. 'He knew that the ship was gone and that we were already in the disaster stage.' Harb was still on a deck beneath the water line. The captain made an announcement that everyone should make their way up to open decks, but it was too difficult. The angle of the ship made walking up the stairs 'like walking up a wall'. Harb was stunned by the speed and extent of the disaster. 'We could not believe what was happening, we believed in our ship.' The weather was bad, but the weather had been bad before. 'We had survived much worse conditions. It is a mighty ship.' Shocked, trapped, he began to recite his prayers.

On deck 13, the Uruguayans knew they had to jump. They were in work clothes – overalls, heavy boots – and Nicolás told the non-swimmer Guillermo to remove his boots. They would only weigh him down. They 'fell into the sea', a three-metre descent. 'Then we just sat and watched the thing disappear.' Nicolás describes *Danny FII* as sinking 'like the *Titanic*', but that sinking had taken almost three hours. *Danny FII* disappeared in 20 minutes, and became the 37th ship to sink that year.

In the water, Nicolàs saw that someone had managed to chuck a life raft into the sea and that it was 100 metres away, so he swam for it, front crawl. But he found it unexpectedly difficult to make progress. There were huge waves, and later he learned that when you are wearing a lifejacket it is easier to swim on your back. There were cattle in the water. Pounding waves, darkness, people screaming, howling and thrashing beasts everywhere: it sounds like a section of hell that Dante forgot to include. Nicolàs saw a Pakistani crewmate holding on to the tail of a heifer as a flotation device. Ahmad Harb saw this too. He found it as astonishing as the fact that calves can swim. 'A person should know that what is destined to happen will happen,' he said. 'If a person is to live, he will live, and the reason could be a calf!' The man lived, reaching shore at Akkar with his cow-shaped lifebelt.

After about half an hour in the water, Nicolás reached a life raft. He was in a pitiful state by now. He had ingested oil and 'all the other crap' a sinking ship vomits up as it founders. There was oil on his skin, in his throat. The raft he found was full of frozen water, but it had flares, so he threw one up, then another that fell back into the dinghy and almost punctured it. He was an hour on the raft, alone. He heard screaming from another dinghy 100 metres away which had 20 men in it, including a Uruguayan friend, Ruben. Ruben called to him. Nico, Nico, come! He wanted the extra space in Nicolás' raft, but it was so full of ice, it was a deadweight and

Nicolás couldn't shift it. After a while he saw a half-dead Filipino man float past and pulled him into the raft. All the while, they could hear people screaming, and the open dinghy was being thrown around by the storm waves: up three metres, up and up, and then bang, it would fall again 'into the whole of the sea and you couldn't see anything again'.

Nicolás is sure that Alan Atkinson made it into a raft. He remembers seeing him. They were many on board, but they had spent enough time together to know who was who. After three hours the first rescue ship arrived. Nicolás and the Filipino waved and screamed, but everyone was screaming, and their gestures were hidden by the huge waves. Another ship arrived, possibly a car carrier. Nicolás calls it 'a gigantic boat'. He says, 'The gigantic boat went into the area of the sinking to save people. The only problem was that it was so big, instead of rescuing them it ran over them. Then it went away.'

After eight hours, Nicolás and his companion were rescued by an Italian naval vessel that flew a UN flag. Others were picked up by Lebanese naval vessels. A Royal Navy helicopter had also arrived from Cyprus to assist. The Italians gave their guests good and immediate medical attention, thermal clothing, food and hot-water baths, then sent them by helicopter to Tripoli. There, the ship's managers paid for a hotel, but most survivors had arrived with no possessions beyond rubber boots given to them by their Italian rescuers. Luckily the Uruguayan ambassador provided his citizens with clothes, enough for them to donate some to their Pakistani and Filipino shipmates, whose embassies gave them nothing. Only on the last day of their time ashore did Falcon Point International, the owners, provide a pair of trousers and socks and shoes for each survivor. Forty-three men returned from the foundering of *Danny FII*. Alan Atkinson, Gary Baker and Captain John Milloy did not.

*

There are tales and rumours about the sinking of *Danny FII*. Ahmad Harb said that when the ship started tilting, Gary Baker 'stood in the middle of the ship and lit a cigarette. I looked at him, but he just waved with his hand saying that he doesn't care any more, he wanted to go down with the ship.' As for Captain Milloy, Nicolás Achard had a second-hand story from the Filipino second mate, who had approached the captain and offered him a lifejacket but Captain Milloy refused. He said, 'No, I am staying here until the end.' Ahmad Harb thought he was injured. 'I heard the captain calling mayday. He recited the complete distress call, and said that we are 13 miles away from Tripoli port. This is where the captain went into silence, his voice disappeared, and I think that he got hurt.'

In a poignant video tribute to his father, Owen Milloy called his dad 'amazing' because he saved so many lives. He showed a box of mementoes: photos, certificates, memories. He held up the watch that his dad wore 'for about 15 years', and which was found when his body was recovered, the day after the sinking. They had to cut it off him, said Owen, but he was glad to have it.

He sounded so proud of his dad. The ship's captain, going down with his ship. It seems such an old-fashioned heroism, one that belongs in the nineteenth century with shipwrecks and flogging, until something happens that proves we still expect our captains to be heroes. In 2011, Italian cruise-ship captain Francesco Schettino was widely and violently vilified for leaving the cruise ship *Costa Concordia* when there were still hundreds of passengers aboard. Not only had he not stayed on his ship, let alone not gone down with it, but he had fled with indecent haste (and done so by 'falling into a lifeboat'). Perfidious captains are remembered: when the cruise liner *Oceanos* foundered off South Africa in 1991, its captain Yiannis Avranas was among the first to depart the sinking ship. Afterwards, he was not apologetic. 'When I give the order abandon ship, it doesn't matter what time I leave. If some people want to stay, they can stay.' Two hundred and twenty-five passengers were left on board after the lifeboats had been launched. Their rescue was co-ordinated not by a crew member, but by the the ship's entertainer. When Moss Hills, having managed to call the coastguard from the bridge, was asked to identify his rank, he replied, 'I'm not a rank, I'm a guitarist.' This is a curious thing about ships: when something goes wrong, every staff member must become a safety expert, even if usually they paint nails or dance twice-nightly in a show.

On 18 December 2009, police came to the Atkinson house in Ayr-shire. They told Alan's parents – Fergus, 85, and Rebecca, 81 – that the ship was in trouble and that a search-and-rescue operation was happening. That was 24 hours after the ship had gone down. The police assured the Atkinsons that everyone was on life rafts. It was the worst thing that could have been said to Alan's mother, because she hoped for months afterwards that it was true. At the Milloy house nearby, the family – two sons and the captain's wife – had been told the same thing. That night, Owen said, it was hard to sleep. 'I just kept tossing and turning, thinking, what if, is he dead, is he alive, he could be in a boat somewhere, a lifeboat. It was painful.' The next day there were news reports. Some said his dad was dead; some said he simply hadn't been found yet. Owen didn't know what to believe. 'I thought, this is horrible. Getting told the story before the police have been told anything? It's fricking disgraceful.' It wasn't until later that day that confirmation came. Captain John Milloy, found dead.

For three days after the police visit, the Atkinsons were given updates by the UK Foreign and Commonwealth Office (FCO) and Falcon Point International, the ship's owner. The information was always the same: the sea conditions were terrible. It was difficult. The animals in the water were making it even more difficult to see survivors in the storm conditions. But the search and rescue was still going on.

Later, the shipping agent's representative came to the funeral of Captain Milloy. On the way back he visited the Atkinsons. He said bodies were turning up in Turkey, Syria, all up and down the coast. He wanted DNA. That's easy, said Martin, because he was an identical twin and was willing to donate. He told this to the FCO, again and again, but nothing happened until February, when he gave a blood sample at the doctor's, and the Turkish authorities rejected it because 'it wasn't in the right format'. By then the bodies washing up had increased threefold. On 25 January, Ethiopian Airlines flight 409, intending to fly to Addis Ababa from Beirut, had crashed into the sea after takeoff, 12 miles south of the airport. Ninety passengers and crew died. More bodies washing ashore, more confusion. I read the press reports about the crash and learn two things: that the wife of the French ambassador to Lebanon died in the crash, and that the Lebanese Transport Minister immediately began an investigation. Why didn't he do that for *Danny FII*? Because he couldn't. It sank in international waters. Its flag made it a tragedy belonging to Panama, even though it carried Lebanese crew. This was a shock for Martin. He was used to the possibility of fatalities in his firefighting job. He knew that if anyone lost a life there would be an immediate investigation. He expected the same would happen for his brother's workplace, but he was wrong. Legally, Alan worked on a small part of Panama, floating in no-man's sea. If Panama didn't want to release the results of its investigation, there was nothing Martin could do about it, and nowhere he could go to protest.

In the early 1920s, two American cruise lines were faced with a difficulty. They wanted to serve alcohol on their ships, but it was the time of Prohibition. Their ships flew a US flag, and according to maritime law, this meant they were governed by US laws no matter where they sailed. They were, as ships have been for centuries, a floating chunk of the nation state, even in the *mare liberum* of the high seas. A nation issued flags, kept a register of its ships, and offered sovereign protection and oversight. That was the deal. It was a flexible one: ships could run up a different flag if it was politically or geographically convenient, if they found themselves in the wrong place during an inconvenient war. After the Second World War, Greeks and Italians bought the ships that had been built for war and were now surplus, and realized they could avoid taxes, crew salary standards and draining union requirements by flagging their ships 'out'. The 'out' was Panama, and then Liberia, a West African state with strong US links, and which used the US dollar as currency, considered itself Little America and did what the United States bid. American business interests were behind Liberia's new flag registry, because they thought Panama too corrupt, however convenient. Honduras and Costa Rica followed, and then the rest of the world. Why not? For a nation, an open registry brings welcome income and can require little work. Today, 68 per cent of ships fly a flag that does not belong to the country their owner is from or resident in. Those two American cruise lines started a practice which has dramatically changed international shipping as much as the box.

The people who run open registries detest the term 'flag of convenience', a phrase devised by the International Transport Federation in 1948, when it launched an ongoing campaign against the practice. But there is no doubt that convenience is something an open registry offers in abundance. If you flag your ship out, you will be able to register your ship with any nation you please, despite not being a citizen of that country. This can be done quickly and easily, sometimes within 24 hours and by email; your crew can be chosen from anywhere; you pay lower taxes; and there are fewer labour restrictions or pesky union diktats. All these things are the accepted attractions of a flag of convenience, and they add up to an unbeatably good deal for ship owners in a competitive industry. In 2011, the US Department of Transport compared the costs of running a foreign-flagged and a US-flagged ship. Because of labour laws, wage requirements and other red tape, it cost 2.7 times more to run an American-flagged ship. Manning costs – because American crew were mandatory – were 5.3 times higher. Flagging out an American ship can save millions. It is a brave or rich ship owner who resists.

The Law of the Sea attempts to counter this by requiring that a ship have a 'genuine link' with its flag nation. Debates have raged for years over what this requirement consists of: company premises in the flag state, perhaps, or an annual report. It does not mean that the flag registry must be located in the state that owns the flag. Liberia may have a Liberia International Shipping Corporate Registry football team based in Monrovia (it changed its name from Barcelona FC in 1990), but the registry itself is run from Vienna, in Virginia, USA. The nearest most Liberians get to the entity that brings their profoundly impoverished country millions of dollars a year is a day out watching football. Kiribati, a tiny Pacific island that set up a registry in 2010, chose the Singapore-based Sovereign Ventures as an administrator, despite the company having previously run Cambodia's flag, flown by ships found to have trafficked cocaine and weapons and people.

Port state control is supposed to be another regulatory brake on open registries. Various port authorities now issue a White List, comprising flags judged to be responsible, and a Black List of ones that are not. The Paris Memorandum of Understanding, an association of European port authorities, included Liberia and Panama on its latest White List, as it has done for years. In the depths of the Black List, as you'd expect, swim North Korea, Libya, Sierra Leone and Montenegro. The principle behind these lists is sound: port authorities have the power to detain unsafe ships in their ports. They home in on ships flagged to Black List countries, regularly detaining the rust buckets and unsafe ones, so that it becomes more trouble than it's worth – and too expensive, because of detention fees and lost income – to flag to Black List states. Academics call this a 'race to the middle', whereby the pressures of repeated detentions push bad flags to get better. It happened to the Marshall Islands, a lax and dodgy registry when it began, but now respectable and respected.

Anyway, registry spokespeople say, the distinction between good and bad open registries is mistaken. Plenty of national flags that don't qualify as convenient ones have poorer standards than the White List. Liberia's general counsel, Brad Berman, wrote that Liberia, despite its desperate development statistics and GDP, 'mandates that its registry is more than a small office manned by a clerk and a pet dog trained to carry registry documents to the local post office'. Liberia is certainly no longer in the dark time of the war criminal and former president Charles Taylor, who diverted flag registry income for his personal use, that is, for funding rebels in neighbouring Sierra Leone. Rebels like Issa Sesay, whom I met inadvertently one evening in the Rwandan prison where he is serving a 50-year sentence; we had a polite conversation about his chicken supper before I realized I was talking to a man whose troops had amputated the arms and legs of babies, children, anyone. Then I hoped the chicken choked him.

Most ship owners operate decent ships that are safe, and pay their crews properly. But if you are unscrupulous, there is no better place to hide than behind a flag. The ITF calls flags of convenience a 'corporate veil'. *The Economist*, a supporter of free markets, and so surely a supporter of this freest market of all, calls them 'cat's cradles of ownership structures'. I call them a back door, easy to slip through if necessary. This facility was best exposed by the oil tanker *Erika*, which broke up off the coast of Brittany in 1999, polluting 250 miles of French coastline. The tanker had been chartered by French oil giant Total, but its owner was unknown. As expected, French authorities immediately began an investigation to track him or her down. They first found a company named Tevere Shipping based in Malta. But Tevere Shipping had outsourced *Erika*'s management to a company named Panship Management and Services, based in Ravenna, Italy. Panship had chartered the ship to Selmont International, registered in the offshore haven of Nassau, which was represented by Amarship of Lugano, Switzerland. Thirty per cent of Tevere Shipping's capital was owned by Agosta Investments Corporation of Monrovia, Liberia. It goes on and on, a dizzying Russian doll of ownership. By the end, French investigators found 12 shell companies standing between the ship and its 'beneficial owner'. Many of the companies were a brass plate in a Maltese or Monrovian street, but that brass plate can act as a mighty drawbridge, hauled up, when flag states provide such anonymity. All the power of the French judicial investigators could go no further. When *Erika*'s owner finally came forward weeks later – he claimed he had been skiing and had not realized he now owned an environmental catastrophe – he was revealed as a London-based Neapolitan, Giuseppe Savarese. The BBC reporter Tom Mangold later asked Savarese why his ship's ownership structure was so complex. I only read the transcript of the interview, but I can hear the shrug in Savarese's voice. 'That is normal in shipping.'

Total, Savarese and RINA, the Italian classification society that had certified the ship as seaworthy, were convicted of moral and environmental damage by a French court in 2008. An appeal two years later upheld the decision in a devastating 487-page ruling that is one of the best autopsies not only of a ship but also of the shady practices of some ship owners, including Savarese. He was found to have knowingly skimped on the quality of steel used to repair *Erika* (although RINA still classed it safe). The striking thing for investigators was not just the complexity of the ownership structure, but how easy it was to put in place. A report by the Organisation for Economic Co-operation and Development (OECD) found anonymity of ownership to be a feature in many flag states, including Liberia, Hong Kong, Cyprus, the Marshall Islands and 28 others. Sometimes, such as in Liberia, this was due to corporate rules in the nation rather than the registry. Usually anonymity is sold as an attraction. All this amounts to what the report called 'a multi-layered approach' and a 'cloaking device'. Total has already paid out nearly €200 million to injured parties, including the French state, environmental groups and Monsieur Cormier, a boat taxi operator who abandoned tourism after the spill; or Monsieur Lambion, who could not work as a fisherman for three months and was given €1500 for moral damage. The flag state of Malta, which had overall responsibility for *Erika*'s seaworthiness, pleaded diplomatic immunity.

Erika had passed all the required safety checks. Yet still she was corroded and poorly repaired, and her hull came apart at sea. I once wrote about *Erika* in a newspaper and was invited to lunch at Lloyd's Register, in an elegant building in London that presents a Georgian façade to the street, and hides behind it a modern building of glass and steel. This is the headquarters of a business that began in 1688 in a coffee house in Lombard Street, when Edward Lloyd began providing the shipping news along with coffee. Now Lloyd's has a staff of 8500, offices in 78 countries and a turnover of $1 billion. It also has a fine boardroom and good food, over which I was politely educated out of my mistaken views. *Erika* happened, but North Sea rigs make serious oil and gas spills about once a week and get away with little scrutiny. *Erika* happened, but much has changed since: the EU has tightened all sorts of safety requirements and regulations. Checks and balances have been strengthened and improved. *Erika* will not happen again, and anyway, *Erika* was only one ship among the 100,000 or so at sea on any given day going about their business safely, securely and vitally. My hosts were courteous. They offered to help my research in any way possible, and kept their promise. They were persuasive.

Yet there are numbers to puncture that persuasion. In 2001, 63 per cent of all ship losses at sea were registered to only 13 flags of convenience. The five worst performers were Panama, Cyprus, St. Vincent, Cambodia and Malta. Matters had slightly improved in 2009: only 58 per cent of ships lost at sea belonged to 13 flags of convenience. There are suspect registries that are not classed as flags of convenience by the ITF, such as Sierra Leone. Include those, and 70 per cent of all ships lost are flagged out. The top four registries according to tonnage lost are Panama, Liberia, Sierra Leone and Mongolia.

For months, Martin Atkinson didn't know where his brother was. There was no body for his family to mourn. Frustrated, Martin mastered the internet, and found the site *www.uglyships.com*. This, oddly, was where relatives and survivors of *Danny FII* left messages of support for each other. This was where someone unknown left several messages saying that he knew for sure that eleven missing Pakistani crew members were being detained by the Israeli Defense Forces. And he was believed: for months, I received emails from a Pakistani man named Ali, whose father worked on *Danny FII* and had not come home. Ali's English was not fluent, and his emails sometimes read like hallucinations, but they were haunting. He wrote that 'accident is old for world'. He said that he was convinced his father was being held by Israelis. There was room for him to believe that when there was no official report to tell him otherwise. His father was old, a handicap on a sinking ship, where strength is as useful as luck. He almost certainly went down with the ship along with Captain Milloy and Gary Baker. Ali wrote that the Pakistani government had offered no support, and nor had the shipping company. He wrote, 'this world are door close for the missing crew and families'.

Martin learned that bodies were still being washed ashore. He kept phoning the FCO: are the bodies from *Danny FII*? From Flight

409? He researched survival rates: the water temperature was 18 degrees, which is half normal body temperature, which means Alan would have lost his body heat quickly. He thought there was a chance his brother had survived, but it was small. In fact, Alan's body had been found on the day the airliner crashed – 25 January – in Samandağ, Turkey. It had been classed as unidentified and was buried in March. By the time Strathclyde Police eventually enabled Martin to give a DNA sample in an acceptable format, it was May. The DNA was matched, the body was exhumed and then flown home, and it arrived in a sealed lead coffin. 'There was no way we could have had an open coffin,' said Martin. 'So that's what we got back.' His twin brother had been in the sea for a month and six days, through Christmas, through New Year, through all that waiting and hoping for a mythical life raft, for another miraculous open boat. Then his parents died, one after the other, within two weeks of Alan's funeral. Their death certificates list a physiological cause, but Martin is sure it was grief. He had no-one left, and still no clarity into this massive tragedy that had descended on the family. He didn't know whether his twin had died from hypothermia, drowning or trauma. How had his brother died 13 miles from shore, on a ship provided with safety equipment, when there were rescue vessels and helicopters and the might of several states searching and rescuing? He wanted answers, but whom should he ask?

He began to do his own research. He learned, slowly, about flag states and how shipping works, and understood that his brother had been a Panamanian subject, really, while he was at work, however inconceivable a notion that was to a firefighter with his feet on the ground and never at sea. He wrote to his MP and to the Prime Minister. He kept contacting the FCO. He wrote to the Panama Maritime Authority via its website. He had no reason to doubt that Panama would immediately and comprehensively investigate his brother's death, and explain why a ship classed as safe had sunk.

He looked on the website and saw the headquarters of the Panama Maritime Authority, an imposing office building in Panama City. He followed the links – with difficulty, as most of the English-language site of the world's largest shipping fleet is still filled with dummy text – to a list of casualty reports. There was nothing on *Danny FII*, all the way through 2010, then all through the next year, then the next. For three years, all his enquiries got nowhere. Other interested parties were also trying to get answers, from the FCO to Nautilus International, the UK seafarers' union of which Captain Milloy had been a member. Still nothing appeared, because there was nothing to oblige Panama to do anything.

The procedure that should follow a marine casualty is clearly laid out by the United Nations Convention on the Law of the Sea (UNCLOS), the International Convention for the Safety of Life at Sea (SOLAS) and the International Convention for the Prevention of Pollution from Ships (MARPOL), all the major instruments of international maritime law. All specify that flag states should carry out prompt investigations into any accident involving loss of life. MARPOL is the most insistent, requiring a report of an incident involving harmful substances to be 'made without delay to the fullest extent possible'. The European Union has more stringent legislations governing casualties within EU waters, but *Danny FII* was not European. Martin appealed to the FCO, but *Danny FII* was not British. There is no higher authority that Martin Atkinson can call on to force Panama to release a report.

Knowledge would be a comfort, but he has only competing stories and theories. Were there animals in the water? Nicolás Achard and Ahmad Harb say there were; the FCO says there were not. Was there a wash-down? Nicolás says there was; Kathleen Baker, daughter of Greg and a former employee on *Danny FII*, told Martin there was no way the captain would have authorized a wash-down in storm conditions. Martin reads what he can, even in Spanish, in

Uruguayan newspapers that report crew members jumping into the sea holding on to a table. 'Modern safety!' says Martin. 'OK, they lost a ship, but they should have been better prepared. They had nothing going for them.' He is a calmly spoken man, but his anger is effective when quiet. 'Everyone I talk to says, oh, what do you expect with Panama? They say it's a get-out for lower standards. It seems to me it's such a casual thing that they expect so many people to die on ships. If it had been aeroplane safety something would have been done about it.'

Behind the scenes, there has been no lack of pressure on Panama. Diplomatic approaches, union pressure. I spent a year writing to and phoning the flag state, its ambassador, and had no answer. I tried back doors, industry associations that Panama belonged to, other more reputable flag registries who might find Panama's behaviour embarrassing. The director of one registry responded with frustration. 'Many of us have struggled unsuccessfully to put some teeth into the international regulatory process that supposedly mandates prompt publication of flag-state casualty investigations.' He said Panama was one of the worst offenders at lax publication and investigation (the *Economist* calls Panama 'delinquent'). Publicity, the director continued, was the best disinfectant until something stronger was in place. 'Naming and shaming is the best tool we have.'

Nicolás Achard now works ashore and plans on staying there. He has just married and wants to stay home, although he took one more trip on a livestock carrier to blow away the ghosts and the fear. 'I was scared and freaking out, but I had to do it.' He and other Uruguayans are suing the agency that employed them, the Uruguayan Agencia Schandy, for the loss of their personal possessions. They are doing that because Schandy never bothered to contact them after they got home. 'We would never have gone into litigation. But they never showed their faces and they behaved badly. All the companies claim they have no responsibility.'

Martin has concluded that life must be cheaper at sea. 'There's something like two thousand people a year getting killed at sea but it's not grabbing anyone's attention. Once you're outside the 12-mile limit, you do your own thing.' He knows this now but still he checks his computer daily for a sign that Panama will finally tell him whether his brother's death was due to accident, chance or neglect that should have been picked up by the flag state. Ali still emails me regularly for news of his father, as if I can help where no-one else will. They are two men adrift.

The Suez Canal: 100 miles long and worth £3 billion a year

5.   SEA AND SUEZ

A Ditch in a Desert

We have turned the bottom corner of Europe, passing through the narrow passage in front of Gibraltar that was a favourite hunting spot in the Second World War for U-boat packs that waited there to pick off merchant convoys. In the 12 miles of territorial waters wrecks are marked; in international seas they are not. The United Nations Educational, Scientific and Cultural Organization (UNESCO) estimates – because it can't do any more than that – that throughout the oceans there are three million ships or bits of ships on the seabed, beached or abandoned. They are common obstacles but also common treasure: diving companies can easily buy access to sunken merchant ships, even ones containing wartime dead. They are not automatically protected by war graves legislation, although naval vessels are. In 2006, two daughters of a British man who died on SS *Storaa*, sunk in 1943 with a cargo of pig iron, steel slabs and tank tracks, fought up to the High Court to have their father's wreck declared a military war grave, and to keep it safe from recreational divers and treasure hunters, from underwater desecrators and busy-bodies. Its salvage rights had been sold to a John Short for £150 in 1985, despite it sinking with 22 men.

These are sad seas in other ways. South of Sicily the captain tells me to look out for dolphins and flying fish, but I am also watching for small boats filled with desperate African migrants, because this is where you find them, if they are found. It is not in the captain's interest for me to spot any, because he would feel honour obliged to attend to them. This is not always the case: when a boat filled with 72 people escaping the war in Libya and problems elsewhere ran out of fuel, a NATO ship failed to rescue it. A helicopter dropped water then flew away, although women were holding up their babies in offering. 'The helicopter did not save us,' said a survivor. 'Are we not human beings?' In 2009, a boat attempting the same passage from Africa to Europe was not picked up by Maltese authorities who spotted it, although passengers were clearly emaciated after 20 days adrift. Only five out of dozens survived. Navi Pillay, the UN Commissioner for Human Rights, in language as angry as a diplomat is allowed to use, said afterwards that 'human beings adrift at sea are not toxic cargo'. As usual, when I read a story about something that happens at sea, I wonder how many multiplications of the incident you would need to make to get the true figure of what happens in the wild place out of sight.

Even for me, delighting in landlessness, seven days without a port is a stretch. There is television, suddenly, as we near Sicily, but it is Italian and dreadful. I have been ignoring the invitations of engineers for days but it is time to go below. Mike, the second engineer, is becoming insulted. For days now our dining conversations have spanned the tasteless sadness of modern vegetables (and the beauty of his garden tomatoes in Romania, so large, so fresh), and the daily offer of a tour of his engine room. I can't postpone it any more, and besides, I want to see the sewage system. Down to Upper Deck, then, and through the door marked 'Beware: when engine fans are running, this door bites'. Mike seems delighted to have a guest to break up the noise, yellow light and constant beeping, pinging alarms that fill his engine-room world. They have been filling mine too: the last supernumerary was a visiting engineer, so for weeks the alarm panel in my room has continued to beep about such emergencies as a disturbed oily waste separator or a bilge pump in distress.

Mike offers tea and earplugs: he has a drawer full of them. Most engineers double-plug their ears with foam inserts and then ear defenders because the engines are three decks high and produce more noise than I have ever heard. They also make appalling heat. Sometimes the engine-room temperature reaches 50 degrees Celsius, yet the men still work in boiler suits. The maximum temperature in which engineers are allowed to work, according to Mike, is 'until they keel over'.

He is proud of his machines. 'Think how much cargo they have to push through water. This ship is a small island. There is enough power here to power a small town.' He does some calculations and watches approvingly as I take notes. The engine produces 51,480 kilowatts, which is 80,000 hp. This is equivalent to 1000 family saloons or 80 Formula One cars. Maximum engine power can create a speed of 25 knots, which on land would be 28 mph. At that speed, it would take us several miles to stop. All this power requires 260 tons of heavy fuel oil a day which, at current prices, costs between £18,000 and £33,000 depending on market movements. For this reason, we are only going at 14 knots, slower than an 1850s tea clipper, which could make 17 knots without all this fury and fuel. There is a term for this, and it is not 'backwards'. 'Slow steaming' is now common practice. Travelling more slowly through water reduces drag and friction and cuts down on fuel. So it saves money. It could also help to heal the planet.

*

Compared with planes and trucks, ships are the greenest form of mass transport. Shipping contributes 11 grams of CO_2 per ton per mile, a tenth of what trucks produce. Air freight flies way ahead, emitting 1193 grams per ton-mile. Sending a container from Shanghai to Le Havre emits fewer greenhouse gases than the truck that takes the container to Lyon. The Natural Resources Defence Council calculated the emissions involved in the journey of a typical T-shirt from a Chinese factory to an American back. This imaginary TEU was packed with 16 tons of cotton in Urumqi, Xinjiang, and sent to Denver, Colorado. If it went by truck to Shanghai, by air to Los Angeles and by truck again to Denver, its emissions were 35 times more than the same journey using rail and sea. On the ocean leg only, a retailer could save 99 tons of emissions by sending the cotton by ship and not plane.

The International Maritime Organization (IMO) calls maritime transport a 'relatively small contributor to atmospheric emissions'. It would be, if the industry weren't so successful. Shipping is not benign because there is so much of it. It emits a billion tons of carbon a year and is responsible for nearly four per cent of greenhouse gases (although rival sides have different figures). That is more than aviation and road transport. A giant ship can emit as much pollution into the atmosphere as a coal-fired power station. Add shipping to the list of polluting countries and it comes sixth. Ships create more pollution than Germany. And yet for decades nobody noticed.

In Joseph Conrad's *Narcissus*, the *Narcissus* has to be hauled out of Bombay harbour by a steam tug which 'resembled an enormous and aquatic black beetle'. On the surface of the sea the tug leaves 'a round black patch of soot… an unclean mark of the creature's rest'. Today the coal is gone, along with the black gangs who worked in the engine rooms in their underwear, shovelling the black stuff in the same type of clothing as the men who had dug it out of the earth. Ships burn bunker fuel now, which takes its name from the coal bunkers it used to be stored in. They have left themselves behind in language as a noun and verb: 'We will be bunkering in Rotterdam' (or filling up with fuel); 'bunkers were completed at 3 a.m.'

Residual fuel oil, to give bunker fuel its real name, is dirty but cheap. Even now when fuel is ruinously costly – £370 a tonne – bunkers is still the cheapest. But it is horrible stuff. It is so unrefined that you could walk on it at room temperature. Even the spokesperson for Intertanko, an association of independent tanker owners, calls it 'crud' and 'one step up from asphalt'. Burning bunker fuel releases into the atmosphere gases and soot, including carbon dioxide, nitrogen oxides, carbon monoxide, volatile organic compounds, sulphur dioxide, black carbon and particulate organic matter. In 2009, it was calculated that the largest 15 ships could be emitting as much as 760 million cars. On the high seas, *Kendal*'s smoke is disturbingly black.

Mike has endless environmental rules to follow. SOLAS requires shipping to 'prevent, reduce and control pollution of the marine environment from any source'. MARPOL entered into force in 1983 and has been ratified by 136 countries. It has rules that govern the discharge of oil, garbage and sewage. *Kendal* has rules that govern the discharge of paper (permitted 12 miles out) and plastic (never permitted). Sewage sludge can also be discharged 12 miles out, which is fine for a crew of 20, but this rule also applies to cruise ships, which can carry 6000 people, the population of a small town. Sewage can add to ocean nitrification and the vastly increasing number of dead zones where excessive nutrients – present in sewage and agricultural run-off – have sucked oxygen from the sea, creating deadly anoxic dead zones where fish and other life can no longer live. In 2003, there were 146 dead zones in the oceans; by 2008, there were more than 400.

Seafarers have cause to pay attention to the admonishing binders of eco rules. When ship owners can slip away behind flags and anonymity, the captain and crew are often the most visible people to blame for disaster. In 2007, the *Hebei Spirit*, carrying a cargo of 250,000 tons of crude oil, was anchored off the port of Daesan, Korea. Its captain was Jasprit Chawla, whom I met at a nautical seminar on a tall ship in Glasgow's docks. He was a wiry and fizzing man: the fizz was the anger he still felt at having been imprisoned for something that wasn't his fault. *Hebei Spirit* was doing nothing untoward while at anchor but waiting for its pilot and for the weather to change. Chawla watched as a Samsung Heavy Industries barge approached on a collision course and kept coming. He sounded the whistle five times. He got on the radio to the Daesan authorities. He tried to call the barge and got no response, then watched in disbelief as the barge hit his ship, fracturing all three cargo tanks. Suddenly there he was in the middle of an environmental disaster 'with hydrocarbons all around us'. Imagine that the ship was an aeroplane. Imagine, for example, that it was US Airways Airbus A320, landed on New York's Hudson River by Captain Chelsey Sullenberger in 2009. Although fuel oil was discharged into the river, Captain Sullenberger was an immediate hero, because all lives were saved.

No-one died either in the collision between the barge and *Hebei Spirit*. Yet Jasprit Chawla and his first officer were immediately thrown in jail. Chawla had been at sea for 16 years without incident. He was kept in isolation for a month, denied access to a lawyer, and imprisoned for 18 months. He became half of the Hebei Two, and the cause of an unusually coherent and powerful lobbying campaign by shipping industry associations. It worked, eventually, despite the fact that the barge was owned by someone with intimate connections to the South Korean government. A court found that Samsung was responsible for 10 per cent of the pollution. On the tall ship, Chawla said, 'I salute the entire shipping community who came to support me when I thought I would never see my family or children again. Your letters were a great help in keeping my chin high.'

When the oil tanker *Prestige* broke up off Spain in 2003, 20,000 tons of fuel oil spilled into Spanish waters. When it was finally towed to shore, its captain, a 67-year-old Greek named Apostolos Mangouras, was arrested and jailed for 83 days, despite having begged Spanish authorities, when the ship was in distress, for a port of refuge (disgracefully, they chose to send it further out to sea in gale-force winds). The case finally came to court nine years later. 'The ship was cracked and they sent it out to the ocean,' Mangouras told the prosecutor, who sought to send this 77-year-old man to jail for 12 years. 'It was the worst alternative. They sent us in a floating coffin… to drown.'

No-one has yet been imprisoned for the environmental damage caused by ships, because the IMO has only just released regulations to increase energy efficiency and reduce emissions. That release took years of negotiation. The IMO is a member organization that rules by consensus, and with 170 members, its pace can be slow. The new regulations require new ships to have a 10 per cent increase in efficiency by 2015. Developing countries (including Liberia and Panama, the two largest ship registries) can apply for a waiver until 2019. By then, shipping will have grown still more, along with its emissions. Already the warming Arctic is freer of ice and freer for shipping. Russians have been sailing through the Northeast Passage for centuries. *The Oxford Companion to Ships and the Sea* refers with no irony to the 'northward-thrusting men of Novgorod' who pushed their boats through seasonal thaws in the twelfth century. Now the ice retreats more in summer, so all-comers who can pay Russia's fees and hire their ice-breakers will come, more of them, and more.

In 2006, Daniel Lack, a researcher at the US National Oceanic and Atmospheric Association, was aboard the NOAA research vessel *Ronald H. Brown* in the Gulf of Mexico, testing an instrument he had built that could measure black carbon in the atmosphere. It was frustrating because he kept running into ships' plumes. Lack was getting annoyed but then realized that he had some unique data. Before his accidental plume gathering, only six or seven ships had ever been measured for the particle contents of their smoke. Modelling studies led by James Corbett, marine policy professor at the University of Delaware's College of Earth, Ocean and Environment, produced startling data in 2007 showing that shipping emissions of particulate matter (including what laypeople call 'soot') 'are responsible for approximately 60,000 cardiopulmonary and lung cancer deaths annually'. Seventy per cent of the pollution occurred within 250 miles of land, near coastlines giving onto busy shipping lanes in Europe, East Asia and South Asia. In Los Angeles, half of all smog from sulphur dioxide comes from ships. Corbett's predictions were dismal: annual mortalities would increase by 40 per cent by 2012.

Yet when he looked into existing research, Lack found that only ten engines or so had been taken from manufacturers and assessed. And despite the hundreds of thousands of ship movements in coastal areas into ports that were barely a mile, sometimes, from human settlements and the air their inhabitants breathed, that was it. Lack didn't realize the importance of his data. He had never really paid much attention to ships. But now he learned about bunker fuel and that it burns inefficiently. He knew already that the more inefficiently a fuel burns, the more black carbon particles are emitted. Only forest fires produce more black carbon than bunker fuel. Under EU regulations, for example, bunker fuel is permitted to contain sulphur content to the rate of 45,000 parts per million (ppm). Low sulphur diesel for cars is supposed to contain 10 ppm.

The sulphur is converted into acid rain. 'To combat the acidity,' Lack says, 'vessels have to burn lubricating oils, and not all the oils get burned.' He sums up scientifically. 'There is such a large amount of particle emissions.' The timing of his research was good. The IMO was just beginning to notice emissions, as were the European Union and many ports. Before, nobody had enough data, and now they did. Lack was deluged with calls. People from local air resource boards. Non-profits that had been trying unsuccessfully to put pressure on the shipping industry for years. People working on scrubbing technology that reduces emissions at the source. Coastal peoples worried about their lungs. There was a hunger. 'The industry realized it had got away with a lot for a long time,' says Lack. 'They grabbed on to my study as a new start.'

For a long time, protesting against the environmental impact of maritime transport was a lonely job. The 1997 Kyoto Protocol didn't even consider ships. Even the big environmental groups had no marine teams, as they focused on aviation and cars. With those more obvious forms of transport, they had had time to become inventive, strategic. They matched people who cared about emissions with people who cared about noise. They launched initiatives for people to 'adopt a resident' who lived near an airport that might expand. But shipping presented a unique difficulty: it kept moving. When a ship leaves one port, calls at a dozen more, and ends up on the other side of the world, which country is responsible for its emissions? Who should be lobbied?

As with other regulatory challenges in this slippery mobile in-dustry, this one fell to the owners of the coastline, which doesn't move. Emission Control Areas (ECAs) that limit the sulphur con-tent of fuel now stretch 200 miles from the entire US coastline. They were already in place in the Baltic Sea and the North Sea. This will please the authors of a 2010 UK parliamentary committee report, who were shocked at the 'lack of urgency' shown about reducing shipping emissions by industrialized countries, and by the 'blocking actions of developing economies'. The IMO, they noted, did not announce a timetable of meetings to deal with greenhouse gases in shipping until 2006, and the first meeting took place only in 2008.

All shipping-themed conferences now have some sustainably themed components. There are clean ships, green ships. People are excited about wind power again, either with sails or kites. Why not? Even during the Second World War, windjammers such as the *Joseph Conrad* still crossed the Atlantic carrying supplies. But sailing ships need the right winds. They would be useful only to a modern supply chain with old-fashioned patience. Perhaps the answer is different fuels: *Maersk Kalmar* set sail in 2010 powered by two containers full of Soladiesel made from microscopic algae. Or cold ironing, where ships don't keep their engines running while they are in port, as they do now, but are powered by shore-side electricity. There is some interesting thinking around the peculiar systems in shipping. Richard Branson's Carbon War Room initiative now enables charterers to choose ships based on their efficiency rating, like a fridge or a house. It makes sense: charterers pay for the fuel, but before now have been ill equipped to choose the most efficient ship to burn it. Fuel-efficient ships, narrates a comfortably northern voice on Carbon War Room's predictably groovy video, can save the industry £45 billion a year and cut emissions by 30 per cent. Every tonne of fuel cuts CO_2 emissions by three tons. Going at 15 knots instead of 20 can save millions.

Slow boats to China, back to the future.

Until we reach the High Risk Area on the far side of Suez, watch officers have relatively little to watch or to watch out for. This is how Marius describes his watch-keeping job: 'You look at the radar, nothing. The sea, nothing. The sky, nothing.'

Sometimes there is more excitement, when cadets come up to the bridge with their mobiles, ready to grab a signal, because there are so many lights they think they are near a city. They find instead masses of fishing boats lit by their candles or torches. You won't see them until you are almost upon them, and then they light a candle or flash a torch at you, and you must get out of their way, with your ship that takes at least a mile to stop. Also, fishing boats have decided that passing in front of the bow of a big ship brings good luck. The closer they get, the better the fishing. 'So you see them,' says Marius, 'and you alter course to avoid them and suddenly they alter course and you think "Shit!" and they pass in front of your bow.' But only just, and all the time. How many collisions are there? 'Who knows? You'd only know if you found the boat.' In a forensic investigation into the loss of the scallop trawler *Lady Mary* off New Jersey, Amy Ellis-Nutt asked a mariner the same question. He replied, 'There are no skid marks on the ocean.'

Otherwise, among all that nothing, there is time for bored watch officers to cause mischief with a radio handset. These are the seas of name-calling.

Marius tells me a Merchant Navy joke. A US submarine captain sees a signal on his radar that is in his way, so he gets on the VHF. 'Signal on my radar, you must change course.' No, says his inter-locutor, I'm not moving. The submarine insists; so does the other voice. The submarine's threats escalate, but the other voice still refuses to move, until the submarine threatens extreme measures of the firepower kind if the other vessel won't change course. Here, a comedic pause. Then, 'I'm a lighthouse, captain, it's your call.' The joke was borrowed by Swedish navigational equipment firm Silva for a 2004 ad. It is not really anti-American but anti-supremacy. No-one is supreme on the ocean but the ocean. Marius tells another story about how dumb warships comms (communications) people are, so that you have difficulty believing that they are comms officers and not the junior baker stepping in during a toilet break. They call him and ask him to identify his ship. OK, that's normal. Sometimes they ask him the ship's port of registry, and he says, 'London.' 'Can you spell that?' 'L.O.N.D.O.N.'

These days, ships are meant to broadcast their AIS signal as a rule, unless to do so would put the ship in danger. Navy ships are allowed to stay electronically unremarked. In principle, technology has removed much of the uncertainty relating to the movements of what Captain Glenn generally calls 'other silly buggers'. He is constantly alert for stupidities, for navigation officers who don't know the rules of the road or who, if they do, will not follow them. The VHF is to be used for navigational purposes as a last resort. VHF-assisted collisions are common when officers waste valuable time on their radios trying to figure out if they are talking to the right ship rather than looking at the radar or using collision regulations and common sense. Consequently, radio procedure is set out in rules and regulations. VHF must always be left on standby: Channel 16 is a hailing channel and for emergencies. You make contact on Channel 16, then agree to switch to another channel. In practice, that doesn't always work, particularly in calm waters and deep seas. Marius likes to listen to Channel 16 because all sorts happens on it. It's the closest a seafarer gets to TV. Sometimes, you hear Chinese being sung. Often you hear Indian voices yelling 'Filipino monkey!' The captain finds this unpleasantly racist, but Filipino voices often retaliate. 'Indian, I can't see you but I can smell you.' Or, 'Does anyone know what IMO stands for? No-one? It stands for "Indian Monkey Organization".'

Any merchant seafarer who passes through this sea is used to such radio-wave vandalism. The US Navy apparently is not. In 2008 a US warship almost fired at Iranian ships in the Strait of Hormuz when it heard someone broadcast the message, 'I am coming to you. You will explode in a few minutes.' This, the *Navy Times* concluded, was the work of 'a locally famous heckler known among ship drivers as the "Filipino Monkey"'. A retired Navy commander was invited to speculate on the heckler's identity. 'Who knows? He could be tied up pier side or on a merchant ship somewhere.' Or he could be any watch officer, anywhere, bored enough to make crank calls by the only means available.

Usually the VHF mutterings are beyond my understanding. Then I hear someone say, 'Miaow, miaow.' I look at Marius, who is on watch. 'Did someone just say miaow miaow?' 'Yes.' 'Why?' 'I don't know.'

For a while, after piracy started up again in 2004 on routes to and from the Gulf, pirates played music over Channel 16 just before they attacked, both to unsettle seafarers and to block the channel so ships could not seek help. Marius has spent many a night listening to weirdness. Round these parts too, he tells me, you hear ghostly voices shouting 'Mario! Mario! Mario!' Friends of his on other ships have heard the Mario-shouter too, but no-one knows who it is or the meaning of Mario. I don't think they want to know. Strange things happen at sea, and so they should.

I spend hours reading the charts. I note the names I find there. Terrible Bank; Herodotus Rise; Hecate Patch, a scrap of sea named for the goddess of dark places. Investigator Bank; Wadge Bank; Kurchatov Seamount, named, I suppose, after the Soviet Union's atomic-bomb creator. Wadge is a mystery. Igor finds my interest in the charts unfathomable and asks about it. It is because of their words, I tell him. It is because I am romantic about the sea, and I like to think of men who sailed through emptiness and scattered anchors of names across it. Fairy Bank, King Arthur Canyon, Shamrock Knoll. Aren't they beautiful? 'Words!' he says with scorn. 'For us, it is just work.'

Marius's job is now to update the charts with 300 changes that have arrived by email, so I can usually find him bent over a chart, intent with a pencil. What changes? It depends. Sometimes the depth reading, sometimes there's no traffic separation scheme any more. For example, he says, on the Cap Bon chart, a depth has been crossed out. Some measurements date from the 1940s. Neither the sea nor the earth stays the same. Today's chart travels from Ra's at Tin to Iskenderun. Those names excite me – I think medinas, Turkish delight, spices – but I am most excited about Suez. A channel dug through a country by a Frenchman, where 40,000 ships pass every year, although it costs nearly $300,000 per transit for a ship the size of *Kendal*; which removed for everyone the terror and weather of Cape Horn, as long as they could pay for this new, shorter passage. A magnificent effort of engineering that removed 10 days from the usual 24-day journey that ships would have to make under Africa and up again to Europe. The canal takes 14 hours to transit and has existed in some form ever since Pharaoh Senusret III, ruler in 1874 BC, chopped through the land mass to make a passage between open seas. It was built by Egyptian labourers working to the design of the French engineer Ferdinand de Lesseps; 20,000 new workers had to be drafted in every 10 months, according to the official Suez canal website, 'from the ranks of peasantry'. Alongside its banks runs a railway and a 'sweet water canal'. I write in my notebook that somewhere nearby there is a vegetable oil pipeline marked on a chart, but I never find it again. The Suez Canal took 10 years to construct, is 100 miles long, and earns the Egyptian government £3 billion a year.

Right, say the crew. But it's still just a ditch in a desert. Even the laconic Vinton finds something to say about it, although the something is not much. 'Sand, sand, sand.' They go through Suez once a month, and it's a pain. Suez doesn't have locks like Panama, which at least provide some interest, and the scenery is duller too.

First, we park. Ships go through Suez in convoy. The channel is only 200 metres wide, and so can only hold one-way traffic. Our entry will be timed and staggered: first we have to wait 13 miles out because we have a deep draught. Another Maersk ship approaches while we are heading to our anchorage. It is doing 11 knots and tries to overtake, then messes up and has to go behind us. The captain shakes his head wearily. He says, 'It's "mine is bigger than yours", isn't it?' The other ship wanted to steal our anchorage space. It was the maritime equivalent of nipping into a supermarket parking space, and as pathetic.

There are other ships waiting. CMA-CGM, MSC (Mediterranean Shipping Company, though its nickname replaces 'Mediterranean' with 'Mafia'), Evergreen, China Shipping. French, Italian, Taiwanese, Chinese. The cogs, wheels and motors of the world and all its stuff. All these ships are rated Suezmax and above, according to the vital statistics of shipping, in which ships are sized by places they can fit through or round. Panamax is smaller than Suezmax, although Panama is now widening its canal in an expensive but surprisingly on-time development programme known as the Big Ditch. *Kendal* can't yet fit through Panama, nor can E-class like *Emma*. Maersk may build a modified version that can if the Big Ditch ever becomes a Bigger Canal.

We stay in green waters until the order comes to move south, to the canal lay-by of Great Bitter Lake. By now the convoy numbers 30. They sit here, fishing boats or leisure boats dotting and darting between them. An Egyptian warship moves past lazily, maybe back from the dangerous Gulf at the canal's exit. When I walk the deck, I avoid the starboard side now because we have taken on Suez crew, a requirement for any passage. They have their own cabin – the Suez Crew Room – that is used for only 18 hours a month, but well used during that time, because the crew hardly leave it, as all they do is eat, drink, listen to tinny pop and try to sell souvenirs. When they leave at the other end of the canal, they lower their boat into the water, but stay attached for a mile or two, as if they don't even have the energy to let go.

The Suez crew is somewhat of a scam: they are supposed to board every ship in case the ship has to tie up. Apparently they have particular rope skills. There is also a special Suez electrician whose job is to tend to the searchlight that is also obligatory and placed on my fo'c'sle perch. The captain has never had to use either electrician or rope-skilled crew in 42 years of coming through here, and views them as an income-generating scheme to add to the already significant fees. *Kendal* must also take a Suez pilot. He is fat and sleepy. At lunchtime, he asks what is for lunch, so the captain rings down to the galley and conveys the menu: split-pea soup (without pork, after a previous cook caused chaos with Muslims), spaghetti bolognese, fishcakes, chips.

'Yes.'

The captain is nonplussed. 'Everything?'

'Yes, everything.'

A folding table is unfolded next to the pilot's chair, and he eats. Apart from that, he sleeps: on the sofa, on the captain's chair, on the watch officer's chair. He is like a uniformed bridge cat, moving around in search of sun. Marius has to keep waking him up for instructions. Still, he is cheap, because he asks for food, but not much else. Suez is known as the Marlboro Canal because for smooth passage, every ship's captain has to have a ready stock of Marlboro to dispense. Immigration, port health, police, security guards. The port captain takes four, to share. The shipping agent takes a few. The electrician gets four packets; the boat crew gets six. Sometimes they want more than Marlboro, and the captain must go to the bond locker when an agent or port official asks for 'chocolate for my babies'. Not the Cadbury's Fruit & Nut? 'No, I give them the plain crap.' Each voyage, the captain dispenses £400 worth of cigarettes. The cigarettes are listed on the ship's budget as 'entertainment, port authorities', or 'gratuities', and accepted by company accountants as a needed expense.

I point out that they already have chocolate in Egypt, and coffee and cigarettes. 'Yes. They want it for free.' In West Africa, officials come on board with empty shopping bags, and empty the bond locker. The toll varies. The captain only pays seven cartons in Port Klang, for example, and none in Singapore. You don't dare give entertainment expenses in Singapore. The captain calls it the 'fine city' because it fines you for everything. *Kendal*'s crew like the Suez team as much as they like the canal. They say, 'The Egyptians can't have built the pyramids, there was no Marlboro then.' But the tobacco is worth giving out, because the penalty could be immense: any annoyed official could easily delay the ship with pettiness. When *Kendal* costs £20,000 a day to run, Marlboro is cheap.

I wake from a nap to find we are in the ditch. The water is green; the banks are sand. From D-deck I gaze at the desert, at an irrigated patch of green trees and plants that form a streak of freshness and life in the middle of the beige, at the homesick cadet on B-deck below me, leaning on the rail to get some signal bars on his mobile phone, photographing and phoning. There are great ships in front of us, stretching along the channel, and more behind. We are a slow sandwiched procession, squeezing through sand.

No-one else is out here photographing. They have all seen it before, and they need to save energy. Going through Suez means staying awake for pilots and port controls, and judging when to get into the convoy. Suez is exhausting. The captain stays particularly alert. He would anyway, but once a pilot set the ship aground in the canal and he has never forgotten it. By the time the captain realized they were going to run aground, they were beached on sand. He got the ship off 'with skill and ingenuity', and went to the toilet with relief. 'When I came out, I said, where's the bloody pilot? Then I saw his head popping up. He was on the deck, praying.' The captain felt sorry for him then. Being fired is a big thing for a pilot. So is grounding a ship.

Our passage seems so stately and secure through this canal. It seems that danger is impossible. Wrong, says the captain. Even the best captain can lose all his deck cargo. You never know. Boxes go overboard all the time. Ten thousand is the usual figure for the number of boxes lost at sea, although I find this number hard to reconcile with an industry that would lose commercial advantage by publicizing any losses. The European Union calculates that 2000 containers are lost every year, that 15 per cent come ashore and that 15 per cent remain floating at sea, causing a serious hazard to small boats. Some boxes become notorious, such as those containing bath toys that were discharged from the Greek-owned, Evergreen-operated *Ever Laurel* in the Pacific Ocean between Hong Kong and Tacoma; the contents are now remembered as yellow rubber ducks, although they were in fact plastic and there were red beavers, green frogs and blue turtles. There were the 78,932 Nike shoes that were set adrift from the *Hansa Carrier* between Korea and Los Angeles, then subsequently tracked by the oceanographer Curtis Ebbesmeyer, assisted by a worldwide subculture of people who collect flotsam.

By tracking the movement of shoes through oceans, Ebbesmeyer established the route of two ocean gyres. From his work, I learned that sports shoes generally float with the tongues facing upwards (unless they contain feet, which is not unheard of); that containers filled with computer and television monitors can discharge lead, mercury, cadmium and other heavy metals into the water. Eight pounds of lead for each monitor. Some lost boxes are painfully expensive, such as the fifteen 40-foot boxes that in 2004 fell from the *Med Taipei* off California in bad weather, with their contents of wheelchairs, hospital beds, ribbons and cardboard. The owners of *Med Taipei* didn't report the loss, a common practice – who would trust a company that can't keep its cargo? – but the accident happened in the Monterey Bay National Marine Sanctuary, and a box was found by a remote-controlled submersible belonging to the Monterey Bay Aquarium Research Institute (MBARI). Boxes have traceable numbers, and the owners were found and fined. The settlement was $3.25 million.

The money helped fund more research by MBARI: seven years later, the sub returned to the container. It was in good condition and presented a remarkable opportunity. No-one knew how lost steel boxes and sea life interact. That is not surprising: there are species this far down in the ocean that have no names yet. Using a robot with long arms, tethered on 4000 feet of cable, the researchers, led by Dr Andrew DeVogelaere, shot 8000 hours of video and saw scallops they had rarely seen, all over the container, and snails that would lay six-inch egg stacks. 'It's interesting,' DeVogelaere told a reporter, 'in that when this container fell into the sanctuary there were negotiations with the shipping company about mitigating damage. They were arguing there was no impact because there was nothing living down there.' They were wrong. The MBARI team don't know yet if the container's presence on the seabed is positive or damaging. Other artificial reefs, such as two million tyres bunched together across the ocean floor off Florida, have been disastrous. The tyres attracted hardly any sea life and detached themselves, floating away to pollute ocean gyres, on beaches, wherever they ended up.

I hear about missing containers in passing comments. The Atlantic was bad five years ago, says the captain. Lots of damaged goods. But then they put stabilizers on ships and it got better. I see the disasters on YouTube videos, crazy stacks of containers, leaning and squashed and wrong. I find missing boxes in the pages of lawsuits. In 2003, *Canmar Pride* was sued by a division of the Ford Motor Company, which claimed that the *Pride* had lost containers filled with its automotive parts that were worth $6 million, after rough seas in the mid-Atlantic. More precisely the *Pride* lost containers that were 'stuffed' with automotive parts. I like this word, sneaked in among dry legal language like a pomegranate seed in dust (it is actually a common freight term) as much as I am pleased to be introduced to the word and concept of a prothonotary, a chief clerk in the courts of ancient Byzantium and in modern Canadian ones. In the 'precedents' section of the case, I can dream up stories of what it is that disappears, from the names of the companies suing shipping lines. Magic Sportswear Corp. (trainers?) *v.* both OT Africa Line and *Mathilde Maersk*. Incremona-Salerno Marmi Affini Siciliani *v. Castor* (bathroom tiles?). Antares Shipping Corporation *v.* The Ship '*Capricorn*' et al. (Greek marbles!).

Arranging 6000 or so heavy steel boxes into a logistic balance according to their weight, stability and contents requires enormous skill. It is always the job of the chief officer. Vinton is remarkably relaxed in manner, and it is a surprise, when I ask him how many boxes are on board, that he can always answer sharply and precisely, though every port changes the number. Stowage is no easier, just less manual. The rampant mechanization of shipping has not sanitized it. Everyone has a story about stowaways. Vinton found one hidden inside a bunk. The man had drilled holes in the wood for air and hidden beneath the slats. Vinton says that you hear stories all the time. 'There are so many. Particularly to transport, how do you call it, flesh.'

On *Maersk Maryland* there were five stowaways who hid in the rudder tank. This is a tank around the rudder that doesn't necessarily fill up with water as long as the ship isn't too low in the sea. The five men knew to go there; the crew think it was organized. When their food and water ran out, they started banging, and when some Thai crew found them, they were taken hostage by the stowaways.

No, that's not right. It was the steward who was taken hostage because he was bringing them their food.

Right. And at Algeciras the Spanish authorities wouldn't let them set foot on Spanish soil. It was a literal ordinance: they could go to the bottom of the gangway but no further. The gangway was British territory protected by the Red Ensign. The company offered to pay for their flights back to Dakar and to pay for security guards, but the Spanish refused. No foot on Spanish soil. So they were taken back to Dakar by ship, 'and they went mental. They fashioned knives and took the steward hostage and at one point were doing tribal dances around him.'

I listen greedily to these stories and I don't mind if they have holes. How many times can a steward be taken hostage? There have been proven stowaway stories crazier and sadder than knives and tribal dances. In 2010, Ghana's authorities arrested three Chinese crew for throwing overboard three Ivorians who had hidden on their freighter. Taiwanese officers of *Maersk Dubai*, when two young Romanian stowaways were found aboard in 1996, put the young men to sea in an improvised raft. They were never found. The killing of eight African stowaways on MV *Ruby* by her Ukrainian crew became *Deadly Voyage*, an HBO/BBC film that starred Danny Glover.

Those were extreme reactions – or maybe not. Read the IMO's stowaway database and you will start to calculate the probabilities: if these are the number of stowaways caught, how many are not? In the more porous ports of Europe, where migrants think they will find a ship sailing to America, the dry database reads like an onslaught. One port: Igoumenitsa, Greece. One ship: the ro-ro (roll-on/roll-off) cargo vessel *Ikarus Palace*. On 3 February, one Somali. Three days later, one Afghan. A Palestinian a week later. On 10 March, one Albanian. And then:

13.3.2010, 1 Palestinian
20.2.2010, 1 Albanian
10.3.2010, 2 Eritrean, 1 Palestinian
27.3.2010, 1 Afghan

31.3.2010, 1 Afghan,
07.4.2010, 1 Albanian
17.4.2010, 2 Albanian
24.2.2010, 1 Afghan
28.4.2010, 2 Tunisian

I wonder, what is going on in Igoumenitsa? And I know what is going on in Igoumenitsa. Ships call and ships leave and people see their movements as escape, as they have done and as they always will.

Kendal's crew doesn't seem to mind stowaways. They are a headache, and the crew would rather not be taken hostage. But they are a part of life at sea. They are what happen. In Africa, you get worried if you don't find them.

Vinton must always keep an eye out for strangers on board, and now he must watch for strangers overboard too. We are not yet in the danger zone, but pirates are already infecting our passage. Stowage has to be calculated to accommodate the risk, so some boxes shouldn't be stored aft where pirates can fire at them. Imagine a rocket-propelled grenade (RPG) meeting that metal, those self-heating chemicals inside the box: what a prospect.

The time and place for such considerations is approaching even while we steam through this quiet green water pacifically, a majestic daisy-chain of sedate ships. I don't know if steaming is the right way to describe our movement. Driving sounds wrong, despite the engines. Steaming is inaccurate, unless that black bunker smoke counts as steam to someone. Sailing is daft. It is a small point of vocabulary, but I have time to make it big during these listless days and 1986 nautical miles so that it becomes a grand theory about how we haven't bothered to modify our language to keep up with these modern ships, because the bigger they have become, the further away they have travelled from us. Fancy. Clearly there is an empty space in my brain that needs filling. It is too hot to be on deck, it is too dull on the bridge now that I've seen 12 hours of desert and canal and the rest of the miles look the same. There is nothing to do but wait. Steaming on, heading for danger, going south.

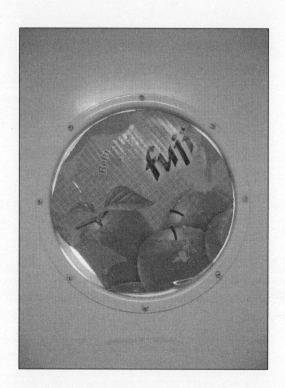

Pirate watch

6.   HIGH RISK AREA

Which Way is it to Somalia?

The high seas shall be reserved for peaceful purposes.
—United Nations Convention on the Law of the Sea

This kind of heat sucks breath from bodies. We are in the Bab al
Mandeb Strait, a narrow opening that marks the beginning of the
Gulf of Aden. It is July now, and almost monsoon season. Monsoon
weather is bad for nausea, but good for anyone scared of pirates, like
me, because they travel in small boats that are upset by the Force 6
waves that *Kendal* dismisses with ease. We are taking precautions,
but much of our protection is weather.

On the internal email system, the captain transmits two daily
news digests – Tagalog for the Filipinos, English for everyone else –
and a security alert from an agency named Securewest. By now, all
the news is pirate news. The Yemeni Coast Guard has seen pirates
move out of the Gulf of Aden and northwards into the Bab el Mandeb Strait and lower Red Sea. In three weeks, pirates have attacked

10 Yemeni ships and one oil tanker. All the assaults were repelled by armed protection teams travelling on the ships. But we don't have armed guards. Maersk doesn't allow it.

Instead, we have pirate watch. The ship has changed: the deck-door portholes on every floor of the accommodation house have been blocked with circular pieces of cardboard obviously cut from cartons from the bond store and Pinky's supplies. One porthole is now blocked by Benson & Hedges; another by an image of rosy red apples. By sundown, all cabin windows must be covered with blackout blinds that are fastened into place with snaps, and a junior officer is assigned to patrol every evening at dusk, to monitor compliance. He does a lot of snapping. Pirate watch will last until we reach our next port, Salalah, beyond the far end of the Internationally Recommended Transit Corridor (IRTC), a 492-mile dual-lane sea highway skirting Yemen's southern coast that ships are advised to take. The corridor begins south of Aden near the island of Elephant's Back, ending just before Oman. The IRTC is patrolled by military ships from three coalition counter-piracy forces: one from the EU, one run by NATO, and the Combined Task Force (CTF-151), led by the United States, with a membership of nations that is described as 'fluid'. Besides the task forces, there are other navies acting independently of coalitions, including those of Russia, Korea, India, Japan and China. It is the first major deployment of the Chinese Navy since 1433, when Admiral Zheng came here, visited the Sultan of Malindi, and took home a giraffe. The Chinese Navy is on piracy patrol, but it is also well placed to support its growing economic presence in Africa. If you want a window into future geopolitics, the Indian Ocean has a good view.

Since some Somalis took to piracy in the mid-1990s, their range and nerve has grown. At first staying close to the coastline of Somalia, they now operate across the Indian Ocean over to India's southern tip and south of Tanzania's. This 'High Risk Area' is 2200 nautical miles by 1800. It includes the IRTC, and also routes of 70 per cent of global oil traffic and 50 per cent of container ships. Of these, fewer than two per cent are successfully hijacked. But that is no comfort when my portholes are blocked by apples and my imagination is running as wild as the waves.

Until we reach Oman, no-one is allowed on deck without a radio. There are no radios spare for the supernumerary, so this means no more ocean-watching for me. For the cadets and crew, there is nothing but watching, because the risk means two men are needed to stand extra lookout duty on the bridge wings day and night, and there aren't enough officers. It is a boring and overheated task, particularly for the ones who for some reason choose to stand in 40-degree heat in heavy engine-room boiler suits. The captain allows the watchers to come at reasonable intervals into the cool of the bridge. 'Within reason,' is how he defines a reasonable interval, but he can hear from his cabin when the bridge-wing door is opened and closed, and he knows that they take advantage. I'm not sure how useful the lookouts are, given the ship-sized blind spot caused by the containers, but I don't mind, because I am nervous.

One of the first things the captain asked me was: 'Why do you want to go through pirate zones when you don't have to? Are you mad?' It is only now that I think the answer to the second question is yes. During the first night of pirate watch, I stay up until 2 a.m., as if that will help. If I am awake, they won't come. This makes sense to me in the same way that if any of my clothes are inside out in my suitcase, my plane will crash. Pirates like to attack in light anyway, either the first or last of the day. They understand how to play with light and sunshine; sometimes they approach in the shadow cast by the ship; sometimes they arrive in the glare. I sleep finally and wake hours later to the sing-song bong-bong that is the ship's alarm call. The ludicrous cheeriness of it would better suit a holiday camp, but I still jump out of bed in a panic, expecting the sunny bongs to be followed by an 'Abandon Ship' or a call to the safe room where we have agreed to muster in an attack. Nothing happens but crackle. It's someone phoning home again. Someone always presses the wrong buttons on the satellite phone and makes an inadvertent public address.

Later, I tell Marius about my uneasy night. He laughs. He is convinced that we are protected by the size and speed of the ship. Even so, there were two alerts during his night watch. First, two fast craft, one ahead and one astern, doing about 20 knots at 2 a.m. That could be either pirates or smugglers. Drugs, diesel, weapons, alcohol and humans flow illicitly across the Indian Ocean. *Kendal* shone searchlights on them, a passing US helicopter did a fly-by, and the suspect craft flashed lights back. Marius thinks they were friendly; the captain is more sceptical. Sometimes they pretend to be friendly. They lure you in. The captain's daily orders, written instructions that are kept on the bridge, require his officers to stay four miles away from small craft if possible. He has written, 'Trust no-one.' Once, the captain was having dinner when the first officer made an announcement over the PA. 'Captain to the bridge.' This is not an announcement a captain ever likes to hear. He thought, 'Oh, shit,' displayed no outward alarm, and took the lift up to the wheelhouse. Two fast skiffs, coming alongside. Finally they veered off. 'I'm sure they did it to wind us up. They don't do it now, there are too many Navy warships around.' When the second incident happened during the night, Marius didn't alert the captain and now regrets it. 'I was thinking, if we're hijacked then I don't want to spend three months in Somalia with 22 crew saying, it's your fault, you didn't call him.' There were two fast boats again, doing 18 knots, coming too close. He shone the lights on them, and the boats turned tail.

There is a US warship off our port beam. I look at it through binoculars and Marius says, you may as well wave. They have stronger binoculars than us. They can see you. He says that when the Americans first arrived in the Gulf of Aden, they wanted to get involved in everything. Anything that looked worrying, off they would go to check it out. Once an American voice came over Channel 16, trying to hail something. 'Merchant vessel, this is the coalition warship, what is your position?' Marius could see who they were trying to reach: a boat going about four knots, which means it was hardly going at all. It was obviously some little fishing craft puttering along. Anyone would know that. But the warship was new and kept calling to the merchant vessel, until someone took pity, got on Channel 16, and said, It's a dhow. It won't have VHF or GPS. They navigate by the stars. The story still makes Marius laugh. 'I pictured it like this giant, huge guy leaning over and shouting at a tiny mouse or something.'

Still, I'm glad to have the warship nearby, especially when Marius pencils in the information from Securewest on the chart, and writes that MV *Golden Blessing*, carrying a cargo of glycol ethelene and 13 Chinese crew, was hijacked the day before. It is now on its way to Somalia. *Golden Blessing* was typical pirate prey: a low and slow tanker with no armed guards. Pirates have never captured a ship our size because our 10-metre freeboard (the height of the ship between water line and deck) is daunting. It is already difficult to climb onto an unwilling ship from a small boat, even if you have done it before, even with good grappling hooks and ladders. But there are still weak spots. Some points at the poop deck are more accessible, so those are barred with heavy nets. Astern, there are hoses port and starboard, jetting water to repel boarders. From the wheelhouse the hoses look like a pathetic deterrent, and I assume that a damp pirate can still perform piracy, but the jets are more powerful than they appear. 'Even so,' says Marius, 'I'm not going out there when they've got AK47s, whether there are hoses or not.'

The tension of pirate watch is hard on the crew. Some are genuinely unnerved, and being unnerved for a week in every month is not nothing. The captain received an email from the company inviting its fleet to order barbed wire for protection. He duly did so and was told that his ship was too big. It didn't qualify for barbed wire, and his order was cancelled. This infuriates him. There is always a first time. Most of *Kendal*'s officers favour armed guards as the best deterrent. At dinner one evening, I remark that the ITF has organized a petition against piracy. Igor nearly snorts into his soup. 'So what do we do with a petition?' he says with scorn. 'Send it to Somalia? "Please stop attacking us!" The only thing to do is to send the petition with an A-bomb in the envelope.'

Marius keeps quiet. Before he transferred to *Kendal*, he was on a smaller ship doing the run from Salalah down to Mombasa, Kenya. It was a sister ship to *Maersk Alabama*, which was captured by pirates in 2009 and whose captain was taken hostage and dramatically rescued by SEAL snipers who killed three pirates in darkness through the doorway of a closed lifeboat. Murderous, but impressive. The sister ship did the same route and was the same size and flag, but its captain was different and so were its tactics. Marius's ship stayed 600 miles offshore for as much of its journey as possible, as company guidance dictated. *Alabama* didn't and was known for sailing only 300 miles off Somalia's shoreline. When Marius left the ship, he was sure he would see *Alabama* in the news. He was right. *Alabama* is still in the news: its crew is suing Captain Richard Phillips, although he became a national hero, for ignoring company policy by sailing too close to shore, and risking their lives and ship.

Marius is not worried by pirates. But even he does not reach the profound calm of Able Seaman Archimedes, to whom I talk one afternoon while he is on pirate-watch duty on the bridge wing. It is the day after the near-attack, and he is dismissive of anyone who expressed concern about it. Scared of fishing vessels! So nervous! He would not have been scared because, he says, even three years ago, they would stop for a few days in the Gulf of Aden to do some fishing, with no trouble. (Ships have been known to develop convenient engine trouble in good fishing zones.) So Archie doesn't believe in pirates.

'What do you mean, you don't believe in pirates? Like fairies?'

'I don't believe. Suspicious craft, yes. But I won't believe until I see them.'

I am not sure how to respond to this. It is such a bizarre thing to say. I tell him the latest figures of piracy: 544 seafarers taken hostage in the first six months of 2010, with 360 still being held. Thirteen ships hijacked. 'Yes,' Archimedes says. 'I know all that. A friend was held hostage for three months. But it was good. Double pay! Overtime!' The Greek owners paid for three months' holiday afterwards. The captivity was fine, the pirates were harmless. Harmless with guns? He grins again. Guns just for protection. They don't want to shoot you. Julius, a fellow AB, is also tranquil. 'These pirates are not like Rambo or the Taliban. Then I would be afraid. But they are just normal people with guns.' They only want the ransom. It is only business.

I had forgotten this when I asked the captain how pirates would reach the top stacks of containers. He was quiet for a second while adding that to his mental list of daft supernumerary questions. 'They won't. They're not interested in the cargo. They only have beaches in Somalia, they can't even unload it.' All they want is the ship and the crew. Expensive cargoes mean higher ransoms, though, so they would never turn down a tanker.

Forty-two thousand merchant vessels come through the High Risk Area every year, and the distances to patrol are dizzying. An EU-NAVFOR commander compared his force's task to patrolling Western Europe with a couple of police cars whose top speed is 15 miles an hour. In testimony to a British parliamentary committee, Major General Buster Howes said, 'Are we able to police the entire area effectively? No we are not. What a [modern warship] can actively survey and influence in an hour is about a pinprick. If it has a helicopter, it is about three times the size of a full stop.' A 'suspicious approach' can become a successful hijack in only 15 minutes. If a ship has a sensible reaction plan, if someone can cut the engines and someone radio for help, if the crew can stay out of danger so that a rescue is not risky, then drifting might give the Navy time to arrive if it is in the same pinprick. But if an approach becomes a successful assault, and pirates have hostages, most navies will not attempt a rescue. When British yachting couple Paul and Rachel Chandler were taken hostage in 2009, they watched as the British military supply vessel *Wave Knight* stood off, uselessly, from *Kota Wajar*, the pirated merchant ship where they were briefly held before being transferred to Somalia. '[The pirates] did not think they were going to be attacked,' said Paul Chandler. 'You can read something into the fact that they were standing on the deck of *Kota Wajar* firing AK47s at a warship.'

On day three of pirate watch, I rush up to the bridge when the ship starts rolling, in case it means something. It means only that we have left the sheltered waters of the Gulf of Aden and are in open sea, where the monsoon swells are stronger. Swells are good. The captain is on the bridge, as he is there most of the time in pirate waters. At midnight, he is concerned about a tanker that has left the IRTC. But he consoles himself. 'He's heading for Singapore so he's probably just set off that way.' He just worries in case the tanker knows something he doesn't.

I don't know what is going to change things, says the captain wearily at dinner. Not some bloody petition. He and his crew will continue sailing through this danger, month in, month out, and that's that. 'I told you. Merchant Navy. Scum of the earth.'

Vasco da Gama, a Meko-class frigate in the Portuguese Navy, is on pirate duty. It is carrying 217 people, some marines, a helicopter and copious weaponry. It is also about to carry me for a week from Mombasa to Mogadishu and back, no port calls and hopefully no pirates.

Vasco da Gama was the current flagship of EU-NAVFOR, so also carries an international staff of 13 who run operations, and who live on the flagship, whichever country it belongs to. When I asked EU-NAVFOR if I could watch them hunt pirates, *Vasco da Gama* was the option offered. The usual practice would have been to put me on a British ship, but there were none in any fleet. The flagship was already carrying internationals and could handle one more. The embed was strategic. EU-NAVFOR felt underappreciated and publicity could help its case, showing that it is doing good and being useful while costing €8 million a year. To get on an EU warship, I had to head for the unlikely setting of Northwood, a north London suburb usually described as 'leafy'. This is a fair description. The enormous Northwood Headquarters is located in the kind of place – quiet and bucolic – I least expected to find the base of the British Army (all of it) as well as NATO's Commander Naval Forces North, the Commander in Chief Fleet, and EU-NAVFOR, the newest tenant. The base is huge, but not large enough to house some of EU-NAVFOR's staff, who have been living for months in a Ramada hotel in Watford. If you know Watford, you know that such endurance counts as proper service to your country.

Wing Commander Paddy O'Kennedy was EU-NAVFOR's spokesman when I visited. He didn't stay long in the job: spokespeople do six-month rotations, as do the ships. As he is a fluent speaker of Arabic, Hebrew and sound bites, his next post would be as the British embassy's defence attaché in Tel Aviv. For now, he was working for EU-NAVFOR despite belonging to the Royal Air Force, and his job was to talk piracy and counter-piracy. He had a talent for it. Even before we reached his office, he had told me that once he was in the shower when his wife shouted up. 'Paddy, there's someone on the phone, he says he's a pirate?' They phoned him all the time, because the spokesperson's number is on the EU-NAVFOR website, and although Somali pirates come from a failed state, they still have smartphones and internet cafés. Pirates can Google. They are known to read up on their crews and hostages, so it becomes dangerous for any information – a family photo of a captain standing in front of a decent house, for example – to be accessible online. A decent house could mean pirates push for a high ransom. Any excuse for a higher ransom.

The wing commander's desk was in a large open-plan office, but he spent much of his time in the operations room, where lines of Finnish, Italian, German and other European military spend hours in front of a giant screen that displays Mercury, an information-sharing programme used by EU-NAVFOR, other coalitions and other interested parties. Another screen showed a map of the High Risk Area. It was a real-time map, and as we entered, the screen showed that a ship had just been attacked. The crew, it was hoped, had taken refuge in a citadel, a panic room that ships are now encouraged to set up. There are good and bad ones. Decent citadels are supplied with food and water to last for days, allow the ship to be steered from within, and cannot be penetrated by oxy-acetylene torches, dynamite or other violent means. If the crew are secured inside a citadel, a ship can be safely boarded by a naval patrol even when pirates are aboard. A poorly designed one can become a tomb. On MV *Arillah-1*, seafarers endured 30 hours inside their citadel while pirates burned ropes and wood near the ventilation grilles of the citadel, trying to choke them out or to death.

At his desk, which held a copy of *Pirate Latitudes* by Michael Crichton – a Christmas present from his wife, still unread in March – Paddy said, OK, everyone knows the general situation in Somalia. Or they have watched *Black Hawk Down*, which they think amounts to the same thing. War, chaos, failed state. No meaningful government since 1991. By 2011, the Transitional Federal Government was nominally governing the country, but only as President Hamid Karzai – nicknamed the Mayor of Kabul – was ruling Afghanistan: partly, and with backup. On the TFG's side was the African Union Mission in Somalia (AMISOM), an African Union peacekeeping force that also wages war; and on the other side was Al-Shabab, Somalia's group of native terrorists, affiliated with Al-Qaeda though without its global ambition. Al-Shabab beheads, bombs and terrorizes, it steals humanitarian aid, but it stays at home to do it. Between those two forces there are Somalis, including two million who require humanitarian aid because they are either underfed or starving. Consequently, EU-NAVFOR was formed in 2008 as a result of UN Resolutions 1814, 1816, 1838, 1846, 1918 and 1950, to serve a dual purpose: to escort humanitarian supplies into Somalia and counter Somali piracy. Stopping illegal fishing was added later.

Paddy didn't call them 'Somali pirates'. He was careful not to do so. Most are Somali, and they mostly operate out of and in Somalia, but some are Yemeni. A few may be Kenyan. Perhaps there is a Tanzanian or two. Nationality is not the only issue about their identity. When Canadian journalist Jay Bahadur interviewed pirates in Somalia, they called themselves *badaadinta badah*, or 'saviours of the sea', rather than *burcad badeed* ('ocean robber'). Somali pirates understand PR, and this is their myth: that they are the descendants of the pirates of piracy's Golden Age in the early eighteenth century, when men like Edward Teach – better known as Blackbeard – and Henry Avery governed the waters of the Caribbean with considerable violence, but also by operating ships that ran democratically. Captains were elected, and kept in check by quartermasters and a council of crew. Piracy was violent and awful, but it was also the best escape route from the more terrible life of a merchant seafarer, where there could be no respite from tyrannical, violent captains.

The US Congress has called piracy 'violence against maritime navigation'. As long as there has been maritime navigation, there has been violence against it. Augustine wrote of an encounter between Alexander the Great and a pirate. The emperor challenged the robber: what did he mean by keeping hostile possession of the sea? The pirate responded: 'what thou meanest by seizing the whole earth; but because I do it with a petty ship, I am called a robber, whilst thou who does it with a great fleet art styled emperor.' I find this smug, but Augustine thought it 'just and apt'. The Romans saw piracy as a threat to trade and therefore to empire, but there were still enough practising pirates for Plutarch to write that they 'already at that time controlled the sea with large armaments and countless small vessels'. When Julius Caesar was travelling to Rome from Bithynia, pirates captured him for 38 days, and Caesar, 'as if the men were not his watchers but his royal bodyguard... shared in their sports and exercises with great unconcern'. Once his ransom of 50 silver talents (equivalent to a modern £1 million) was paid, his equanimity became revenge: he equipped a fleet, hunted down his captors, and crucified them. Carthaginians preferred to dispatch pirates by flaying them to death.

Piracy may seem straightforward. Surely it is nothing more than the ugly business of taking the possessions of others through violence? But it can escape easy categorization. What were privateers but pirates with permission? They travelled to rob foreign ships, just with authority from the nation states who had dispatched them. The early American colonies, forbidden to compete with English ships for trade to and from Europe, found pirates brought useful income, as long as the violence was done against far-away maritime navigation. Colonel Frederick Philipse, who founded one of New York's great fortunes and families, funded a pirate base in Madagascar and sent privateers on revenue-generation voyages. Piracy is a matter of opinion. In a café in Mombasa, a local man says to me with genuine contempt: 'You have been on a warship called *Vasco da Gama* hunting pirates? But Vasco da Gama was a pirate.'

This slipperiness, this shifting of shapes has made room for myths and theatre. Blackbeard knew that drama was an effective way to spread terror. His flag featured a skeleton stabbing a heart while toasting the Devil. He wore his black beard in pigtails and somehow set off sparklers around his face when he boarded hunted ships. Pirates knew the importance of spreading stories of their brutality, but also of their bravado and rage against authority. Just before one was hanged in 1718, he was asked to repent. 'Yes,' he said, 'I do heartily repent; I repent that I had not done more Mischief, and that we did not cut the Throats of them that took us.'

I haven't read of any humour coming from Somali pirates, although they did hijack a ship named *Buccaneer*. The way they treat hostages is not funny. But they also understand the power of telling stories. They have their own origin myth: after Somalia's law and order fell apart in 1991, chaos broke loose on- and offshore. There was no police or functioning army on land and there was no coastguard at sea. Somalis prefer to eat camel meat if given a choice, but fishing is a common coastal occupation. Into the authority vacuum sailed foreign fishing vessels, come for booty. The pickings were good: there was lobster, tuna, shrimp. Local fishers, lobster divers and other coastal professions found their living stolen by Taiwanese, Spanish, Russian and Thai trawlers that scraped the bottom of their seas with shameless abandon and took all they could without licence or payment.

Then, in the words of Abdirahman Mohamed Farole, president of Somalia's semi-autonomous northern region of Puntland, this is what happened next: 'The violation of Somali waters by foreign trawlers expectedly triggered a reaction of armed resistance by Somali fishermen [who] linked themselves with local warlords for protection, placing armed militiamen on board the trawlers.' He calls this new breed of fishers 'fishermen-turned-pirates'. They then targeted unarmed commercial vessels, 'inhumanly taking hostages for ransom and disrupting international maritime trade routes'.

There are other versions of their origins. For Robert Young Pelton, who ran the Somalia Report news agency, pirates emerged originally from the Puntland coastguard. When the national government fell, the coastguard turned pirate 'in about a day'. A London-based Somalia expert told me modern pirates had never been fishermen or coastguards. He thought they came from inland criminal gangs. It was a protection racket. Mombasa-based Somalis were anyway in the habit of selling illegal fishing licences to foreign operators. You can do that in a failed state when foreigners used to a rule of law know no different. The foreigners, he said, would come and start fishing, 'and the [Somalis] would make their presence known'. He meant that they demanded money. 'Then they realized they could make more by pinching the ship.' Thus the template was formed. 'We would get a report of a vessel seized, journalists would ring up fishermen and get quotes about foreigners raping the seas and [were told] that Somali fishermen were furious. That becomes: Somali fishermen are doing the piracy.' In fact, the UN Monitoring Group on Somalia estimates that only 6.5 per cent of pirate attacks have been against fishing vessels.

What is certain is that in the first few years of the twenty-first century, pirates began to set out in fast, small boats called skiffs. They had powerful outboard motors, but could only carry what fuel fit in their boat. They were hampered by distance, fuel and weather: the rougher waves of the monsoon meant that even launching from a beach was difficult, never mind approaching a large ship at speed and throwing a grappling ladder at it. They had no GPS or charts. In the words of former EU-NAVFOR commander Major General Buster Howes, a man with a silky turn of phrase, 'they navigated by guess and by God'. In this Genesis story of piracy, these were 'subsistence pirates'. And then something changed. Either inland Somalis got involved, or those inland Somalis organized criminals, or it was a natural escalation of the blindingly obvious. Pirates began to hijack *dhows*, larger fishing vessels that could serve as mother-ships, that can carry dozens of passengers or hostages, travel further and hold more fuel barrels. Now the pirates could hunt for weeks not days, towing a couple of skiffs with them, so that they stopped being pirates, and became a PAG (Pirate Action Group). They could travel as far as India and down to Mozambique. They could travel 1000 miles. They could be anywhere.

The truth about much of Somali piracy, although it is about solid weapons and solid violence, is as shimmering as Blackbeard's beard. Tales are told; myths shift. Facts change as fast as tactics. What is clear is that the second half of the first decade of the twenty-first century was another golden age of piracy, just as 1716–1722 was the golden age for Blackbeard, Bartholomew Roberts and colleagues. The Oxford English Corpus has noted a fourfold use of the word 'pirate' since 2007, with *Somali* being the most common modifier. Behind the shimmer are some plain facts. Men, as a job, take other men hostage while they do their job, for doing their job. Other men and women try to stop them.

You will like *Vasco da Gama*, a colleague of Paddy's had told me. There is no sauna, as on Swedish flagship *Carlskrona*, but the Portuguese have long lunches and wine. As I see when I approach the gate at Mombasa's port, where a sleek pale green warship is waiting, there will also be officers who wear Ray-Bans and look like models. Lieutenant-Commander Pedro Silva Barata is in charge of communications for the international staff. He wears his name on a Velcro name-badge, along with his blood group. I understand the military practicality of wearing this on your chest, but it never stops seeming oddly intimate, like seeing underwear.

Three crew members salute as we board. Pedro salutes back while I shuffle. This is my first formal encounter with military life, and only the first episode of awkwardness. The last time I felt this socially inept was in front of the Crown Prince of Bhutan, when I hid a water bottle behind me as if it would dirty his royalty. I would have had no idea what was expected even if I hadn't been arriving sleepless from London, sick to my stomach on malaria pills, and still trying to absorb the fact that Mombasa's airport road is now called Barack Avenue, and the sounds of hundreds of people emerging from the Linkoni ferry next to the warship, their noise like a storm of oversized insects. The ferries still do good business, because part of Mombasa is an island, but the port has suffered otherwise. Since piracy began properly to grow in the early 2000s, cargo ships have stopped coming, even though Mombasa, Kenya's only seaport, serves five landlocked East African countries. Cruise ships also stay away, particularly after *Seaborne Spirit* was attacked in 2005, and pirates were only repelled with high-pressure hoses and a sonic weapon. Four years later, when pirates attacked MSC *Melody*, they were assaulted by deckchairs thrown by furious passengers. In 2010, a local shipping reporter tells me, there were 43 cruise-ship calls into Mombasa. By summer 2011, there had only been five. Still, the coalition navies are some compensation. They bring money and they spend it. When the US ships come, girls arrive from all over Kenya, and Mombasa clubs fill with ship's officers and crew. R&R on a military ship consists of more than a disconsolate trip to a local overpriced shop or a lonely seafarers' mission. Hence the Ray-Bans.

Vasco da Gama has come to Mombasa from the Seychelles, where the crew had beach parties and got suntans. Before that it was patrolling the IRTC, the path for prudent merchant ships. Prudent merchant ships are advised to do a lot, these days, for better protection. They should report to the Maritime Security Centre for the Horn of Africa (MSCHOA). They should travel at maximum possible speed. They should employ 'hardening' methods such as high-pressure hoses to repel boarding, the use of barbed wire, and the placing of dummies in strategic positions to bulk up small crew numbers. They should be prepared to answer any suspicious approach by clever navigation: zig-zagging is best. All these things come under the label of Best Management Practices, empty-sounding jargon for what is a set of good advice. Some of the advice has precedents. Some of the techniques advised are tried and tested, such as using speed: ships avoiding U-boats in the Second World War were safe enough to travel independently of convoys if they could do 15 knots. Manoeuvring: every wartime captain knew that zig-zagging a ship made it harder to target. But despite these efforts, ships have been brazenly hijacked in and near the IRTC, three miles outside Salalah's docks, and off the coast of India. Like all asymmetric forces, pirates can change quicker than complicated coalition naval forces governed by regulations, rules and law. They can respond and dictate. They learn.

Vasco da Gama is crowded. There are 214 people on board a ship half the length of *Kendal*. With more people and less space, I learn to walk differently. First, I brace my knees to counter the greater motion of a smaller ship. (Warships are no place for knee problems, because you are constantly exerting your joints.) Then, I learn how to lean into the bulkhead to pass people in crowded passageways. *Vasco da Gama*'s crew do this sinuously and with skill because the passages are usually crowded on a 24-hour ship. At all hours I could encounter people on the narrow, steep iron ladders; on the black-as-night weather-deck; at the sharp corners; in the hydraulically sealed deck exits that can take your arm off if you don't withdraw it quick enough, but that keep out nuclear, biological and chemical contamination and flies.

Supplies are also taking up room because refuelling of all sorts is being done in Mombasa. This is down-time after the tension of the IRTC, of the proper piracy work. Not that this week's job is not being taken seriously, as it consists of providing a military escort to *Petra 1*, a bulk cargo vessel carrying humanitarian supplies into Mogadishu. *Petra 1*'s top speed is 12 knots (nearly 14 miles an hour on land) but her usual pace is four. She may as well have a target painted on her side, particularly as the supplies are for AMISOM, the UN's military presence in Somalia, and Al-Shabab's enemy. It was because *Petra 1* had been fired upon doing this supply run that the French military began providing informal escorts, and from that came EU-NAVFOR. Trouble isn't really expected, although the Spanish frigate SPS *Infanta Cristina* was attacked while on escort duty in 2010 by MV *Izumi*, the first merchant vessel to be used as a mother-ship – a floating headquarters – by pirates.

My accommodation is in the sick bay. It's the only free space on board. Only senior officers don't share cabins, and some cabins are so small that only one person can change clothes at a time. Privacy here is prized because there isn't any. The sick bay is impressive, with comforting clinical steel, six bunks and the only bath on the ship, useful in case of burn victims. Unlike *Kendal*, *Vasco da Gama* has a doctor and nurse, as well as six cooks and levels of staffing that would make merchant seafarers envious.

My visit has been carefully planned because it can be useful. 'The Navy has to get better at publicity,' says Pedro. He tells me that the Portuguese Air Force is always in the news back home, because they do something derring-do and then send press releases. In Portugal, as elsewhere, the Navy remains the silent service. (Not the most silent, though: in Tony Parker's book about lighthouse-keeper life, one wife says that compared with the lighthouse service, 'the Navy's a bunch of chattering monkeys in a monkey house'.) The schedule involves a 'walkaround' of a different department each day. There will be interviews with the flag commander, the captain and all department heads and anyone else I choose. Four departments are run by lieutenants – logistics, weapons, mechanics and operations – and the fifth is run by the XO, the Navy name for the chief officer. The fifth department is the entire ship, so the XO is in charge of the crew's welfare and of mine. He is a shaven-headed man with a sunny temper but also a gravity that emerges in his delight in conveying things accurately, so that he will return hours after a conversation with a fact about Catherine of Braganza, or the proper definition of Portugal's Exclusive Economic Zone. I tell him my needs, which are for vegetarian food and some pirate action. The ship is already catering to two Muslims on board – the bridge happily tells the Djiboutian translator which way Mecca is, when he asks five times a day – so a vegetarian is manageable. The pirates: who knows?

From the safety walkaround I remember little except the amount of Velcro sticking everything to every wall everywhere. 'If we throw the ship against a wall,' my escort tells me, 'it will stick.' The logistics walkaround is a shock after merchant-shipping parsimony. It would make Pinky weep. The logistics chief, a harried lieutenant-commander named Semide, won't tell me how much the budget per head is, only that it is more than $7. From his expression, it is much more than $7. The ship is crammed. We walk over boxes of orange juice. A carton of vin de pays has spilled and smells. Semide kicks it with disgust. 'What a mess. It doesn't normally look like this, but we have no space.' He has to store food supplies with machine spares. Tomato juice with wing-nuts. As for the plenty, 'marines can eat 12 bread rolls for breakfast. Some guys eat five times a day. You have to calculate for who you have on board.'

The logistics department is also responsible for feeding and clothing any detained pirates. A small group of detainees would be kept in the nuclear, biological and chemical decontamination compartment next to the hangar. More than a dozen would have to live out on deck, in a space beneath the hangar hemmed in by nets. They would be given clothes if necessary, though not the crew's fireproof overalls: they cost too much. Semide talks about pirates in the future tense, as *Vasco da Gama* has never yet detained any. There have been encounters though. The closest was with a suspicious dhow departing a known pirate beach in Somalia. The XO describes the incident as part of the mission that 'contained many heartbreaks'. The ship fired its main gun. Boom! It landed in front of the dhow's bow. 'For half an hour we fired. They didn't stop. They got on the radio and said, "We are in national waters. You can't stop us. If you want to stop us, come and get us."' This powerful warship was handicapped: it couldn't send its rigid inflatable boat (RIB), a fast, zooming dinghy, because the distance was too great and the RIB could not be protected. It couldn't use the helicopter because a rotor was damaged. For snipers, they have to be within 300 metres.

When they can get close enough, their choices are to detain, destroy or disrupt. There is a notorious video showing how the Russians, one of the independent naval forces, destroy and disrupt by putting pirates back in their dhow and then apparently blowing it up. The pirates were actually removed before detonation, but other independent naval vessels have been less scrupulous. *Vasco da Gama* can't do that, being bound by law and convention. Even if it does detain pirates, it is always difficult to meet the burden of proof that prosecution requires. There are known signs of pirate activity: grappling hooks, ladders or too much fuel. All these things are now called 'tripwires', signs of pirate behaviour or intent. But it is not a crime to travel the Indian Ocean carrying ladders. Most fishermen in these parts carry weapons, and the ones with weapons who are not fishermen can easily throw their arms overboard.

Even if there are enough tripwires, and *Vasco da Gama* ends up with a clutch of pirate prisoners netted on its deck, the chances of finding a nation state to prosecute them are low. EU-NAVFOR releases 80 per cent of detained pirates because it can't find willing courts. For now, the Portuguese can fire at fast outboard motors or destroy pirate equipment, both imperfect solutions. The XO keeps a slow Honda outboard motor on deck that he will swap for the pirates' faster one when he gets a chance. He knows, though, that pirates who are neutralized simply go home and fetch more weapons, however slow their boat. After enough outboard motors were destroyed, pirates began stationing men near the motors. When the navies started firing at the skiffs towed by pirate action groups, the pirates stationed men in the skiffs.

They are not dumb, or not always. A US embassy cable reported that Seychelles officials had detained 11 Somali men in three skiffs near Marianne Island. 'Someone must have briefed them on what to do when intercepted,' a coastguard officer said, 'because they dumped their guns and surrendered once we approached.' The men were malnourished. From that, and from the supplies in the skiffs, the coastguard decided that 'the motherboat must supply the pirates with all needed equipment and tell them not to return without a captured vessel'. The same group, the cable continued, had approached locals taking day-trippers to Marianne Island and asked, 'Which way is it to Somalia?'

The only likely action this week will come from drills and exercises designed to keep the crew alert. Marines get easily dulled and the warship's specialized diver has been relegated to his other job doing the laundry. I see him laden with T-shirts near the laundry room sometimes, and he never looks pleased. Also, there are many skills to be kept fresh, if a US marine's list of all the elements of his anti-piracy training is accurate: surgical shooting, combat conditioning, diving, high-altitude low-opening (HALO) and high-altitude high-opening (HAHO) parachute operations, rappelling, fast-roping, climbing, hand-to-hand combat, communications, knife-fighting, combat trauma, explosive and intelligence-gathering. Some drills are more interesting than others: a ship fire is demonstrated with dramatic smoke. 'It's water vapour. They use it in nightclubs.' The XO is keen to keep his journalist alert, so he will let me have a trip in an RIB, a quick joy-ride on the most dangerous waters in the world, and a flight in Bacardi, as the crew have named their Lynx helicopter. I come to think of Bacardi as the ship's pet, though one with nifty flexible rotor blades so that it can fold in on itself to fit in the hangar.

The RIB goes out, and I come back with exhilaration and a bruised forehead from steel safety bars combined with a choppy sea state 6. Bacardi is more fun and less painful. First, because the flight crew like to keep their morale up by playing 1980s pop, my serious safety messages – if we ditch, jump into the sea on the right-hand side, because the pilots can see you better – are delivered to a soundtrack of 'Karma Chameleon'. The flight detachment has the best deal in this *Petra 1*-escorting down-time, as they fly reconnaissance missions over Somalia and out to sea almost daily. Loudspeaker messages – 'pipes' – announcing that the flight hangar is in use, and that smoking is therefore banned on deck, begin at 5 a.m. most days. I guess at most of them, as they are always in Portuguese, which sounds like Italian and Russian have been put in a blender. Hardly any of the international staff speak Portuguese, but there is rarely any translation provided. 'I hear something,' says a French member of the international staff. 'But I have no idea what it means, so I look at someone Portuguese. I think, he's not looking worried, the ship is not sinking, it's just that I'm allowed to smoke outside again.'

Up in the helicopter, we fly over *Petra 1*. A crew member comes out on deck and waves. 'That's how we know it's not a pirate,' says the co-pilot over the headphones. 'Pirates don't wave. They're always in a bad mood.' He is joking, but knowing the difference is vital for the helicopter crew. It determines how close and low they can go. An RPG has a range of 500 metres. So they must get close enough to get good intelligence but not so close that they regret it.

The flight crew does regular reconnaissance missions over pirate camps ashore, usually easily identifiable: huts on a beach, skiffs beached nearby, SUVs coming and going. Sometimes Bacardi gets close enough to see faces. There is no shortage of intelligence in counter-piracy. All the coalition task forces know where the hostaged ships are anchored, off Eyl or Haradheere or Garacad, pirate hotspots along the coastline. Pirates don't need to hide when they have human shields. The camps have been given code names. Great Pumpkin. Van Pelt. Spike. I see these names on maps in the operations room, a place of darkness and screens where I am asked not to look too closely. Next door in the comms room there are dozens of tape cassettes decorated with skulls and crossbones and labelled 'Piratas'. They hold recordings of boardings of suspicious craft and 'other counter-piracy stuff, mostly flight operations', says my escort. 'Quite boring.' The skulls and crossbones are for fun. What is the point of all this information if you can't do anything to the pirates? The communications officers shrug. 'We share information. That's all.'

In the quarters that he has taken from the captain, the flag commodore – the chief of the EU-NAVFOR fleet – is everything I expect a flag commodore to be: talkative, weary and sophisticated. Alberto Manuel Silvestre Correia knows what I will ask. Yes, counter-piracy work is frustrating. Yes, of an assumed pirate workforce of about 4000, at least 1500 have been held in Navy warships and released. Some have been captured two or three times. If they were prosecuted, it would make a difference. If those 1500 Somali men disappeared from coastal society, it would make a difference.

These are shameful statistics, and bewildering: if piracy holds no risk and capture promises nothing more daunting than three meals a day and a ride home, then it will continue. Correia knows this. He says, as everyone says, that the solution is onshore. There are no Kenyan, Tanzanian, Mozambican pirates because they have coastguards and law. Somalia must be rebuilt. Somalia must be saved. The commodore says that pirate attacks have diminished, which is true. Successful attacks are also down: at the time of our meeting, no ship has been hijacked for three months. In the Indian Ocean, by the summer of 2011, this is considered a great achievement. But the warships are handicapped by state cowardice as well as law. The UK has never prosecuted a pirate and nor has Portugal. The United States has: in 2010, five Somali men became the first pirates since 1820 to be convicted under US piracy law for an ill-advised attack on US frigate USS *Nicholas*. The following year, Abduwali Abdiqadir Muse was sentenced to 34 years' imprisonment for his role in the taking of *Maersk Alabama*. His crimes were hijacking, kidnapping and hostage-taking, not piracy.

Mostly the job of prosecuting falls to locals: Kenya and the Seychelles have both been persuaded to prosecute pirates, with aid given and new prisons built. Seychelles' prison is run by a former governor of HM Parkhurst on the Isle of Wight. Its staff include two former Parkhurst officers who, one tabloid delightedly wrote, usually guarded sex offenders. 'There was a stampede when this job was advertised.' Pirates must be better than paedophiles. When Seychelles inmates rioted in 2010, the 11 detained pirates were careful not to join in, locking themselves in their cells and refusing to co-operate. They were described as model prisoners.

Correia does not talk of eradicating piracy. He is realistic. 'We have to contain it to a tolerable level of piracy. It is difficult to define what is tolerable.' It is not difficult to define what could change things. 'We have to provoke any effect that discourages them to fight. We have to produce an effect on their centre of gravity.' He thinks this is difficult for a civilian to understand, but I understand it fine. Everyone has a weak point on their poop deck. All arrests should lead to jail. There should be meaningful risk. He read that the average lifetime earnings of a Somali are £9000. 'With one piracy action he can get double that. So why not take the risk?'

The media often writes of a war against pirates. But although most ships are insured against piracy by war risks insurance, for the frigate's crew this is no war. They bristle at the word. 'War is a very strong word for the military,' says the XO. 'We are acting as policemen.' In official language, the counter-piracy coalition is a constabulary operation, and the frustration is familiar to any police force attempting to police an inner-city area, where you stamp out trouble and it moves elsewhere like a bubble in an air mattress. It is like any asymmetric encounter, where guerrillas win through flexibility.

'We are being useful,' says the XO. 'We destroy their equipment. The frustration comes when I have 17 pirates for 12 days and no-one wants to take them. I have to leave them on a beach to be pirates again, two weeks later.' The military often sees repeat offenders despite the harsh conditions at sea. When the Danish warship *Absalon* kept 13 pirates on board for 38 days they all put on two kilograms in weight: weeks stalking ships at sea can easily become a starvation diet. I see an arrested pirate on TV whose legs are sticks. It is not an easy life, spending weeks of waiting, running out of food. Perhaps this is why the XO has a strange sympathy for their quarry. 'You have to understand,' he says, 'they are not just pirates. They are human beings. By the Geneva Convention we have to take care of them.'

We are due to reach Mogadishu by 5 a.m. The ship is in alert stage 2. Not quite battle stations (alert stage 1), but prepared for trouble. I get up at 5 a.m. – easily, thanks to the pipes – and go to the bridge, but there is only darkness to be seen. *Petra 1* is due to be escorted into Mogadishu's port – which has only two berths, though I am surprised it has any – by two AMISOM armed teams in fast boats, but they are late. Three hours later in the ops room there is an air of alertness. This is more action than they have had all week: in the time since I got up and then went back to bed, shots have been fired from the shore. No-one is unusually worried: shots are always being fired from Mogadishu. At whom? 'Who knows?' says a lieutenant. 'Just because they want to, probably.' Suddenly two fast boats emerge from the harbour and now there is concern. For some reason, the boats don't identify themselves. I ask why not, and get a shrug. We listen to the crew of *Petra 1* calling the boats on the radio, using agreed code names. *Vasco da Gama* is Fox; *Petra 1* is Hound. Eventually the fast craft identify themselves as *Guardian 1* and *Guardian 2*. They are armed boats, but our armed boats. The comms officers manage to sound professional rather than frustrated. 'Message to Hound: you can proceed to port over.' Hound comes back: 'Thank you for your very kind co-operation. We are happy with you.'

Petra 1 delivers its supplies safely. A few more boring days trundling back to Mombasa, and *Vasco da Gama*'s escort job will be over. Whether the supplies ever reach the people they are supposed to reach is not the escort's concern. Al-Shabab has controlled the port before and may do so again. *Vasco da Gama*'s boarding parties have seen humanitarian supplies in pirate skiffs. 'There is no-one here who is not crooked,' a shipping person tells me in Mombasa, and he means in East Africa.

In Mombasa, I see the crew around town now and then, on their generous R&R time. (At sea, a box outside the sick bay holds anti-nausea pills, free for the taking. When the ship is alongside, the pills are replaced by free condoms.) Some have gone on a two-day safari north; some wander around the old town, or have un-ship food in seafront restaurants, as I do. My goal is Mombasa's heavily touristed Old Town, but not for the usual attractions. The courthouse is a few hundred metres from Mombasa's historic fort, and this is where pirates will be. I want to see what they look like, even though I can guess: thin, and Somali. I have made no appointment, but a court official welcomes me into his office. 'You want pirates? We have several on trial.' They have dozens awaiting judgment and others in Shimo Latewa prison, already convicted. Seven presumed pirates are being tried for an attack on MV *Polaris* in February 2009. The court official finds me a chair and lets me take notes from a dossier marked 'Kenya Penal INSOC 69 (1), 13/07'. As attacks go, the only unusual thing about *Polaris* was that there was enough evidence to detain the attackers. They are still suspects two years on because trials in Kenya are slow, and because midway through this one, Kenya's Supreme Court decided it didn't want to try the world's pirates after all, and that there was no domestic law to justify trying foreign pirates who attack foreign ships and who are detained by foreign navies. This caused some international panic. If Kenya wouldn't try them, who would? After diplomatic bargaining, a Memorandum of Understanding with the EU was signed instead, and now Kenya will try pirates on a case-by-case basis.

Prosecuting a pirate is difficult. Naval forces must do the job of the police but without being trained for it. They have not usually been trained in evidence gathering (although this is changing). Everyone involved in a pirate trial except the detainees is frustratingly mobile: the crew have long since gone back to sea, along with the naval force. People must be recalled. Flights must be taken. None of that is simple or cheap. In the *Polaris* case, witnesses did come back to testify, including an NCIS (Naval Criminal Investigation Service) agent from US *Vella Gulf*, the warship that detained the suspects. In his testimony, he listed the damning baggage he found upon boarding the skiff:

Seven bags of personal belongings
One handheld GPS model no. 13476207

Four 1000 shilling notes [Somali shillings]
137 rounds of ammunition
Six magazines
Five AK47 rifles, serial numbers weren't readable
One pistol with a magazine with 5 rounds of ammunition
One rocket propelled grenade launcher
Three Nokia cell phones
Sim card and phone charger
In a separate bag, 19 1000 shilling notes
Family photo and address book
One hook [attached to] a rope
One revolver with three fired rounds. Rounds were unsafe and we discarded them.
Two rocket propelled grenades. We were unsure of them as they were damaged so we photographed them and discarded them.

The following day, the case has a 'mention' – a brief summary that seems to serve no purpose – in the old courthouse. The judge is a large man who rarely looks up. From the *Polaris* dossier, it's clear why: he is furiously writing, because the entire official record of the case is handwritten by the judge. Kenya's judicial system is founded on the rule of law, but it operates with the rule of biro. The accused sit in the dock. They have an interpreter and a lawyer, although only just: the attorney, Francis Kadima, had abandoned his charges, complaining that they couldn't pay him. He was now back in court on their behalf because the EU was paying his fees. The suspects are skinny. They complain, through their interpreter, that the prison food is bad, that they have contracted tuberculosis. 'I feel pain all over,' one writes in the dossier. 'Especially the bones.' Kadima does not inspire confidence or liking, but he has created a shrewd defence. They are Somali, his clients say. They attacked a ship from the Marshall Islands and were arrested by US forces. 'The government of Kenya did not arrest us. We were told that the UN will take care of us as we are poor fishermen with no money.' The mention is swiftly concluded and I am none the wiser, except that the suspects are going on hunger strike to protest at their treatment and lack of human rights. The judge seems shocked by this. 'We are not animals,' he says in his summing up. 'We have no interest in keeping anybody in custody.' (The two years of detention say otherwise.) The alleged pirates file out and mill on the porch with their lawyer. A policeman stopped me taking a photograph earlier, so I daren't try again. Instead I sit on a chair and look at them.

On my final day on *Vasco da Gama*, I roamed the ship asking the crew what they thought of pirates. Their answers were surprising. A cook: 'Pirates are human beings with problems.' A helicopter pilot: 'When we've been flying, we see the poverty that rules in Somalia. I don't sympathize but I can understand how things started.' The scariest of the marines: 'Pirates are doing this because they are poor and don't have money. It's a way to get power.' I found this compassion astonishing. I look at these hungry diseased men who probably pointed automatic weapons at the crew of *Polaris* and terrified them for financial gain, and I don't care about their poverty or problems. I glare at them. And one notices me, stops talking to the lawyer for a moment, and glares back at the white woman who thinks he is a pirate, when he knows he is a poor fisherman.

Vasco da Gama marines train in counter-piracy tactics, Indian Ocean

7. NO MAN'S LAND

Veiled Faces in the Water

Pirate fishing, pirate radio, terrorism, environmental activism, down-loading songs from the internet: none of these is piracy, according to a presentation given at ICOPAS, the International Conference on Piracy at Sea, which meets annually in Stockholm and should not be confused with ICOPA, the International Congress of Parasitology. Pirates are violent criminals. You wouldn't know that from their usual appearance in film, in newspapers, at school sports days, where they are lovable rogues, child-friendly buccaneers, swashbucklers. They provide jokes: the Somali team at the Olympics didn't realize shooting and sailing weren't the same thing. They are saleable: a Mombasa firm that offers armed escorts to merchant shipping has called its pirate-chasing craft *Jack Sparrow*. Even EU-NAVFOR's communications with ships are sent on letterhead featuring pirate skull and crossbones, to stand out among all the tedious stuff that is constantly spat out in ship's offices.

People love pirates. They are cartoons and harmless. I wouldn't mind the comedy peg-legs if the distortion didn't continue into more serious quarters. I lose count of the number of articles and documentaries that focus on the pirates, on their motivation, on a one-sided story. Tabloid newspapers delight in the arrest of a pirate who has six toes on each foot. With that information, the *Sun* of course produces the headline 'Yo-Ho-Toe'. Here is another thin Somali in a yellow jumpsuit, talking to a BBC documentary maker in Hargeisa prison, saying it's only business. 'There is no problem taking a ship. It will only be taxed and released safely. There is no harm.'

For most of the last decade, it has been accepted that modern piracy is the bloodless kind. These pirates are rational economic actors who understand that every ship is insured and that insurers will pay. They will not harm the crew, because the crew is their leverage. They operate according to understandable business norms. I read studies that analyse piracy as a 'market-dependent crime'. They decide that it operates best in a stable environment, not anarchy, which is why many pirates come from the less chaotic areas of Somalia like Puntland. Stability is needed to get supplies. I read that the average profit margin for piracy in 2010 was 25–30 per cent, that pirates are 'the very essence of rational, profit-maximizing entrepreneurs described in classical economics'. In 2010, Harvard Business School chose Somali piracy as the best business model of the year.

Breakdowns of the pirate economic model have been done. One suggests that it costs $300,000 to kit out a pirate attack, including $2000 for weapons and ammunition; $14,000 for skiffs and outboards; $1200 for curved ladders; $4000 for GPS receivers and radios; $7000 for food; $30,000 for miscellaneous equipment; $180,000 for bribes. Once hostages are taken, guarding costs are $15,000. That must be the luxury version: a pirate financier interviewed by the British documentary-maker Neil Bell was cut-price by comparison: $30,000 to finance a Red Sea attack; up to $40,000 for the wider Indian Ocean. He could get an RPG for $800 and ammunition for $200. There is no shortage of weapons for sale in Somalia's markets, along with infinite supplies of *khat*, leaves of a plant that is chewed by millions in Arab countries, and on Africa's eastern coast, because it contains cathinone, which produces effects similar to amphetamine. It is cheap, and it is an efficient lubricant for violence. Pirates, Paddy O'Kennedy of EU-NAVFOR told me, live on *khat* and milk. They are high when they attack ships because that dulls the fear. Navies that apprehend pirate groups often find clutches of fifteen-year-old boys in their number, small boys protected by weapons that reach their thighs, and by an armour of intoxication.

Who runs these boys? There is talk of behind-the-scenes control from internet cafés in London; Dubai; anywhere where the huge Somali diaspora, spat out by chaos and sent running, has ended up. Each year, *Lloyd's List* catalogues the 100 most important people in shipping. I thought the most illuminating feature of its 2010 list was that it included only one woman. But attention focused on the fourth place on the list, because that was given to Garaad, one of the three most notorious pirates.

Here is another number: 67, which is how many hostages died between 2007 – when Somali piracy began to flourish – and 2010. Here are the hostages killed in 2011 by this harmless business activity: Marie Dedieu, Christian Colombo, Jean Adam, Scott Adam, Phyllis Mackay, Bob Riggle, David Tebbutt, Wu Lai Yu, Captain Akbarali Mamad Sanghar, Jakku Suleiman Sandi, one bo'sun, 12 unnamed sailors. Some were killed by pirates; some were shot by navy crossfire in lethal 'rescues'; at least one jumped overboard. In this rational business activity, attack rates on seafarers exceed violent assaults in South Africa, the country with the highest level of crime in the world (697.5 per 100,000 for seafarers; 576 for South

Africans). Pirates holding the Taiwanese trawler *Shiuh Fu* amputated the hand of its captain, Chao-I Wu, to force a ransom payment. On at least one occasion, a captive seafarer was keel-hauled, a sweet name for a terrible thing. A sailor is tied to a rope and dragged under the ship, from one side to the other. It is an old practice, but even modern keels have barnacles and things that rip and shred, particularly on ships that have been static for months. If the man is not flayed, he will probably drown. That is the dramatic abuse; malnutrition and extreme mental stress are routine. Between the contours of this rational business activity, there is too much blood.

Shipping likes conferences; you could easily attend one a week, on financing, chartering, sustainable shipping, hull design. Supplying the world with nearly everything is an enormous and complex job: there are things to discuss. Maritime security and piracy conferences are now the fashionable ones to attend. This one takes place at the Museum of London's Docklands branch. It is a handsome building of high ceilings and old bricks that sumptuously preserves an echo of the warehouse's old role while sanitizing it – along with the rest of Docklands – into a public-friendly waterfront where no docker need set foot because no ships come to call.

The museum is running an exhibit on Captain Kidd, a famous Golden Age pirate. The show features historical documents as well as swashbuckling, treasure and violence. A laughably hokey trailer for the exhibit is narrated by a man whose voice is meant to have Hollywood-style gravity but doesn't. Kidd, it says, is the man who inspired the pirate movies. He is the truth at the heart of the pirate myth. In a press release, the show's curator continues this tourist-enticing theme. 'The story of Captain Kidd helped create much of the pirate mythology we've known and loved since the Golden Age of Piracy.' I don't love pirates. The House of Commons 2006 report into piracy was written by people who don't love them either:

'We must be clear what piracy involves,' its authors write with dry anger. 'Kidnapping, theft, assault, rape, wounding, murder. There is nothing remotely "romantic" about the perpetrators of these appalling crimes, or their detestable activity.'

Today's seminar is about detestable activity. For once, people are gathered in a room to talk not about the men who fire guns but about the ones who face them. A Maritime Humanitarian Response Programme is being launched to improve assistance to the families of hostages while their relatives are held, and to the hostages once they are released. The discussion panellists, squeezed behind a long table and trying not to look uncomfortable, are two Vatican priests, one representative from a seafarers' union, one psychologist, one NATO rear admiral, and one former pirate hostage, whose name is Chirag Bahri.

The rear admiral says what I expect him to say: that the solution to piracy is on land, not at sea, but no, he doesn't know how to fix Somalia; that the military solution is no solution; that he is not convinced that pirates are deterred by prosecution because the benefits of the risk-taking are so high and 'because they have nothing to lose. Their motto is "do or die".' I doubt this. I don't think this is in the pirates' cost–benefit calculation; they hope, as anyone would hope, that they will do or fail, but that they won't die.

The unionist is Roy Paul of the ITF. He is a large, plain-speaking man with a fatigued frankness. He laments, as the rest of the panel laments, that hostages released from pirates are left adrift. When they do seek help, the help is inadequate. He describes a released hostage who sought counselling. 'The first time he came, he explained to the doctor what a ship was, and he explained what had happened. The doctor had no concept of maritime life. The second time he came, he had to do the same thing. He didn't go back.' When you work in an invisible industry, you get tired of the effort required to pull it into the light.

Roy shows pictures. They are different from the images that usually accompany piracy stories, and there aren't many of those to begin with: Somalia is a difficult place to be a journalist. Local reporters are frequently assassinated; foreigners get kidnapped. Colin Freeman of the *Sunday Telegraph* was kidnapped on his way to the airport by his own protection team, and lived for 40 days in a cave.

The most popular piracy image is by Agence France Presse. It's the back view of a man holding an AK47, gazing at a picturesque blue sea, the silhouette of a hostaged ship offshore. Everything about the image is calm. Even the weapon is draped without menace on the man's shoulders. I have not seen images that Roy is showing now, of what ships look like when pirates have finished with them: wrecked cabins, filth, the comprehensive and violent theft of everything worth thieving. One image shows pages from a notebook kept by a hostage on a captured Thai trawler. They express an anguish that is not usually heard.

> Dream to the day Release Us.
> I want to back home.
> Help me please!
> Thank you for Soy Sauce made us do not starve to death.

Soon it is Chirag's turn to speak. I have never encountered a former hostage until now. I look at him with fascination, at his smart suit and neat hair, as if he is a specimen. He is young – 29 years old – and speaks a strongly Indian English. His emotion is making it more accented still. Anger is a rare thing to see, as a hostage is a rare thing to see. Some sign non-disclosure agreements with their employers. Some tire of telling their stories and never want to see a clipboard or voice recorder again. Many go straight back to sea because that is their life. What else can they do? Chirag tells his story briefly.

He makes people laugh when he tells how the pirates wanted him to convert castor oil to motor oil. How stupid they were. 'We are not supermen,' he told them. 'We are seamen. We are just doing a normal job. What have we done?' He is passionate; he is politely furious. 'It's very, very awful. I would request from my heart that something should be done with immediate effect.'

Chirag's anger has pushed him into becoming a public ex-hostage, a spokesperson for the 4000 men and women who have been captured by pirates to date. It is an important position to hold. Sometimes, for fun, I ask friends and acquaintances – educated, sophisticated ones – how many hostages they think are being held by pirates. Usually they suggest a dozen, when it is actually 40 times that.

I arrange to meet Chirag the next day at ITF headquarters in south London. We sit in a small room and I try not to think that what I am about to do is indefensible, because I want him to tell me in great detail what he lived through. You can stop talking when you want, I say. I don't want to ruin your day. He nods. The interviews the day before were difficult. 'Everything came in front of my eyes again; I was tied up, I was crying for help. I got a little bit emotional.' He is also nervous about his safety. This sounds far-fetched in a secure, comfortable room on a noisy London road, but he is serious. Pirates have contacts and connections in London. Someone in the shipping industry told him he could still be attacked. You never know. But he will talk anyway: his world is so ruined, it doesn't matter if the day is. The first thing he says, with flat bitterness, is that he is getting divorced 'because of the great Somalia'. Behind his smart suit and anger, his life has been unmoored.

Chirag is from Ghaziabad in Uttar Pradesh. This is as landlocked a town as you can find in India: it is more than 600 miles to the nearest coast. But Indians have a strong maritime tradition, with good maritime schools and good English that makes them popular with manning agencies. Becoming a marine engineer seemed like a good career choice. So in 2003 Chirag went to sea, and by 2010 he was on his thirteenth ship, a tanker named MV *Marida Marguerite*. He was the second assistant engineer, about to be promoted to second engineer. 'But then, piracy…' He is quiet a moment. 'Unlucky fellow.'

The tanker's owner was OCMI, a German company. It flew the flag of the Marshall Islands and carried a crew of 19 Indians, two Bangladeshis and one Ukrainian. On that run, they were taking benzene from Kandla Port in Gujarat to Belgium. They had called at Salalah and were 120 miles out, eight days into May, at noon, when they saw what Chirag calls 'veiled faces in the water'. It is a common belief among seafarers that pirates don't like to attack in full sunlight, but pirates know better than conventional wisdom. The crew were not unprepared. They had razor wire to repel ladders and boarders. They knew about and followed the latest version of Best Management Practices. But still, they were mostly dependent on luck, like all ships that travel slowly and without private security or nearby warships. That day, luck was somewhere else. *Marida Marguerite* was doing 13 knots; the two skiffs were doing 25. The visibility was good enough to see for five nautical miles, but the pirates could neutralize that advantage. They knew that the funnel casts a shadow on the sea, that if they approached through that shadow the radar couldn't see them. Chirag was in his engine room when he was told that skiffs were approaching. It took only 15 minutes for the approach to become an attack. So fast and terrifying. I watch a video of an attack on another ship: the speed and unrelenting nearing of the skiff have a menace that penetrates my computer screen. This must be the fear felt by the hunted, the kind that reaches your throat first.

Marida Marguerite began to follow a prearranged plan. Evasive manoeuvres and zig-zagging first, so that Chirag was on his toes in the engine room, running up and down to push his engines to maximum power. Outside, the attackers launched two RPGs at the ship, and fired their AK47s. Non-stop, clatter clatter.

I ask him where the RPGs hit. No, he says, you don't understand. They deliberately miss because they don't want to harm the ship. It is just for the scare. I remember the pirate financier in Puntland, and calculate it to have been a $1000 scare. The pirates put their ladder mid-ships and climbed up to the deck. Chirag doesn't know how they got through the razor wire, but it was either with agility or with wire cutters. Then they headed for the wheelhouse. The crew had removed the outside ladders because they expected this, but the pirates climbed pipes. The captain watched them climb for the three minutes it took them to reach the bridge doors, which were locked. You will let us in, said the pirates, or we will heat you out of there. I don't know what Chirag means by this, but it doesn't matter, because the fear is the important thing to be conveyed, and he is doing that easily.

The doors were opened, and the crew were told to assemble in the wheelhouse. There they all were, then: 22 men who knew they were in a high-risk area, who sailed with nervousness but thought they might escape because of the balance of probabilities or the size of the sea. A Danish family sailing a yacht from the Maldives to Oman thought the same thing. They hoped to 'sneak through', they said after they were released from six months of pirate captivity. (A tabloid newspaper ran a gleeful article about how one of the pirates wanted to marry the 13-year-old daughter, although rumours already ran in military circles that she had been raped.) This Danish family seemed so stupid. Who sails a yacht here any more? The hijacking of the US yacht *Quest* a few weeks earlier, and the murder of its four crew, had been unmissable news. NATO now advises yachters to put their boats on a ship to travel through this ocean. The Danes thought they were protected by geography. So did Paul and Rachel

Chandler, the most famous kidnapped yachters. 'When you explain to people that it's like sailing out of Falmouth, and the pirates are based in Lisbon,' said Paul Chandler after their release, 'you can see their minds thinking, oh, well, that's quite a long way away.' That is an empty sea, he said. Just not empty enough.

There is still debate about whether pirates counter the vastness of their hunting grounds with planning. Most piracy experts think they linger and hunt by chance, waiting for a ship. George Kiourktsoglou, a piracy researcher at the University of Greenwich, thinks that they target certain flags. Perhaps this is because he used to be a nuclear engineer and does not believe in chance. According to Kiourktsoglou, pirates prefer to target ships flagged to registries that have no naval presence in the Indian Ocean. So ships flagged to France, Turkey, UK, Malta and Cyprus, for example, run only a 0.26 per cent risk of being attacked; for flags from Singapore, Marshall Islands, Antigua and Barbados, the risk runs twice as high. The starving pirates who are captured, their legs brittle and like sticks, reveal another reality: that the hunters are sent out with supplies and they don't come back until they find a ship or run out, and sometimes the calculations let them down. There are no firm figures for how many pirates starve or drown while out at sea, but some do. Major General Howes of EU-NAVFOR has calculated that 50 die each month. It is not a bloodless business for them either.

On the *Marida Marguerite*, the crew didn't have a citadel prepared. There was nowhere to hide safely, so the crew stayed on the bridge as they were told, and watched six pirates, pissed off and hyped up, shouting at their captain to sail towards Somalia, 600 nautical miles away. What could the captain do? He had followed procedure: he had radioed a distress call on Channel 16. He had alerted the UK Maritime Trade Operations Centre in Dubai. In the past, some ships failed to do this when attacked, so the UK Hydrographic Office now issues an Anti-Piracy Planning Chart, where all the procedures and necessary numbers are listed alongside a stern warning not to use the chart for navigation. But these pirates had been too quick, or the crew had been too slow. By the time a naval helicopter flew overhead, the pirates were secure enough to fire into the air. This is our ship now. The helicopter withdrew.

When Chirag arrived from the engine room at the bridge, the pirates shouted at him. Sit! Sit! 'I was terrified. For me to see these six monkeys with ΛK47s: I thought, my god, this is the end of the day.' All the crew members were now sitting on the bridge floor. Some were crying. Others were comforting their crewmates, saying, no, they won't kill us. This is business. Some started talking about fighting back. There were only a few pirates: it could be done, surely? But the senior officers disagreed. At least one crew member would be killed. They would have to capture AK47s then fire them at night. They were merchant seafarers, for God's sake, not soldiers. They were unused to weapons. The idea was quickly dismissed.

So the crew watched the pirates and the pirates watched the crew, while the ship steamed towards Garacad, a small harbour town in north-central Somalia, where it was anchored four miles offshore. Here, the guard changed. The boarding party left and were replaced by 40 pirates, a mixed group of teenagers and young men. This division of labour is common in piracy: good ship-boarders are prized and not wasted on months of guarding. Half of the *Marida Marguerite* boarding party were on their third hijack, and off they went to try for a fourth. The new crowd brought a negotiator, an older, bearded Somali who spoke English. At this point, Chirag began to feel hopeful. Negotiations would happen; ransom would be paid; they would not be kept for long. He was wrong. At the time this happened, the average period of capture was 250 days. This had changed over time. In 2005, charter rates were higher and fuel costs lower. It cost $150,000 a day to charter a tanker, and charterers paid that whether the tanker was freely sailing or captive off Somalia.

A month of captivity could cost a company more than $4 million, making it imperative to solve any hostage situation quickly. One-million-dollar ransoms were freely paid and captivity times were in months, not years. Now, charter rates have been decimated by the recession. When it's only $10,000 to charter a tanker, companies can afford to let negotiations endure.

The modern history of negotiation has been associated with land-based kidnappers. Only recently have expert ransom negotiators like John Chase learned to talk to pirates. Chase is a 'response consultant' for AKE, a company offering services in Kidnap & Ransom (K&R) situations. He is dressed casually when we meet in a London café; he looks young for his 50 years, and speaks quietly so that afterwards, the recording of our conversation has the sound of coffee cups clinking in the foreground, and the intricacies of bargaining for human life behind that. His workload is unpredictable – he could be called once a year or once a month – and it is in the interests of the insurance company to which AKE is contracted as negotiator for him not to work, ever. In practice, that means he gets a good salary to spend plenty of time with his children, then has to leave them suddenly, for weeks and months, for as long as it takes. Chase has been working in K&R for 30 years, and he has gripping and gruesome tales, about such things as the Mexican gang known as the Ear-Loppers, after their favourite bargaining technique. The Ear-Loppers took exception when a rival gang also started chopping off hostages' ears, and annihilated the other gang for stealing their brand identity.

Chase is pragmatic. He expects hostages to lose body parts sometimes. 'We always say to clients and families, people may lose an ear but they are alive, they can lead a normal life.' He has only had two failures. One involved a hostage who tried to escape and was shot in the back. The other happened in Iraq, when forces loyal to Saddam Hussein executed 60 hostages, all at once, after Saddam was hanged. That was unusual, because once there is money on the table kidnappers negotiate, a truth that applies to Colombian jungle rebels, Mexican ear-loppers and Somali pirates. Chase's first piracy case was in 2000. He soon learned that pirates behave more like land kidnappers than Blackbeard or the lovable Captain Kidd, who would kill crew when it suited, and easily. The prize for Indian Ocean pirates is the ship with the crew. Either on its own would not have the value of both.

This is the procedure, usually, once a ship is taken. Chase, or someone like Chase, will fly with a team to the headquarters of the company that owns or has chartered the ship. A crisis management room is set up, and far too many interested parties will want to be involved. At this point, culling is required. 'The crisis management team has to be nimble enough to deal with a piracy case. Often they're built for, for example, if a tanker hits a reef somewhere and there's a spill. We pare down the crisis team to three, four or five people to take decisions.' This can involve trickery. 'You always get some senior director saying, I need to be a part of this. We say, that's great, but we are going to be in this room for the next 30 days, 24/7. They usually say, oh, I was going to the cottage next weekend and suddenly they're not there.' He really does mean 24/7. Frequently the team members can be sleeping under the boardroom table for a month. They are rotated out every 30 days: that is considered the maximum time before mental and physical exhaustion begin. Chirag and his crewmates, humans confined in a small space, dependent on other humans confined in a small space.

The opposing sides in these negotiations have much in common. Each puts forward a special employee to do the talking. On the response-team side, actors are often used. They can read scripts well, and they are always reading from a script. There is no ad-libbing in ransom negotiation. On the pirate side, there are now sophisticated, erudite translators. It is a new career opportunity for

Somalis who left their wrecked country for Europe or the Gulf, who have come back with their overseas education and language skills. Chirag won't tell me the name of the translator or of any pirate, although he knows them. It is not worth the risk. He says only that the translator was English-speaking, Somali, and that he had spent time in India and knew some Hindi. He had also been to the United States many times. Negotiations began, 'but he didn't get any fruitful result'.

Probably the expectations were too high. By 2010, the size of ransoms demanded was escalating. Pirates were asking 'crazy sums', says Chase. It is his job to manage expectations. Each region has its own known going rate and expected negotiation time. In Afghanistan, for example, the ransom paid is usually half a million US dollars, and negotiations will take 100 days. It makes no sense to deviate from that, to offer a million, because then the kidnappers hold out for more. If a million is offered within two weeks, but the accepted length of negotiation is 100 days, then kidnappers will start wondering: is my hostage wealthier than I thought? Does he have government ties? Chase calls this putting the 'expectation comfort zone out of whack'.

For the first few years, similar understandings operated with piracy. Then some ship owners gave in too soon, or too high: there are no formal guidelines or rules, so competing negotiators do their own thing. The maritime lawyer James Gosling, who has been involved in plenty of negotiations for shipping clients, gave a talk at the Vatican in 2012 about the peculiar economics of bargaining. These are not, he said, 'what you and I would call normal commercial negotiations. You don't start with one figure, counter another and then finish somewhere roughly halfway in between.' If an owner gives too high a figure, pirates will retract on figures that they have already agreed on, and go back to a higher ransom demand. Gosling called this the 'yo-yo effect'. Paying ransoms that are too high skews expectations, so that pirates now expect to get $10 million for a small ship owned by one family who simply cannot pay that. When many ships are heavily mortgaged, and owners rely on daily charterer fees to keep going, a hijack is disastrous: the charterer stops paying, but wages must still be paid, along with mortgage payments. Several owners, said Gosling, have had mental breakdowns or heart attacks when their ships have been taken. Some have gone out of business. For Chase, whacked expectations mean negotiations take longer, hostages are held longer, and more are getting hurt or killed.

Chirag didn't know that there were these rules and expectations. All he could see was the day in front. It was good that he could still work. A ship's engines always need maintenance, even a ship stalled by the limbo of a kidnap. The sea is still sea and the salt is still corrosive. Some ships released from captivity have sunk. Some of the sinkings no doubt suited ship owners who were anxious about the cost of repairs to a ship damaged by months of immobility, and who possessed adequate insurance. Others were genuinely corroded, wrecked and diminished. Chirag began to stay in the engine room for 12 hours a day, keeping things going. The pirates didn't follow him down there. They didn't like the dark or the noise. Once the engineers understood this, they deliberately set off engine alarms any time a pirate came near. Also, for the first weeks, they hid beer in the dark spaces of the engine room. A small triumph.

After 12 hours, Chirag would return to the bridge and chit-chat if possible, 'if the pirates were OK'. He became an expert at pirate-watching, at guessing their moods. He soon learned that they were predictably unpredictable. Supplies were brought aboard from the shore, and the supplies often included goats, which were slaughtered on the main deck, to Chirag's disgust. He thought his captors were filthy, that they had skin conditions and STDs. But he also complained that they used all the water from showering. He was wary of the *khat* they were constantly chewing, which he tried once and didn't like because it changed the taste of his mouth and his mood. On the ship, afternoon was doping time and by the evening they were high. Chirag learned to read more carefully when their eyes turned red. They became paranoid that a naval vessel or a rival pirate gang would dare to attack them; that the crew might call the Navy somehow.

After 20 days, the hostages were allowed to move into cabins. Time passed with difficulty, but it passed. Chirag says things like 'for the first six months', as if it were nothing. I suppose he wants to forget it, but this empty time interests me. What happens to a brain over months of fear? Colin Freeman, held hostage in a cave by his Somali armed guards, put it like this: 'You realize that your mind, already tired and stressed, is not the limitless sanctuary you might expect. Rather than passing the time with intellectual, life-affirming insights, I increasingly found I could only manage things like listing old pubs I'd visited in my youth, and ranking the girls I knew in order of attractiveness.'

At least there was food. At least there was more than soy sauce. The pirates brought their own cook, who prepared goat and more goat. The captives' diet was potatoes and bad rice containing stones that fractured teeth. If they were lucky, the pirate cook made them chapatis. Supplies were meagre although there were regular boat taxis bringing food and goods from the shore, indicating that Garacad tolerated the pirate activity off its beach. This is not always the case. The northern Somali town of Bargal posted STOP signs with messages that piracy is *haram*, or against Islam. The town council presented its local pirates with a list of demands, then posted an 80-strong police force on the beach. When pirates came shopping as usual for *khat*, they were turned away. Other villages and towns in Somalia have also banished pirates.

But still pirates have no difficulty finding refuge. Perhaps they are good for business. Dr Anja Shortland of Brunel University wanted to answer this question by measuring normal economic indicators, but on the ground, research in Somalia is difficult. Instead, she used Google Earth, studying satellite images of areas where pirates were known to operate. She was looking for evidence of construction and electricity as indicators of prosperity and progress. Shortland compared images from 2005 to those from 2009. None of the notorious pirate towns – Eyl, Hobyo – had enough light to show up, then or now. They had the darkness of unelectrified poor places. Then Shortland looked at walls. Somalis like to live in compounds. If they have money, they build walls. They do home improvements, like anyone. By 2009, compounds in Eyl and Hobyo had grown in size, and more had cars parked outside, suggesting 'a combination of a rising value of stored goods and increasing community tensions'. The walls and snazzy compounds showed that pirates were prospering, but that common good – in the form of electricity – had not been shared among other residents. There were no other visible improvements to infrastructure. Being a pirate town did not pay.

There are plenty of tales of wild parties, prostitutes, drug-taking and more. But in Mombasa, a local shipping journalist thinks he knows where the money goes. Into that new apartment building, and that money-changer's office; into that block of offices; and that villa there. The journalist had bought a piece of land for 330,000 Kenyan shillings in 1993, and in 2010 a Somali offered him 1.5 million shillings (about £11,000) for it, in cash. He didn't sell. He doesn't know for sure that the buyer was a pirate, but the rumours are powerful around these men with such cash from such a poor country. 'Some who have done piracy several times are here.' He says the godfathers – the land-based pirate controllers – come here to spend their gains, that the money-changers are mostly Somali-owned. 'The government turns a blind eye, maybe because of corruption. They can make you not see them.'

*

There is no need for secrecy in piracy. John Chase's negotiators often communicate by Skype. It's not like in Afghanistan or Iraq, where you are trying to negotiate out of sight of governments who want to rush in and rescue. Somalia is different. 'The pirates will talk on the phone for hours at a time. Everyone knows where they are, it's not an issue of trying to locate them.' Everyone knows where the hostages are, but no-one is rushing to rescue them. Bryan Toki, a maritime security consultant, once rescued an Indian ship that had been held for 332 days. He was 'haunted by the sight of Chinese sailors, rail-thin with beards down to their waists, waving for salvation on a nearby ship'. He wanted to fire at them 'to open up on those bastards who were holding them and free those poor souls'. 'But,' he said, 'I had to remind myself, this is a business.'

On *Marida Marguerite*, the beatings began at the end of August. This was when the negotiations began to go badly. The second officer had turned turncoat, whispering information to the pirates about the size of the company, the value of the ship and its cargo. The pirates seemed to believe him. In Chirag's description of his captors, they are part knowing and part gullible. They knew enough to research Chirag's name on the internet, to bring him a printout of a letter his sister had written to the Indian government begging them to do something to release her brother. But the Indian government would do nothing when the ship flew the flag of the Marshall Islands. 'They can only pressure the owners. German owners, Marshall Islands flag, crew members from all over, cargo from some other country going to some other country, vessel of some other make. The problems are bad because of that.' When the pirates sequestered every mobile phone on board, they knew enough to spurn some because they were old models. But they were dumb, too. They found a phone in a drawer that didn't even have a SIM card, so that the screen read 'Emergency SOS'. 'They saw that and said, you have called the Navy. The captain and chief were beaten up day and night because of that.'

There had been slaps before, if the pirates didn't like the crew talking. But at the end of August, they began the torture. The captain was first, then the chief engineer, then down through the ranks. On 9 September, the pirates came to the engine room again. They saw the intercom phones as if for the first time and said, those are satellite phones. (On another ship they thought a coffee-maker was a sat-phone.) They said, you are calling the Navy. You are calling the company and telling them not to negotiate. There was no protesting to be done. There was no point in Chirag saying that of course he wasn't delaying negotiations, he couldn't give a damn how much the company paid, he just wanted to go home. At 6 a.m., he and a fellow engineer were taken to the bridge deck and told to lie belly-down. Three pirates came and tied their ankles to their wrists in a classic stress position. The heat was 40 degrees Celsius by early morning. Then, Chirag's genitals were bound tightly with plastic cable ties. 'They were such torturous people. They used to have fun with that. Lots of crew had their genitals tied up.' Cable-tied genitals and cooking on a hot deck: this continued for four hours. Chirag's left hand was paralysed for a month, and his sperm count suffered too. He knows who decided this new policy of violence. It was a young pirate, under 30, but who looked 15. He was the most dangerous one. Chirag won't say his name but I learn that it was Budiga. Budiga was the Devil. 'Some older pirates had some heart in them. They used to tell the young chap, leave them alone. This is not humanity. The crew have not done anything.' Harassing the crew, they said, would not move the company quicker.

But it might. So there was more slapping, kicking, 'like you would kick a donkey'. The senior officers had worse in this tort-urous period. They were taken to the meat freezer, ice was put in their undergarments, and they were left there for 40 minutes, in minus 20 degrees Celsius. Another was hung by his wrists from a mast. This sounds so antiquated, both the hanging and the mast, like it belongs in the romantic mythology for which we love Captain Kidd. The sailor passed out after two hours.

The longest-held ship so far is MV *Iceberg*, whose 24 crew were reduced to 22 over three years of captivity. Chirag knew about *Iceberg* because he could see it every day, anchored a mile or so away. I am drawn to *Iceberg*, to the absurdly long time it was held hostage, because it was abandoned by its owners, Azal Shipping of Dubai, and by its flag state, Panama. For all its captivity, it was visible off the shore of Somalia. In 2010, British documentary-maker Neil Bell took a handheld camera on board *Iceberg*. In his film *The Pirates of Somalia*, we follow his camera into the ship and into the cabin where 23 men lie shoved together like sausages. Their faces are Yemeni, Indian, Ghanaian, Sudanese, Pakistani and Filipino, and their expressions are dull with despair.

In London's Imperial War Museum, in the small Merchant Navy section, there is a log book from a raft that fled SS *Culworth Hill*, a ship torpedoed in the Second World War. It is written on sailcloth. The words are plain and the wretchedness is clear:

> King, 11pm, 11 April: Out of mind
> 2nd engr 5am 19 April GANGRENE
> Leak, D.E.M.S., 6am Out of mind
> Bolt Army Gunn 10am 19 April Out of mind.

Why does a long-gone raft have anything to do with a Panama-flagged ship? Because *Iceberg*'s third officer, Wagdi Akram, went out of mind. He was Yemeni, a father of four and a well-liked member of the crew. But then he deteriorated. First he disappeared, and his crewmates found him hiding in a ceiling. They chained him up because they saw that their friend had become 'mentally incapacitated'. For three days he was chained, but on the third day he seemed the old Wagdi, as gentle as he used to be. They released him. The next day he went to pray, but didn't finish his prayers. The bo'sun found him in the sea near the anchor, dead.

The crew of *Iceberg* were not allowed to forget Wagdi Akram, because they were still living with him. Bell's camera heads into a room that holds a chest freezer. 'This freezer for fish,' says the crew member who opens the lid. Not for fish any more. He lifts up some packets and there is the calm, dead face, its skin brown and its moustache black, of Wagdi Akram, out of mind.

When *Iceberg* ran out of water (and also electricity, making that freezer of death more dreadful) Chirag was ordered to resupply it with water from *Marguerite's* own stock. He also resupplied other hijacked vessels and 'needy fishing trawlers'. *Marguerite* was the pirate water fountain, supplying 300 tons of water in all to other ships. Chirag describes a strange community of frozen ships and boats, anchored in limbo just off Somalia. *Asian Glory*, *Samho Dream*, *Al Nasir*, *Iceberg*, all captive, all nearby. The artist Allan Sekula, in his book *Fish Story*, writes about Michel Foucault's definition of a heterotopia, a displacement habitat, a place that exists between places. Cemeteries, fairgrounds, retirement homes, psychiatric hospitals. But the best heterotopia is the ship, 'a floating piece of space, a place without a place, that exists by itself, that is closed in on itself and at the same time is given over to the infinity of the sea'. Foucault is wrong. There is a better heterotopia: a ship lying at anchor off Somalia, crippled and crewed by crippled people, visible but untouchable.

Marida Marguerite exhausted its fuel supply after two months. This derailed the pirates' plans to turn it into a mobile mother-ship. This is when they demanded that the engineers turn castor oil into fuel, an impossible request against all laws of physics. Anyway the ship was in no fit state to be sailed. Chirag here smiles. The machinery was not fit because Chirag had temporarily sabotaged it.

'I personally did some small thing. I opened some of the machinery parts and I did all I could to make them feel that the machinery is not in a working state. I don't want my vessel to become a mother vessel.' He sounds very pleased. 'I got some tortures for that but I'm OK with that.'

Chirag elides the next few months. There was hope in October, then more waiting. Somewhere in a conference room where people were sleeping under the boardroom table, details were being worked out. Money was being arranged, as it usually is. John Chase is strict about being strict. 'They'll demand several million and then say, just send $2000, I can buy medicine and food. Of course your loved ones sound sick, you think you need to send this. But for $2000 in Somalia you could feed a whole family for a long time. If you send a few thousand every few months, they will keep going for ever. You have to resist temptation.' Sometimes negotiators have sent food out on a boat when a captive ship has run short. This did not always go smoothly: if pirates ask for halal food, you have to send livestock. But how do you get a live goat up a six-metre sheer side of a ship? With difficulty and dexterity.

The ransom is sometimes not the biggest cost in freeing a ship. John Chase's team charges £2000 a day for negotiation, a fee regulated by the insurance industry. Then there is the drop. Before, when the amounts were smaller, it could be sent out in tugs or boats, like the goats. A million dollars could fit into a rucksack. When the crude tanker *Irene* was released for $13 million, the cash weighed as much as a gorilla.

This is how the conclusion is supposed to happen. Money is arranged, usually from friendly banks in Dubai or in other offshore environments that permit the payment of ransoms to criminals. Both UK and US governments publicly discourage the payment of ransoms, but their laws permit it, as long as the recipients are criminal gangs and not terrorists. This distinction would probably baffle

Chirag, hog-tied on a scorching deck for hours, but fortunately for pirates, no-one yet has linked them convincingly to Al-Shabab. So men with small planes are hired, because the ship is too far offshore for a helicopter to be useful. A pod the size of a mini torpedo is attached to the underside of a Cessna or Otter. The ship is told to set sail, if it can, into the wind and code words are established so pirates don't confuse the money plane for a Navy assault. The crew are made ready: for proof of life, they are lined up on the deck. They wave, sometimes, or stand impassively and hoping beyond human expectation. The pods are dropped into the sea. The pirates go out in skiffs to collect them, and all is usually well.

This procedure can go wrong: in 2010, rival pirate gangs fought over a $5 million ransom that had been dropped on the laden oil tanker *Maran Centaurus*. Only the arrival of Navy helicopters broke it up. With *Marida Marguerite*, it went right. Chirag and his 21 crewmates were on deck, watching nervously. 'It was a moment to cherish. A chartered plane counted us first.' The right codes were transmitted by radio. 'Hellfire calling, beta beta hare or something.' The money was dropped a mile away into the sea and fetched by skiff. And Chirag, who knew his captors well by now, could see that this was a dangerous time, when the paranoia rose in the pirates. 'You knew from their faces. The person who used to smile at us, you see his face and, oh my God, you had better stay away.'

The counting of the money began. This is something that would probably interest Harvard Business School, because it is an organized and complicated business. Pirates use log books and accountants. The accountant on *Marida Marguerite* had been there all along, tallying how many goats had come on board, what the rice was costing, making notes. Chirag reckons 150 to 200 people arrived during the next 24 hours to get their payment. A village-full of people come to be paid for services rendered.

Finally, the pirates ransacked the ship, taking whatever they could find, from cell phones to clothes – but not Chirag's new leather jacket, which he had hidden in the engine room – and left with money stuffed in their pockets, in their stolen clothes, in plastic bags, in the crew's suitcases that the crew no longer needed, because they had nothing to put in them. After eight months, the shock of the home invasion – because that is what hijacking a ship is to the men who live on it – must have abated, only for a final insult. By 10 a.m. on the morning of 28 December, all the pirates had gone. Some had left earlier, saying they had a long way to travel. Then a US naval vessel arrived and Navy Seals came on board. You must have been pleased to see them, Chirag? But he is dismissive. He thinks they took pleasure in the condition of the ship. His pride was damaged.

This was still a dangerous time: there were still a thousand miles to travel to safe anchorage, back to Salalah. Released ships have been attacked by rival pirate groups on their way home. I read of letters of safe passage given to released ships like old-fashioned passports. *Marida Marguerite's* pirates left a phone number instead. Call if any other pirates attack, and they will leave you alone. Chirag doesn't know who the number belonged to and he doesn't care: he says the captain threw the number away anyway. It mattered only that the ship was sailing away and under its own power. When the pirates finally left, laden with money and other people's possessions, the crew got back to work. No way were the engineers going to let their ship be dragged off by a tug. The shame of it. 'Why should I lose money for the company by paying for tugs?'

This loyal parsimony is a surprise. The German owners had behaved decently enough, continuing to pay the men's salaries and 'extra basic' while the ship was captive. They sent a fuel barge to replenish its oil and a fresh set of clothes for every man. Later, the crew were paid $1000 to $2000 in compensation, depending on seniority. I work this out to be about $8 for every day of abuse, fear and loathing. This is not a calculation that I have seen done by Harvard economists.

Chirag does not want to go back to sea. Other released hostages have. At least one crew member of *Maersk Alabama* went back to the same ship on the same route, though never again without armed guards. By now, two-thirds of ships carry armed private security guards, even while the status in law of these rent-a-marines is still fluid, even while you hear stories still, of them dropping weapons in the ocean rather than paying expensive export licences, or worse. They are permitted by several flag states, the IMO, ITF and the UK government. The business is popular, attracting former marines and Special Boat Service men, who leave the service or their post-military mercenary jobs in Iraq and Afghanistan, rushing to this new money zone where they will earn better money than a government salary and not get blown up. There are now thought to be 1500 armed guards working, and a couple of dozen floating armouries where weapons are stored. Now, ships advertise their armed guests in their AIS, so that where the display reads 'destination', there reads instead 'full armed guards' or '3 armed guards O/B [on board]'.

Armed security costs around $50,000 per transit – though security companies are coy about figures – through the High Risk Area, but it is an economical expense: some insurers now reduce premiums if armed guards are on board, by up to 75 per cent. No ship carrying armed guards has yet been hijacked. That is the sea change. Ashore, proper investigation is finally being carried out by the United Nations Offices on Drugs and Crime into the financial flows of piracy, with a view to blocking them. Somalia has a new government stable enough for new prisons to be built, and for pirates to be tried, as the MV *Polaris* attackers wanted to happen, in their own country. Other countries have taken on the pirate task. Yemen, the United States, Germany and Italy have prosecuted pirates. India, meanwhile, wants to prosecute Italian marines who shot two Indian fishermen off Kerala, mistaking them for pirates. As for other shooting of innocent, AK47-carrying fishermen at sea by marines or ex-marines, certainly it happens, and certainly we never know about it. All these efforts have dulled the second golden age of piracy: attacks are down. Perhaps the ex-military men whose messages I read on close protection forums, exchanging information about weaponry and sun protection and how many DVDs to take for ship life (a lot; it can get boring) will do what the commander of the EU-NAVFOR fleet wanted, and keep piracy to a 'tolerable' level. Or the rent-a-marines will move their services to West Africa, where piracy is growing while East Africa's is dimming. And then, cynics say, the young men of Somalia will get back in their boats and set off again, hopeful and hunting.

If seafarers can't come to church, the church goes to seafarers

8.   SANCTUARY

The Merchant Navy Comforts Service

The view – crashing waves, a sandy beach – is spectacular. It is unexpected, because all I knew of the Port of Salalah, in the Gulf state of Oman, was its status as *Kendal's* sanctuary after pirate waters, as the relief at the end of the Internationally Recommended Transit Corridor. I wasn't even sure how to pronounce its name until Captain Glenn told of a girl in the office who pronounces Salalah like 'Ooh-la-la!' (the stress, at least in English, is on the first 'la'). The spectacular view is to be had from the terrace of the Oasis Club, a bar-restaurant on the cliffs above the port. I go there twice in 24 hours, with whoever can grab a few hours' leave to come with me, enough for a quick Skype home; perhaps a drink – non-alcoholic of course – and a meal that hasn't been cooked by Pinky, some fruit that doesn't look as sad as ours.

In the better ports around the world, sailors always head for a mission to use those precious hours. Run by church organizations – the Norwegian Church, the Seamen's Church Institute of New

York and the UK's Mission to Seafarers are the best known – these missions, or seafarers' centres, offer internet, food, drink and a small period of solace and different company to that on your ship. The Mission to Seafarers alone runs 230 centres worldwide, and it is a godsend, because most are in or near ports, and seafarers lack either the time, the money or the visa to go further.

The Oasis Club is not godly; it is a private establishment that has become a de facto mission because of its location near the port, its free transport and its chefs who produce steaks the size of plates. Also, in this dry state, it serves alcohol to those seafarers allowed to drink it, which includes the entire US Navy. I travel in with Francis and a bunch of the Filipino crew. At passport control, Francis begins to speak Arabic to the staff while we look at him in shock. I suppose it shouldn't be a surprise: really he is speaking globalization, because he used to work in Jeddah, one of the satellite destinations of Filipinos' enormous reach. This is the first time that he has seen uncovered Arab women. The bus driver wants to sell him a sword, and Francis fingers the metal and says 'Wow' politely, but doesn't buy it. Overseas Filipinos often take home a box of gifts known as *balikbayan*, a word meaning 'one that is returning home to the country'. A sword wouldn't fit.

The club is packed because a US warship is in port and its crew are making full use of their R&R. There is no table without chasers on it. One sailor swats a fly and says, 'Yeah, baby.' In this atmosphere, you would pronounce Salalah as the girl in the office does, and it would fit. The Filipinos gather around a table to Skype home and to talk; I check emails and wish I hadn't. They are an intrusion into my ship brain, which has become different. It must have, because it regularly and routinely spits out dreams of such violence and vividness that they leave me of a morning on my cabin sofa in a daze, shaking the dreams off like sand. It is rare that I wake up without having dreamt a murder. The crew nod with recognition when I tell them this. They think it is the vibrations, that the noise gets into your head and shakes thoughts asunder.

Instead I head for the club's terrace for some air and some view. There is a drunken sailor already there who is sober enough not to reveal what the warship has been doing, but I presume it has been on anti-piracy duty and thank him with some force, as the keen comfort of seeing a sleek grey ship in Gulf waters – Chinese, Dutch, American, who cares? – is still fresh. The sailor seems to be drinking off months of stress, and so would my crew if Maersk hadn't brought in that no-alcohol policy two years ago. Maersk seafarers aren't even supposed to drink in airports when transiting onto a ship.

Kendal is a ship with high welfare standards: the library is well stocked; the DVDs are plentiful. Providing socializing or solace is apparently more difficult, even for Maersk. The captain laments the demise of the British Merchant Navy, but it is hard to recruit young people to the prospect of months on end of loneliness in company. 'Ships' crews today are subject to constant change,' write the authors of a report into transnational seafarer communities. 'As a result, crews tend to consist of strangers-become-shipmates and consequently the social relations of seafarers' employment are experienced as a series of discontinuous encounters.'

Despite the Oasis Club and the plate-wide steaks, despite the tax-free income and the duty-free goods, despite the view of a glorious ocean that they can't wait to be rid of, this is still an isolating life. Julius and Pedro ask me one day what my purpose is in asking them questions, and I say it is to write about seafarers' lives. Pedro nods. 'The toughest job and the loneliest.' Yes, echoes Julius. 'Definitely the loneliest.'

For most of history, the seaman's life has been one of adventure, perhaps, but also of weevils, awful food, terrible weather, press gangs, pirates, the constant possibility of drowning or injury. Sea life was underpaid, underfed and so often lethal that Marco Polo thought a man who went to sea must be a man in despair. There has always been concern for the souls of seamen, who were thought to belong to a heathen parish. When the English King Stephen sent a fleet to Spain in 1147, the articles of agreement included a priest for every ship 'and the same observances as in parishes on shore'.

It was only in the high times of evangelism that seafarers became a popular cause, when Victorian missionaries, who could travel through the Empire to save souls, instead wandered down to the local docks. Mariners' churches, missions, centres and accommodation houses abounded in the nineteenth century. Naval officers impressed by missionary work in the South Pacific had begun work among the destitute seamen of East London docks in 1827, and opened a Sailors' Home. The Seamen's Church in New York opened in 1835, the same year that an Anglican reverend, John Ashley, fitted out a cutter named *Eirene* to become the first floating chapel of the Mission to Seafarers.

This was not an easy parish to minister to. In his history of the Mission to Seafarers, L.A.G. Strong writes that 'the visitor who was unwise enough to interrupt a card game could expect anything, from the ship's dog at his trousers to a howl of derision and the routine inquiry, "Does your mother know you're out?"' But the rowdiness was misleading. 'Behind their grim exterior, their beards, their tobacco chewing, and the menacing knife at their belts, these Victorian seamen were lonely.' They were also sometimes emerging from months or years at sea in slave conditions. Flogging was only banned on American ships in 1850, although when the Secretary of the Navy asked senior naval officers for their opinion, only seven out of 241 replies wanted it discontinued. It took another 65 years for American seafarers to be protected from other forms of corporal punishment, with the 1915 Seamen's Act legislation – nicknamed the Magna Carta of the sea – which aimed to improve the welfare of the US merchant marine. Until then, captains could and did chastise their crews with 'fists, boots, pieces of rope, brass knuckles, pistols and ship-board items such as belaying pins, marlin spikes, hand spikes and other tools'.

Nor was there peace and harmony ashore. Sailors in a strange port were easy targets for exploitation. Dockland touts known as crimps or landsharks abounded. These were colourful names for unscrupulous people. They were expert at their work: they waited for sailors dockside, or boarded their just-berthed ships to trap them on board. Most sailors wouldn't get their wages for a few days, leaving them with nothing to live on when ashore. You haven't been paid yet? Then have this gin, this woman, this boarding house bed on credit. It's no trouble. After three days of such underhanded open-heartedness, the sailor usually had a bill long enough to push him straight back onto a ship and out of the way of home.

The crimps – they had names such as Timmy, Dutch Charley and Flash Tom – were making the godless world of seafaring worse than it need be, so the Reverend Robert Buckley Burton, a seafarers' chaplain in Bristol, took action. In a scene more *Mission Impossible* than Mission to Seamen, he bundled sailors into a line of waiting cabs and took them to the station and to trains home. Police at the station helped the good reverend oversee the purchasing of tickets and the delivery of seamen onto the trains. 'Victory was complete,' wrote Strong, 'when the trains pulled out of the station, and the crimps stood behind the railings, shaking their fists.'

Priests no longer went to sea. Chaplains were installed instead in overseas ports of empire and trade: Madras, Singapore, Vancouver. In San Francisco, the chaplains were considered so trustworthy that seamen would leave gold coins with them for safekeeping. This was a broad church. The Strangers' Rest Mission in London's Spitalfields catered for West Africans, Caribbeans and Chinese, although the

Chinese were given their own dedicated shelter in the 1900s. There were homes for Destitute Sailors, Coloured Sailors, an Asiatic hostel for Indians, which showed Hindustani films and provided 'native washing facilities'. There were floating boats of worship: the first three churches of the Seamen's Church Institute of New York (SCI) were full-sized chapels attached to a barge that floated up and down New York's waters as required. The Floating Church of Our Saviour for Seamen was, wrote Leah Robinson Rousmaniere in SCI's official biography, a 'pinnacle, Gothic-style church with a seventy-foot steeple'. It was a stunning example of 'ecclesiastical maritime architecture', these days possibly not an overcrowded branch of architectural studies.

Accounts of the early missions abound with tales of not obviously religious endeavours such as chaplains sourcing a piano for a musical captain at short notice, or recruiting compliant – but not too compliant – young ladies for seamen's dances. Some chaplains visited ships carrying lists of Old Testament names for crossword enthusiasts. The third and last floating chapel came ashore in 1910 – tethered to the ground of Staten Island and becoming All Saints Episcopal Church – and by 1913 a magnificent new sanctuary for sailors had been constructed at 25 South Street, flying flags on its roof that in code spelled 'welcome'. By the early twentieth century, it had accommodation for 714 seamen, over 200 employees, and an excellent reputation among seafarers for all sorts of services, some expected, others less so.

The Institute's most famous employee was Mrs Janet Roper, known to all as Mother Roper, well known for her efforts to match families with their lost seafarer relatives and the other way round. Seamen were known for going missing, but Mother Roper located two hundred a year on average. In 1934, she gave a radio interview to Captain Phillips Lord, which ended like this:

Boys who are sailing out on the sea and listening in tonight: find for me – Smoky Joe – his mother is dying. Tell Harry Kelly – Punch Kelly – his father has died and his Mother has got to go to the Poor House. I want to hear from Frank Pazana, Mike Murphy or sometimes called Lemon George – tell Blinky – that's one-eyed Blink Ross, his little girl is sick and needs him. Pass the news to Punch Smith his wife is seriously sick. Shorty McGuire has been looking for his wife and little boy for ten years. Tell him I've finally located his wife and little boy – and they want him back. Goodnight boys – and see that you write your Mother and your sweetheart once every month and let them know where you are. That's only fair play. Goodnight, boys.

What resonates most from Mother Roper, from the archives of all the seafaring parishes, is a constant and unwavering kindness, offered in all weathers and all ports, and for no obvious gain. The Polish sailor Józef Korzeniowski, Joseph Conrad, knew the Sailors' Home on London's Well Street, with its tiers of small rooms offering shelter. It was, he wrote, a 'friendly place… Quietly, unobtrusively, with a regard for the independence of the men who sought its shelter ashore, and with no other aims besides that effective friendliness.' In the Port of London, a chaplain reported taking visiting Chinamen sightseeing, before feeding them supper at his home. This, wrote the authors of the port's 1966 report, was 'men who are strangers [being] taken into a world of friendship'. Two years later, a Chinese-language padre, Peter Kao, reported taking Ng Sing, a chief steward on the *Benvrackie*, on a similar tour. This was a big event: Ng had been with his company for more than 20 years, and this was his first-ever time ashore.

There is much that Ng and Mother Roper would not recognize about today's shipping world, but some things are unchanged. In

2007, a seafarer working on an LNG tanker reported that his regular route – between Qatar and Japan – left him 18 hours in port at both ends. He hadn't had shore leave for 50 months. When Erol Kahveci of Cardiff University asked seafarers how long their average shore leave was, 36 per cent said two hours. Nearly two thirds spent all that time in the port area. Now that 4000–6000 foreign seafarers arrive in British ports every day, the missions have changed their mission. From looking after Britons abroad in a strange land, as they used to do, they now care for the rest of the world coming the other way.

Immingham, a port on the north-eastern coast of England, doesn't look much like a sanctuary. It is not stunning like the terminals of Singapore or Shanghai. Nor does it have the waves or views of Salalah, because it is perched near the mouth of the flat, dull Humber Estuary. I had never heard of Immingham, though I grew up only 50 miles from it. When I researched it, the first story was not about its impressive annual tonnage – it is the largest port in the UK by volume shifted – but about Graham Cardwell, an assistant dock master who faked his own death in 1998 by leaving a lifejacket and hard hat on the docks' mudflats. He was assumed to have been carried out to sea while undertaking routine inspections, but had carried himself instead to the East Midlands, where he lived under an assumed name and worked in a pub, before a passing tugboat captain recognized his voice, having heard it so often in the docks over the VHF radio. Cardwell told police he believed he had cancer and didn't want his wife and children to know. 'A family reunion,' said a police spokesperson, 'is not expected for the foreseeable future.' Perhaps this is a place that sends you mad. You would think as much, if you drove in through its gates and saw the huge refineries and the vast dumps of coal and iron ore, if you wiped from your car dashboard the layer of coal dust that soon settles when the window is open, and saw nothing but flat warehouses, no greenery, nothing but toil and production.

You would think so, but then in the middle of the mucky docks you would reach a modest building and a modest Irish priest who would change your mind. Father Colum Kelly arrived at Immingham as a temporary chaplain for the Seafarers' Centre, on loan from his inner-city Catholic parish in Leeds. It was meant to be a six-month loan, eight years ago. The parish is too broad and the needs are too great, and he is still here. The view from the Centre is nothing much, unless the *Ernest Shackleton* research vessel is visiting, sheltering cut-price in these temperate waters from her Antarctic survey work. Yet Colum waves his arm to the view, to the industry and muck. It was a shock when he arrived, but now, isn't it beautiful?

Inside, the building is warm and spacious and has been equipped with consideration for people who spend their lives among metal. There is a trickling fountain surrounded by plants, pool tables, a large bar and a shop that carries freshly made sandwiches, hair dye, and Fisherman's Cough Linctus, a local remedy. That fishermen require particular cold remedies is not a new notion: Fishermen's Friend lozenges sell billions every year, but were invented by a Lancastrian pharmacist to resolve the bronchial problems of local fishermen working in the freezing Atlantic. Now they are bought by local dockworkers who come for their lunchtime sandwiches – there is no other shop on the docks – but also by citizens of the Philippines, Cape Verde, Russia, Ukraine, Bangladesh, China, India, who regularly arrive in Immingham and head to the nearest source of supplies.

When missions are the only touch of land that seafarers en-counter, they get reputations. Bristol's mission is liked, according to a port welfare survey, 'because it has many phone boxes'. Chinese and African ports are hopeless and sometimes dangerous. Of course African ports don't have facilities offering welfare, wrote one seafarer, because 'how could they provide it for visitors since they don't have it for themselves?' Felixstowe is well attended, but the beer is considered overpriced. Also it is less jolly now: children racing through it used to be a common sight when seafarers could take their families to sea, before the days of piracy. Felixstowe's shop is more popular than its bar prices. It sells London souvenirs to seafarers who will get no closer to the capital than 100 miles distant, but their families don't know that. The shop manager in Felixstowe had studied her clientele well. Taiwanese drink Guinness in the morning with a bar of chocolate. The Italians love Cadbury chocolate, Indians prefer Quality Street. Everyone likes souvenirs that are lightweight and easily packed. Seafarers travel home by aeroplane with the same luggage restrictions as anyone. Felixstowe's manager sourced her souvenirs from a nearby warehouse, so she often found herself following a container from the docks to the warehouse, buying its contents and selling them back to the men who had brought them.

Immingham's mission is popular. Transport can be provided, but the docks are not so gigantic that visitors can't walk to it, or cycle if they have a bike on board, from their ship. The building is spacious and its staff are kind. There are books in the library, and an Argos catalogue that can supply the shopping needs of the hurried at prices far cheaper than chandlers'. There is a small chapel in the corner of the games room, but most seafarers prefer to have Mass on their ship, so it is rarely used. Colum usually has music playing there: Rachmaninov's Vespers are popular, 'and not just with Russians'. When I visited Felixstowe's chapel, it had no music, only a noticeboard filled with modern prayers, including one asking God to help 'with the smooth processing of my son's dependent visa and also pray for my wife's blood transfusions that she will have a Christian blood donor'. Another, from Anonymous: 'What you are doing is so loud I can't hear what you are saying.'

From the beginning, church welfare groups tried to cater to the needs of their seafaring parish. The contact was not necessarily going to be happy, given the Latin prayer *Qui nescit orare, discat navigare*: He who does not know how to pray, let him go to sea. In 1942, the Seamen's Church Institute statistics recorded 106,362 visits to its 138 missions, but only 14,021 attendances at its church services. The Port of London Mission in 1965 fared even worse, evangelically speaking: only 2101 seafarers attended services, but 18,475 used its entertainment facilities.

In her history of the SCI, Rousmaniere quotes an old sailor introducing the Institute to a young boy looking for a ship: 'You can eat there; sleep there; they'll stow your gear. It's cheap and it's clean. They got a job board – tell you what ships are lookin' for a crew. They got it all; and they ain't *too* holy.' The cultural and geographical shift of modern seafarers, though, makes for a more receptive audience for proselytizing: there are Filipino Catholics, Russian and Ukrainian Orthodox, Indian Hindus. Visitors to Immingham's centre can choose from three kinds of spiritual comfort: Catholic from Father Colum, who works for the Apostleship of the Sea; ecumenical from David, a lanky Methodist who represents the Sailors' Society; and Anglican from the Mission to Seafarers' chaplain. He is replacing the previous incumbent, who was prosecuted for immigration offences (he married his own wife twice). The Anglican for now is on holiday, and probably deservedly, as his last posting was the Red Sea port of Aqaba, where he regularly attended to seafarers arriving on ships punctured with pirate bullet holes.

Colum lives above the shop. He is the only residential chaplain of the three and the only full-time priest working for the Apostleship of the Sea. There are a dozen rooms on his floor, but most are empty and forlorn: the centre used to provide accommodation for seafarers, but there is no call for that now. Colum's small flat features décor that has placed function over beauty. There is a utilitarian mismatching of things, though no necessary thing is lacking. He has a single bed suitable for a child or a priest, and one comfortable chair, next to which there is usually a book of poetry. There is something of the ascetic about Colum: he never eats lunch, and forgets that other people do. He is sustained on his own energy between breakfast and dinner. I don't mean that he is an impoverished personality: far from it. The energy he gives off would fuel his boiler, which remains broken despite attempts by a visiting ship's engineer to fix it. Colum says not to worry, he has adequate heating, and indicates a tiny fan contraption that wouldn't warm a flea.

The rooms are dismal, but the view is not. Colum's office faces onto the lock that leads from the outer waters to the inner docks. He looks up sometimes from reading that poetry or working on his computer to see a window filled with a ship sliding by. Today, a wind-turbine ship slowly passes, heading for the North Sea where it will plant wind farms. It has four columns reaching 100 feet up which will drop beneath the ship when it begins its work, perching the ship above the water. 'It's amazing,' says Colum. And it is. He also likes the cable-laying ship that passes through sometimes. Its crew gave the centre a varnished cross-section of cable which is kept behind the bar. It is about 30 centimetres tall, looks like the veins of a giant and is worth £3000. The ships keep him awake at night sometimes, but he loves this place. How could he not? Every day the view is different yet the same. The surroundings never depress him. 'Never. The whole world comes here.'

Colum had no seafaring links. His family in Ireland is not a maritime one. After 30 years in city parishes, though, the secondment sounded like a break. The first step was to go to sea. Apostleship of the Sea training consists of taking a passage on the QEII. Colum's voyage was no sinecure. It was right after the 2004 Indian Ocean tsunami, and the Thai crew were distraught when they watched the TV news and saw 'doors and bits of houses floating through their villages'. It was his first exposure to the modern seafarer's predicament of quick information and eternal impotence. It was then that he understood: even a seafarer on the most advanced, most expensive of ships may still need comfort. He still needs effective friendliness.

Colum's duties are various. A typical day contains nothing typical. He might be asked by seafarers to buy batteries, if they can't come ashore. He might give them a ride to the stores to buy decent coffee, noodles or laptops, where they will encounter a checkout girl who says, making conversation with foreigners, where are you going next? And when the seafarers say Panama or Brazil, she'll say, 'Oh, how exciting,' but she has no idea that their Brazil is different to hers, that hers is palm trees and beaches, and theirs is a concrete dock. An Indian crew arrived at Immingham and Colum went aboard their ship. He asked the captain his usual questions: 'What can I do for you? Shall I take you shopping?' The captain said no, thank you, but he had another request. His crew would like to walk on grass. Green, green grass. 'We have been ashore,' said this captain, 'but most of the time we walk on steel. It is unforgiving.' The priest was not flummoxed. He put them in the centre's van and drove them to a churchyard near Hull airport. 'And they all took off their shoes and walked barefoot on the grass for an hour, then they went back to the ship.'

Batteries are a common request. A battery can mean a lot when you have been for several weeks without one. 'Never underestimate,' he says, 'the value of a small gesture.' He often buys things for seafarers – electrical goods, children's toys – and delivers them to the ship next day. Sometimes he pays for the goods himself and trusts he will be paid back. He looks bemused when I ask if that trust has ever been betrayed. No. Sometimes seafarers give him fistfuls of dollars and send him off to shop for them. The faith is two-way.

His is a ministry of small gestures with great impact. A SIM card, a battery, a gift for a man who has spent yet another Christmas at sea. At Christmas, Immingham's centre delivers 1300 shoeboxes of donated gifts to seafarers. In mid-January there are boxes still left over from the Christmas deliveries, so Colum approaches a group of Filipino seafarers sitting near the fountain. The fountain has toy penguins perched on its edge. They were in the Christmas crib, says Colum, as if that is normal. He asks who was at sea for Christmas, then gives a box to a seafarer named Jude, who seems pleased. He has time to talk, and as is usual with seafarers, big things arrive quickly into the conversation, so that Jude tells us he has yet to meet his youngest son, Elijah, born four months ago. Other than that, he says, life's OK. He works on a tanker and the food is fine. Everything is fine, and now he has a Christmas gift too. The box holds toiletries (toothpaste, shower gel, a hairbrush) and woollen items: a sweater, socks and a woolly hat. All seafarers' charities provide woolly hats and other comforts. In the Second World War, the Merchant Navy Comforts Service, established in 1940, sent parcels containing a helmet liner, two pairs of socks, a scarf, a sweater and woollen gloves to men leaving for convoys and trouble. A man heading for the Arctic convoys received in addition 'a pair of those long socks called sea-stockings which are so essential to his comfort'.

The Sailors' Society runs a Woolly Hat Week every February with the dubious aim of getting the general public to wear a woolly hat to appreciate seafarers. There are now 386 knitting groups listed on the Sailors' Society database, including Pam Richardson from Bedford, who was knitting when I phoned her one evening. A maroon bonnet, since I asked. She tried a balaclava but thought it was a bit too complicated. Pam had been knitting hats for sailors since 2008, although she has no maritime connections. She didn't even like ships: you'd get her on a plane first. She met a priest at the Sailors' Society once who asked her what her involvement was. 'I told him I just knit hats. He said, "Don't ever say 'just'! Wherever

we go in the world, sailors always ask us if we have any bonnets.'"
This is true: I watched one seafarer leap over the ship rail and sprint
down the dock when he saw that the visiting chaplain had a car-boot
full of hats. He was headed for Norway and it was winter. Once, a
seafarer approached the same chaplain and gestured to his head.
He didn't speak much English, and the chaplain wasn't sure what
he wanted. A scarf? A hat? A headache pill? 'No!' said the seafarer.
'Terrorist!' A balaclava.

Jude takes the hat. He appears grateful. But he earns $1390 a
month. He could have bought a hat and everything else from the shop
50 metres away and probably has. That is not the point. 'They can
really help us,' said one sailor to researcher Erol Kahveci. 'They
can share my emptiness.'

The International Labour Organization defines seafarers as a special
category of worker. The seafarer's special identity does not change
the fact that he – or, rarely, she – spends most of his or her working
life stuck on a confined metal box where intimidation is easier to
get away with than in most workplaces. A ship's call in port is then
a precious chance for outsiders to inspect, to enquire, to minister.
Colum does ship visiting daily. He is a man of God in high-viz and
hard hat. He never calls ahead: ship visitors turn up and hope for
welcome and it is invariably given. Any visitor is a fresh face. 'The
chaplain asked me how I slept here,' a seafarer reported to a welfare
survey. Such a simple enquiry, but 'even that was very important for
me. It is nice to hear another person talking to you.'

The first ship is Norwegian. It has a good, sturdy gangway, good
paint, no rust: all the signs of a decent ship. We are a priest and
a woman: each bringing more bad luck than the other in seafarer
superstition, but the AB on gangway watch doesn't flinch when he
hands out ID badges. Colum makes conversation: Where have you
come from? What are you carrying? How long have you been at

sea? Murmansk. Coal. A long time. The watchman is Filipino, as are the three men we find in the lounge area, lounging. Colum's greeting consists of 'What can I do for you?' before he reaches into his pocket for a cheap SIM card they can buy, or gives them a flyer about the centre with all useful numbers, or asks if they need him to buy anything. He can bring it to the ship tomorrow. It's no trouble. They ask if there is a charge for the mission bus, and he says no, it is provided freely, although the centre is funded only on goodwill and donations. That means it is funded with great difficulty. 'There is a voluntary port levy, about £10,' says Colum. 'But you'd be astonished how many companies cross it out. The majority don't give it. £10 on a bill of £50,000, and they cross it out. If every ship calling here gave us £10, we would fly.'

Last year, the centre lost £4000 when someone broke in and raided the safe. Colum knows who it was. Everyone knows who it was except Immingham's port security. It was late one Sunday night. 'He drove here but not a single camera in the whole port picked up his car. We asked security about it. They said that their cameras can't read number plates at night.' Colum and David, his Sailors' Society colleague, form a double act of disdain about the security. Immingham, like all major industrialized ports, must conform to standards set out in the International Ship and Port Facility Security code (ISPS), devised after September 11, 2001 and enforced by 2004. This has various requirements, such as keeping a gangway watch at all times on ships, so that seafarers must be guards as well as everything else, and more guarded gateposts ashore. It is probably most economically summed up by a student at a Swedish engineering college, who wrote in a paper: 'The ISPS code forces the ports, ships and all organizations who work in the marine industry to keep their security gates more tightly.'

Colum drives a gas-converted old Lexus, but he also likes to ride his motorbike in and out of his dock homeland. He wears different helmets, so the guards at the entrance gates can't see his face, but he has never been stopped. Lesley, who drives the seafarers' bus, one night saw two men loading a BMW onto a trailer from a yard full of new cars. Sometimes you see those new cars being driven from Immingham to somewhere else, by drivers wearing dark glasses even in Lincolnshire gloom. The drivers are part time: they are called upon when needed. I like this idea, of a force of drivers in suspended animation, reactivated for a Nissan Micra arrived on a ro-ro from Zeebrugge.

That night, Lesley thought: you don't usually see single trailers taking cars away. She phoned security. 'Where? We can't see them.' But Lesley could, and she followed them in her bus until help arrived. They were caught, but there must be hundreds who are not. For all the tightly closed gates, docks are porous places, though you hear about their holes only through anecdotes.

Colum's combination of dog collar and hard hat puts him in a unique and useful position. He can be minister, but also listener. Often, seafarers tell him things they would not dare tell people they consider to be more official. He is a safe pair of ears. Once, he visited a ship at Immingham and the crew were silent and wouldn't look at him. This was striking. It is rare that he is not made to feel welcome. He left knowing something was seriously wrong, and that evening saw some of the crew in the centre, their day's work done. They saw him and began to cry. They told him, we have just come through the Bay of Biscay in a Force 10 and we know our ship will sink when we go back that way. We know we will die. They begged him to help. They knew that he was in a special and delicate position. Mission chaplains must be careful about their role as human helpline. They cannot be seen to be snitches, or they might be refused access. But they have to be a comforts service that doesn't just provide woollens. Colum phoned someone he knew at the right authority and the ship was officially inspected. A bilge pump, supposed to pump water out, had been put on backwards and was pumping water in. The ship would have sunk. 'But the crew didn't dare say anything on the ship. The captain had called them to the bridge and made them sign forms saying they were happy with everything.' He shakes his head. It's sad. Such exploitation.

Priests, though, cannot be everywhere. The ITF also runs a global network of inspectors from its affiliate unions. Once, on the other side of the country, I visited the port of Birkenhead near Liverpool. It is not an ISPS port, with no visible security. Tommy Molloy is the ITF's man in Liverpool. He works out of Mariners' Park, a retirement community for ex-seafarers that overlooks the Mersey, a wide and majestic river. The park has green lawns and pensioner-suitable speed limits. There are individual houses and a residential centre, where rank is still respected and old mariners call each other Chief and Captain. Molloy's job is to inspect ships that come to call and check on welfare. Some ships have signed agreements with the ITF to pay decent wages and provide proper conditions. Plenty have not. He knows his place: it is to work on the dirty end of shipping. He shows me images of mouldy food, mouldy upholstery, shocking sinks. The crimps may have gone out of fashion but exploitation never does. At sea, Captain Glenn bewails chandlers who supply ships with green bananas that will never ripen, fruit that goes mouldy obscenely fast, sub-standard meat. He swears that he used to see meat stamped with 'For Merchant Navy only', and that it was the rancid kind. Afloat and ashore, seafarers with constricted time, little local knowledge and ready cash are easy marks for all sorts of profiteers. Molloy heard about a taxi driver taking Filipinos into the city centre who swore to them that both tunnels under the river Mersey were closed (a legal impossibility) and charged them £130 for a 50-mile detour on a four-mile trip. Don't get him started on what the men were charged for Manchester United tickets.

There are more serious concerns than green bananas or football. Exploitation of seafarers is easy when an owner can slip away behind his flag and brass-plate company. Non-payment of wages is common and blatant. When Molloy visited one Greek-owned ship, he found that the Filipino crew and officers hadn't been paid for months, and approached the captain about it. 'The captain got on the phone to the company and told me $48,000 was being wired immediately. I said, hang on, but I haven't calculated the total yet, then I did and it was $47,600. They knew exactly what they owed.' When MV *Most Sky* arrived in Liverpool in the winter of 2010, its crew had to club together to buy a loaf of bread. They were warming themselves with a kebab grill. *Most Sky* was a scrappy-looking ship. MV *Philipp*, which arrived the following year, was not: it was flagged to Gibraltar, part of the reputable Red Ensign group of registers, and owned by Vega Reederei, an established German shipping company. Its crew were employed by a Vega-owned manning agency in Manila. Its books seemed to be in order, except that they were false books. Visit any Filipino seafarers' forum and you will find plenty of tales of double book-keeping. One set of salary rates to please ITF; another set of figures that are the true wages paid. On MV *Philipp*, the crew was getting a third of the official figure in the books and was owed $230,000.

Good port authorities have systems in place to detain ships. In the worst cases, they can impound and sell them. The UK's Maritime and Coastguard Authority, regulator of all Red Ensign flags, can detain a ship if it is dangerous or delinquent, or if the owners have abandoned it, but not for unpaid wages. Abandoned ships can be arrested and sold by an Admiralty Court, but that takes at least twelve weeks. Twelve weeks in winter with no heat is a long twelve weeks. Also, for the owners there is usually an escape route eastwards. The

German owners of MV *Philipp* promised to pay the money owed; then a manning official flew in from Manila and persuaded the crew to return it. Molloy kept fighting, and the crew were paid again. Then, on arriving in Manila, reported the ITF inspector there, 'they were bundled into two vans, taken to crewing agent Vega Crewing's office and the money taken from them under duress.' Who could the crew complain to? Blacklisting by manning agencies is a career-ending risk, and common: about 10,000 Filipino seafarers are thought to be blacklisted.

Sometimes, the ships are just abandoned. This is defined in law, rather lyrically, as 'the severance of ties between the ship owner and the seafarer'. It is usually a calculated and cynical economic decision. If insurance premiums or port fees are too high, or the company goes bankrupt, the owner disappears, leaving unpaid wages and a stranded crew. Molloy has tales that might seem preposterous, of seafarers selling blood to earn money – this happened in the United Arab Emirates in 1999 – or worse. The worst he has yet heard was the case of *Ionian Sprinter*, a ship owned by Greek Adriatic Tankers until the company went bust and left its ship and crew in St Petersburg with no money or food, for months. They got so desperate, they caught and ate a stray dog. 'Not because Vietnamese like eating dogs,' said Trinh Vinh Thang, the Vietnamese radio officer. 'We were just too hungry.'

Abandonment peaks during deep recession, but it never goes away. Seafarers often stick it out even when they are eating dog, in the hope of claiming wages they are owed. Often, they have already taken out loans back home to cover the unpaid wages. Molloy remembers the case of *Kyoto One*, a ship owned by Panaygis Zissimatos, a Greek ship owner notorious for the amount of debt he had accrued and for the number of bank loans he defaulted on in the 1990s. The ITF got three months' back wages for *Kyoto One*'s crew and urged them to go home. They wouldn't, and the ship ended up in Durres, Albania, just before the revolution. 'The Russian chief phoned me and said the Sri Lankan bo'sun had lost his mind. I spoke to the bo'sun on the phone and he said, if you send me home, I will cut my throat.' Like thousands of seafarers, he had coped with not being paid by taking loans from moneylenders. 'If I go home without my wages,' he told Molloy, 'the moneylenders will kill my family.' Russians and Ukrainians are more likely to stand up for themselves, in Molloy's experience, but Filipinos will stick it out longer because of blacklisting. Someone easily gets work for four or five years, makes a complaint about a racist captain, for example, and suddenly there is no ship. There is nothing to be done. There is still no international instrument to stop ship owners doing the equivalent of a night flit, although there is hope of setting up a global fund to pay seafarers at least enough to get home. In 2009, the worst year for disappearing owners and stranded seafarers, the International Labour Organization's database recorded that 57 ships and 647 seafarers were abandoned; the ships included the *Tor Atlantic*, left in Argentina, the *Prince*, abandoned at Dubai, and the *Fiona*, left in Ancona, Italy. Hardly any of these cases were ever listed as 'resolved'.

As we descend the gangway onto the docks of Immingham, the air filled with the faint dust of a nearby grain silo, Colum says, 'People get outraged about sweatshops, but they don't realize that once the stuff is loaded on a ship, that can be another sweatshop.' The position of the Fair Trade Association is one of defeat. The complexities and realities of shipping are too great. 'We work with nearly 900 producer organizations in 60 countries across the developing world who ship to thousands of traders in over 20 different markets,' a spokesperson said. 'Incorporating shipping requirements into our standards and certification processes would add to auditing costs.' They would like to have ships that have signed agreements with unions to guarantee good conditions. They would like to avoid flags of convenience. But without any way of monitoring, 'this would be merely an empty gesture'.

In the face of all this, is a woolly hat an empty gesture? This is an industry which thinks it is acceptable to use the phrase 'the human element' to describe its workforce, not realizing that the inhumanity of the phrase scores a rhetorical own goal. It may seem frivolous to confront this hard, fast, pitiless world with woollen comforts or a battery. Colum disagrees. 'Anything we can do to humanize this harsh industry, we should do.' He visits churches and schools to give talks about the shipping world, and hears people wonder that such a life exists 'in this day and age'. They say, I can't believe that people have their wages stolen, or must sail on unsafe ships, or that the crooks can get away with it. 'But these people are invisible. Ports are invisible. We have to make these people matter. They do matter.' If the priests and the unionists didn't look out for seafarers, who would?

Colum is dreading being moved back inland. He won't go. 'I'll do this as long as my knees hold out.' He stays for the times that he walks through what he thinks is an empty centre and hears a strange noise, and finds at an internet terminal a young Ukrainian seafarer singing to his baby for the first time. He stays because the one constant is that his parish will always be different from one day to the next. He stays because the newly ratified Maritime Labour Convention might fill those gaps between paper and practice and make decency required and indecency impossible. But if not, Colum will be there with his hard hat, confronting strangers who come to a strange land that they feed, clothe and equip with effective friendliness and a simple acknowledgement of their worth, such as that in a schoolchild's prayer on the wall of Felixstowe's Seafarer Centre library. 'Make all the people on the ship safe,' wrote the nameless pupil, 'so we can have all the food from the ship that the seamen bring us. If other countries were not so nice, we wouldn't have so much food. Thank you. Amen.'

Whaletown

9. ANIMALS BENEATH

So Remorseless a Havoc

On *Kendal*'s chart table, I leave a note for duty officers. It says, 'Watch keepers, if you see whales or dolphins, please call me on 227.' For days, southward slowly through the Indian Ocean, grazing India, heading for Sri Lanka, the note reaps nothing.

Off Colombo, we drift. Because *Kendal* zoomed through the pirate zones, the captain is left with a day to spare. He can't be early to port because the berth has been booked. The only option is to float back and forth across a square of water he has designated. We are like a strange sea video game: first we steam to one corner, then the engines are turned off so that we meander back, then steam again. Zig-zag.

I go to the fo'c'sle and at first can't figure out what is so unsettling. By now I am used to the powerful stink of the animal hides that we loaded at Salalah, that gets stronger and stronger as I walk forward, a pungent chorus. What unsettles me is not the smell but the quiet. Even in port *Kendal* is noisy. This is the first quiet for four weeks and it is sweet, although sailors would dread such calm, creating a passive verb – to be becalmed – to express the malevolence they felt, as if they were assaulted by something beyond just weather and chance. In *The Mirror of the Sea*, Conrad encounters a fellow captain who has just emerged from a becalming and drifting.

'We had three weeks of it,' said my friend. 'Just think of that!'
'How did you feel about it?' I asked.
He waved his hand as much to say: It's all in the day's work.
But then, abruptly, as if making up his mind:
'I'll tell you. Towards the last I used to shut myself in my berth and cry.'
'Cry?'
'Shed tears,' he explained briefly, and rolled up the chart.

I love the calm. The water is green, blue and clear, enough to display unmistakably a trail of trash coming out of Sri Lanka and heading into the ocean to add to the millions of bits of plastic that roam there already, unstoppable and tragic. I spot a brown splodge. A sponge, maybe, or a plastic bag. It is an endangered sea turtle. It swims merrily, or swims with no thought of my silly anthropomorphic adjectives. On the fo'c'sle now there is also a large dragonfly, golden and black and dead. Perhaps this will be my allotment of ocean wildlife. That accidental passenger pigeon, long disappeared into an Algerian saucepan, a turtle and an insect.

The next day Marius says with careful innocence, 'I saw whales the other day, and hundreds of dolphins.' I ask him what kind of whales. He says, 'The blowing-spout kind.' He tells me that in the Strait of Gibraltar ships are only allowed to do 14 knots so that they don't run over whales. That is considered the maximum speed which allows the animals time to get out of the way. (Actually, it's nearer 10 knots.) On one ship Marius worked on, the captain was doing 18 knots in the Strait and a cadet dared to speak up. 'Captain, we are killing the whales!' There is the odd grumbling from grumpy columnists in *Lloyd's List* about slowing down for little purpose, but in general, seafarers like to see sea life. It makes a change. Some ships carry whale-spotting books. But the captain on that ship was different. He said he didn't care. His ETA was more important.

Did he kill any whales with his 18 knots? Who knows? The only evidence of ship strikes against whales is when injured animals are beached with gashes and horrible injuries, attracting huge crowds and causing headaches for authorities charged with disposing of the carcass. The most notorious whale disposal incident occurred in 1970, when the Oregon State Highway Division was tasked with destroying a 45-foot sperm whale that had arrived on the beach at Florence. Perhaps because of their experience with moving large boulders, the highway officials decided to use dynamite. A crowd gathered, the charges were blown, and then everyone ran as giant chunks of blubber rained from the sky and crushed the Oldsmobile 88 of Walter Umenhofer, who became known as 'the blubber victim' for evermore, to his annoyance. The tale of the exploding whale was singular enough to have been investigated and authenticated by the myth-puncturing website Snopes. It is more singular that the detonation of whales still occurs.

Off Western Australia, for example, in 2010, a whale was exploded. A courteous man named Douglas Coughran emailed me from the Senior Wildlife Office of the Nature Protection Branch of Western Australia to explain why. It was, he wrote, an example of the 'very challenging issue of human/whale interaction'. Whales that are beached on unpopulated shores are left to break down into the nitrogen cycle 'as nature has done for millennia'. A carcass on a more public beach is a health hazard, so those animals are usually removed with ingenuity and earth-moving equipment and buried elsewhere. This particular dying humpback had beached on a sandbank and could not move or be moved. It was too big to shoot so it was dynamited while not quite dead. The Department of Environment and Conservation tried to give reassurance: sandbags would be placed around the whale's head before it was exploded to death, and a helicopter would patrol afterwards to prevent a shark feeding frenzy.

At sea, whales are bashed, battered, gashed, pinioned, stuck. The true scale of trauma is unknown, like much else about whales. The size of big ships means they can hit giant sea animals, lost boxes or yachts and not notice. A bump, maybe, a faint jolt among all the pitching and rolling and jolting already. Visual evidence of fatal encounters is rare enough to draw crowds. When a tanker brought a whale into Baltimore in 1940, newspapers reported that it attracted 10,000 spectators. In June 2012, *Maersk Norwich* arrived in Rotterdam with a whale draped over its bow, long dead.

Off Sumatra, the animals come. I am watching and peering as usual, with little hope, and there is something off to the corner of my eye, and then there they are. A dolphin gang, zipping and zooming beside the bulbous bow right beneath my fo'c'sle perch. Perhaps it is because I have been at sea for a month, or perhaps I would do this anyway, but I talk to them. In fact, I shout. Get out of the way! You will be hit by the bow! I don't want any deathly draping on this ship to provide some preserved horror on YouTube. The dolphins laugh at me. They understand ships. They are fast enough to outpace us, even at 14 knots. So they come and go, racing against the red bow pushing through the underwater, taking turns, propelled by the bow wave. They can feel the action that the bulbous bow makes in the water, flattening it, creating speed and giving them some. Half a dozen gangs come and go, veering and carousing and bow-surfing, using the ship to their advantage. It is fabulous, a treat, a beautiful harmony of animal and machine. This is not how the sea's animals and its machines often get on.

*

In a laboratory about 8000 nautical miles from Sumatra, I am peering again, now at creatures in a plastic specimen container. They are minute but not microscopic. My eyes can see them fine, their little bodies and shrimpy legs that would be terrifying if magnified. They are such tiny things to be linked to such huge matters as devastation, pollution and extinction, of man and beast.

The creatures are copepods. They look like nothing much. When I ask if they have brains, one of the laboratory researchers needs to look up the answer because she had never considered it before. (Yes, they do.) Another researcher says her friends call her the Bug Counter because they think she works with sea bugs and that's funny. The brains aren't of much interest because copepods are fascinating as food. Specifically, the major food source for 50-tonne animals that for some reason have chosen to survive off minuscule, elusive bugs.

Copepods feed the North Atlantic right whale. The right whale's beautiful Latin name is *Eubalaena glacialis* (the true whale of ice), but whalers gave it a more prosaic one because this, they concluded, was the right whale to hunt. It was plentiful, slow, and floated when it died. Also, it contained satisfying amounts of whale oil and baleen, the keratin fringes and fronds that span its huge mouth and filter sea water, and that were, confusingly, sold as 'whalebone', a substance so essential and ubiquitous, it was the nineteenth-century plastic. A Mr J.A. Sevey of Essex Street, Boston, sold 53 varieties of whalebone items, including divining rods, tongue scrapers, plait-raisers and policemen's clubs.

The Basques were the first to hunt the true whale of ice, a thousand years ago. Then came the North Americans, Portuguese, British, French, Danish and Germans. Everyone wanted this whale. For two hundred years, through the high times of whaling, mothers, fathers and calves were harpooned and slaughtered. Whale researchers don't know how big the population was before that, but it was decimated enough for the right whale to be given protected status in 1935. Now there are about 400 North Atlantic right whales left. This figure makes *Eubalaena glacialis* one of the most endangered large whales, and one of the most endangered species in the world despite having no natural predators in the ocean. But it still has an unnatural one: right whales used to be hunted by men on ships, but now the greatest threat to their survival is the ship itself. Because of its habit of feeding and breeding close to the eastern shores of the United States, the right whale now has a new name. It is the urban whale, because its habitat is usually within 100 miles of the US coastline, and in busy shipping lanes.

The laboratory is in Provincetown, Cape Cod. It is off-season now, and the town is quiet. It is so determined in its off-season quietness that its status as a famed hedonistic summer destination – popular with gay visitors because of its tolerance – is difficult to imagine. I like the stubborn seasonality of places like these, in the way that I miss half-day closing of shops on Wednesdays. There is time to breathe.

Provincetown is mostly closed. Though it is early April, the weather is also off-season, with a biting wind on the pier where I wander, stretching car-crunched muscles and shaking off soda sugar, looking into the beach-hut kiosks that are quiet as sentinels. One belongs to the Provincetown Coastal Studies Institute. Its purpose is instructional as well as commercial. A display board educates about the particular, peculiar currents of Provincetown's bay, about the way that the movement of currents brings waves of copepods, which makes whales come every year as punctual as the seasons, to feed their fill. Opposite the booth is a large white boat named *Dolphin VI*, a whale-watcher. Provincetown is where whale-watching began. *Dolphin* isn't yet running, but there are other ways to see whales, even off-season.

My whale-watching facilitator is Stormy Mayo. His legal first name is Charles. I forget to ask him where 'Stormy' came from, and then I think, it doesn't matter. People who are interested in whales learn to accept not knowing something because they soon learn that they will never know very much. The Mayo family is tenth generation in Provincetown, having arrived 16 years after the Pilgrim Fathers. Stormy has inherited land in the East End part of town, and a private beach. It was there, 30 years ago, that he set up a summer school with his wife. This led him to whales.

He knew of them before that. Anyone who grows up in Cape Cod knows that whales come there. Stormy used to go out with his father on boats and saw them. But whales were not his calling. He had a marine biology doctorate from the University of Miami in Marine Ichthyoplankton, so his interest lay in the mid-layers of oceans. His wife Barbara worked on the flora and fauna of the *benthos*, the bottom layer where clams live. After university in Miami, the Mayos returned to Provincetown so that Stormy could build a schooner, a wooden square-rigged sailing boat. He is still building it. But having a family beach, two PhDs, and a clientele of seasonal summer people, Stormy and his wife decided to give outdoor lectures. The title was Marine Ecology and Oceanography; the venue was the beach or sometimes a boat; the dress code was bathing suits. It was successful. Tourists who wanted more than the beautiful light that has attracted artists to Provincetown for 100 years could sign up for a few weeks of instruction in wave action, moon action and the day-to-day activities of clams.

The course did not cover whales. The Mayos didn't think of that. This was the 1970s. No-one was yet saving the whales. Scientifically, says Stormy in his office next to the bug-counting lab, whales were 'a blip on the radar. They were thought to be insignificant in the ecosystem.' He has a spare and dry delivery. When I ask what is in a plastic specimen jar on his desk, he says,

'Well, I'm prepared to call it a blob.' Back in the 1950s and 1960s, he says, 'who gave a damn about whales? Just big blubbery, cow-like things.'

Then Albert Avellar, a Provincetown skipper, noticed that the tourists he was taking out fishing were more fascinated by the big blubbery cow-like things than by the fish. Stormy and the captain didn't get on, because Stormy was known to be an environmentalist, a protector of the ocean. Fishermen were the ones who consumed and plundered. They were supposed to be on different sides. But the captain thought a whale-watching cruise would be a good idea, and having a PhD on board talking about seabirds and whales was an even better idea. Stormy was dubious. How could they be sure to find whales? Avellar was certain. Right whales, he said, come to Race Point every 15 April. And still Stormy doubted. 'I didn't know much about them but one thing I know is, this is a rare animal. But we went out to Race Point on 15 April and there they were.' Since then, the Avellar family has built one of the largest whale-watching operations in the country, and Stormy – his wife died in 1988 – is now head of Right Whale Habitat Studies at the Provincetown Center for Coastal Studies, counting bugs and trying to save whales.

The Coastal Studies boat is RV *Shearwater*. RV stands for research vessel. Often, research vessels are expensive and technologically advanced to be quieter, greener. *Shearwater* is more low-tech. The Center is not richly funded and the boat was a donation from a wealthy inventor, so Stormy took what he was given, and it was a fishing trawler. Modifications were made for its changed purpose, such as the installation of plastic seats on the observation deck for marine-mammal watching, but the engine still belches diesel and smells of fumes. It is not quiet.

Today the research team is all women. The principal investigator, Christy, will decide where to go according to what sightings we get.

We will follow the whales. Up top there is Beth, a former biology teacher, whose task is to help Christy gather water samples to count copepods, and Eliza, a Harvard student interning for her third summer and today's photographer. It is the task of everyone to watch for whales, constantly. The captain is Ted, standing in for the regular skipper. Normally he takes tourists out on dinner cruises from Chatham. He has a calm air that I associate with sea people, though that may be fanciful.

Stormy can't come because there is a conference call to be done. He sits on many boards, task groups and committees, including the Atlantic Large Whale Take Reduction Team. He used to be one of the few official whale disentanglers, which explains the two lacrosse helmets on a shelf in his office. Whales get entangled in fishing ropes and lines and gear with heartbreaking regularity – 75 per cent of right whales have been or are entangled – and humans try to disentangle them. It is extremely difficult to remove ropes and cords from a thrashing 50-tonne animal at sea from a small boat. Things fly at you. There are poles being thrust. The helmets are not to protect against the whale: one flick of a tail, says Stormy, 'and my head and helmet are over here and my body is over there, so it really doesn't matter'.

Today's mission is bug-collecting. The day is fine, the sky is blue, the weather report is not alarming, and we set off, hoping for the right whales. They arrived in January this year, far earlier than their usual appearance, in April. No-one knows why their schedule changed, just as no-one can explain why they are not calving as much as they should, after ten good years. The southern right whale population, which lives in the southern hemisphere, has been growing by 78 per cent every year, but figures for North Atlantic right whales are gloomy. Researchers hoped to spot 30–40 calves by the end of the calving season in March, but by February they had only seen five. Already, northern right whales have a potential biological removal

(PBR) level of less than 1, the number that can safely be removed from their population each year by human causes. When their feeding grounds coincide with shipping lanes – traffic in and out of the Cape Cod Canal towards Boston passes through here – a strike rate of one a year is hardly unlikely.

On *Shearwater*, instructions: if anyone up top sees whales, they should stomp on the roof. The instruction is definitely to 'stomp'. That is the quickest way of getting attention in the cabin and from Ted. The engines should then immediately be cut because propellers can be lethal even if they belong to a well-intentioned boat. There is also an aerial team out today, which will help with spotting from a small aircraft. The whale aviators are seasonal, working only in feeding and breeding seasons. They are also all women. A disproportionate number of right whale researchers are female, says Beth. She thinks it's because women will work for no money. You don't go into right whale research for riches.

We head out of the harbour towards Race Point. The point got its name from two currents that meet here and seem to race each other. Copepods like the currents here and so do the whales. Their favourite food is a variety of copepod called *Calanus finmarchius*, which whales follow to all their known feeding grounds: Cape Cod, lower Bay of Fundy, Great South Channel and Jeffreys Ledge. A chapter in *The Urban Whale*, a compilation of right whale research that manages both to have scientific rigour and to be gripping, is entitled 'Enormous Carnivores, Microscopic Food, and a Restaurant That's Hard to Find'. In it, Mark F. Baumgartner writes that right whales 'are among the Earth's largest animals, but they feed on creatures that are the size of fleas'. Right whales are 50 billion times the size of copepods. It is like humans choosing to eat only bacteria. It makes little sense. Perhaps it's the taste? Beth can answer that. She has eaten copepods blended to a paste, with crackers. They taste like the sea. If they are eaten alive, they zip around the mouth like Space Dust.

Northern right whales are as seasonal as Provincetown summer folk. They have a whole ocean to live in, but they still stay close to us, feeding in Cape Cod and the Bay of Fundy, migrating south to Georgia to give birth, then back up north to feed again. The aerial team reports in. A group of whales has been spotted, 'sagging'. I hear Beth say this and think whale-talk would sound rude to the hard of hearing. Whales can also take a 'fluking dive', with their tails – flukes – the last thing to disappear beneath the water. Sagging derives from Surface Active Group (SAG), which sounds like a Second World War battle formation, but describes a group of right whales getting friendly or frisky. Right whales can dive below for 20 minutes at a time, but for friendly socializing or determined mating, they stay in surface waters. Beth and Eliza point out the SAG in front of the boat. There: look. But there is only a mass of black shapes just under the green water, rolling, seething and rolling. I can't distinguish a whale, and neither can Eliza. She exhorts them to be more identifiable. Come on, she says to the SAG, show me a ped scar. She means a scar – probably from a propeller or boat strike – somewhere along the peduncle, a part of whale anatomy reaching from the tail fluke to the mid-back. But scars mean nothing to me. Right whales have no dorsal fins, so they are just black slabs. Even if I could see them, they would not impress. These are not poster whales. Stormy Mayo calls them ugly as sin. He thinks our fascination with them is a size issue. 'If the right whale were the size of a cockroach, a slimy thing, slippery, looking like that, crawling around behind your cupboards, you're going to tell me that you would take it out and cherish it? I'd say you'd step on it.'

Other whales have more charm, however slippery and slimy. When a northern bottlenose whale swam up the Thames in London in 2006, it drew crowds of thousands. The rescue operation cost £100,000, although the whale died while being transported on a raft back to the river mouth where its doomed navigation had begun.

An *Observer* journalist wrote that he would never forget 'the day a whale sailed through the middle of London; and the people of the city, rather than trying to hack it to death, came in their thousands and lifted it and tried their hardest to sail it back'.

The bottlenose was headline news, but in fact marine mammals strand with dismal regularity. Cetacean-stranding databases list their causes of death and location. Most die of infections. But there is also starvation and physical trauma caused by propeller or a mass of ship. Between 1970 and 2007, 67 right whale carcasses have been reported. At least 24 had died from the consequences of being struck by a ship. No wonder the roof-stomping signal has been devised: our research vessel propeller could cut through whale skin like any other despite its noble scientific intentions. We can approach up to 500 metres from the animals, a distance only granted with a federal permit and not permitted to commercial whale-watchers. Because right whale research is hands-off, researchers used to puncture right whales with identifying tags – Stormy calls this practice 'sticking things into whales' – until they noticed that there were swellings around the tags, that the whale's body responded as if to a wound. Right whales had enough stresses to deal with, and the tagging was stopped.

Identification in the hands-off era comes down to photographs and pattern recognition. Both natural and unnatural markings are useful: propeller scars, but also callosities, patches of rough skin that are white because they are infested with cyamids, lice-like parasites. Eliza thinks she has recognized one of the frolickers from a scar. It's Minus 1.

Pardon?

Minus 1. That's his name. She doesn't know how he got it. All the right whales we know of are listed in a photo-identification catalogue, an effort that is comprehensive, exhaustive and impressive in its scale and in the level of collaboration required to achieve it. Any whale, whenever glimpsed, is photographed and given a catalogue number. As whales become known, they are given mnemonics, names to aid with identification. That sounds sober and rational, but the names can be enchantingly queer. There are the mother and calf Kleenex and Snot. There is Van Halen, named after a callosity shaped like a guitar. There are Yawn and Etch-a-Sketch and Rat, named after a scar on her side that really does look like a rat chasing a ball. Some whales are named for their deeds, such as Shackleton, a young male who swam up the Delaware River into the port of Philadelphia in 1994. Like Ernest Shackleton, he got stuck, though in his case under a pier, and like his namesake, he escaped and survived. Later, Shackleton was understood to be the calf of Eg #1140, also known as Wart. The names are a pleasing hit of colour among scientific rigour, somewhat like scientists who have wild tattoos of DNA chains and molecules under lab coats. But whales would be better off if there were too many of them for names.

Whale fieldwork is a slippery business. Researchers must understand their subjects only by glimpses, bodies on beaches, or by what RV *Shearwater* is doing today, which is taking samples of water, squirting them with formaldehyde, then analysing how rich the water is in copepods, and what that means for the reproduction, health and survival of the right whale.

The SAG splits up. Who likes to be watched while they are mating? I assume that *Shearwater*'s presence is audible for miles ahead, with its relatively noisy engine, but then I see right whales feeding. Their activity is called skimming, because they feed just below the surface. A right whale eats like a bulldozer: open that great mouth, and take in tons of water. The baleen fringes strain out the copepods from the water. We see two right whales skimming, but they do not see us. Or they don't care. I don't know how they give off an air of ferocious intent, but they do: it is something in the directness of their line, in the tenacity of their purpose. Head down, mouth open, go. One theory about why whales keep getting hit by ships – which they should hear coming, when the engines are the size of houses – is that they are too intent on eating, so that nothing will disturb them. Stormy has another idea. He thinks they are tethered and handicapped by themselves. 'They're feeding, they've allowed the boat to get close because they're oblivious, they're moving slowly and then at the last moment when they could apply huge power to diving out, their mouths are full of tons of water and they're anchored just like a sea anchor on a ship.' A sea anchor that reduces their speed to about two knots, too slow to escape a ship. He is not certain though. This is not scientific fact. He calls his theories 'all my imaginations'.

Imagination is important in right whale research, because it fills in some of the unknowing. Some of the things that have yet to be conclusively proved include why right whales have, periodically, disastrously low reproductive rates but sometimes recover; or how whales arrive in feeding grounds that other whales have found. Chemicals? Calls? Smell? We don't know how whales know to go to places that their ancestors have gone to; a young whale named Porter, for instance, was discovered far from usual feeding grounds off North America, in a fjord in Norway. We don't know where they go in winter. We do know that right whales travel for distances that make any human achievement on land seem laughable. When a young male named Churchill became entangled in fishing gear in 2001, $250,000 worth of attempts to disentangle him failed. He was tracked using a tag linked to a satellite. He was called Churchill because he was an obstinate animal. He stubbornly survived, although the fishing gear had wrapped around his mouth and he couldn't feed. The scarcity of right whale food means they can fast for long periods, but not this long: Churchill swam for two months, and apparently unerringly, while starving to death, up to Georges Bank off Canada, into the Gulf Stream, to the Gulf of St.

Lawrence, then back, though not using the Gulf Stream because the current was against him this way. To Emerald Bank, southwest of Sable Island, 186 miles off Halifax, Nova Scotia, which is known for its wild horses and shipwrecks. Then down to the Roseway Basin, known for rich plankton, and back to Georges Bank. There, the dying animal visited the heads of deep ocean canyons that are cut into the north American coastal platform before returning to Georges Bank and, in Stormy's words, 'hanging out'. In two months, this crippled, insulted whale had swum 5000 miles on no food. Sightings showed that he was getting thinner and thinner. The roll of fat behind the blowhole that indicates a healthy whale was long gone. And then, so was he, somewhere off New Jersey. There was no body: dying whales, if they don't strand, sink and drown.

The *Shearwater* team think the whales we have sighted are skinny. Also, they are not as numerous as expected, despite Beth's superior ocean-gazing skills. She sees grey seals – over there! A head like a dog! – then porpoises and fin whales, where I see only waves and water. You get used to it, she says. Your eyes get better. You learn to see what she calls 'funny water', which might mean a whale is in it, and which she calls 'a highly technical term'. The copepods they gather are also meagre, another worry. Maybe the whales aren't getting enough food. It is another stress on them. But one of the greatest pressures on them is not something Beth can spot even with her sea vision, because it is to do with waves, but of an unexpected kind.

Oceans are not quiet. Millions of cruise passengers go to sea for the peace, but underwater and in water there has always been noise. Waves, rain, disintegrating icebergs, other animals. The sea is a place of sound, because when light can only penetrate 200 metres below the surface, sound is the best way to communicate. A great whale swimming in the deep can't see its own flukes, but it doesn't need to.

Because water is denser than air, sound travels faster, further and more resonantly in it. Consequently, marine animals are vocal beings. They can transmit singing, clicking, calling. With sound, they can gossip, search for mates, avoid fishing gear, communicate. They send out clicks and understand from the echo what is around them and where they are going, just as bats do. The humpback sings in complicated sequences the length of a concerto; the blue whale makes great moans; the fin whale sends out pulses that divers used to think were the creaking of the ocean floor. Minus 1 and his companions in that SAG group were probably producing the sounds that have been described as 'scream calls, warbles, gunshots, noisy blows and up-calls', and we watching humans up above could hear none of them.

Sounds underwater can travel astonishing distances: a right whale can hear another from 10 miles away. The ocean has natural sound 'channels', like noise byways: if a sound falls into a channel, it can travel hundreds of miles and perhaps thousands. It can travel an ocean. When a foghorn-like signal was transmitted from Australia in 1991, it was heard off Oregon three hours later. Sound is not the preserve of mammals: Dutch biologist Hans Slabbekoorn estimates that 800 species of fish use hearing. Every species of fish he has investigated has been able to interpret noise, either through an inner ear or by understanding vibrations on its body. I don't know what is more astonishing: that fish can hear or that I never considered such a possibility.

Sound means life for aquatic animals. And now because of us it can mean death. Humans are thoroughly embedded in din, from traffic, people, construction, and research shows that excess or overloud noise can have physiological effects, disrupting concentration, sleep, reproductive patterns. It can bring insanity into a living room or prison cell. There is no reason why noise would not do the same for mammals who live in water where sound has more power still.

How do we pollute the ocean? With plastic and chemicals and sewage, but also with noise. We lay cables across its bed and drive piles into its floor. We fire airguns that have the force of dynamite to carry out seismic surveys. Our fishermen send out constant pings – echolocation – to find fish. Our militaries deploy sonar that induces the bends in dolphins, porpoises and whales, so that they arrive in mass strandings on beaches with blood on their brains and coming from their ears; with air bubbles in their lungs; with all the signs that unfortunate divers display when they rise too soon through water. All this is acoustic smog. It is pernicious, widespread, damaging and preventable.

Modern ships the size of *Kendal* run on machinery that produces noise and vibration above the water but also beneath it. The movement of propellers in water produces something known as cavitation: the constant creation of tiny bubbles that continuously pop. Aquatic bubble-wrap. The cavitation of a freighter leaving Cape Cod Canal can be heard all over the bay. A super-tanker can be heard in the sea a day before its arrival.

Noise research is a recent field for oceanographers. Until recently, the tools required to study noise – underwater listening devices known as hydrophones – were too expensive to be widespread. Only classified military circles could afford them. The first significant civilian research was done in the 1950s, but the data were only analysed 40 years later. No-one had thought to do a comparative study of long-term noise levels before. Researchers had been looking at daily, weekly or monthly noise rates. When they compared levels over a longer time scale, the results were shocking. Ambient noise in the deep ocean was increasing by 3 decibels every decade. Every 10 years, noise from commercial shipping had doubled.

The quality of the noise is a greater problem. A ship produces sounds that fall below 100hz. This is the same frequency used by right whales and other ocean animals to communicate. I ask Russell Leaper, a researcher at the International Fund for Animal Welfare (IFAW), to translate what the noise of a shipping lane might sound like to a whale. He calls it broadband noise. I want more of a translation. He says, 'white noise', background traffic, something like the constant noise of the A64 that I can hear from my office. It depends on the frequency and proximity of the shipping. Up close, the noise of a ship to a whale would be like standing next to a jet engine, or almost in it. In the vast spaces of deep sea, it will be quieter. But in the habitat of the urban whale, in the coastal areas of the eastern seaboard, there are many ships, less space.

There are other acoustic polluters. If the ocean floor is rocky, the noise from seismic airguns – which fire loud pulses to generate waves that can be used to image the ocean floor – can travel immense distances. Researchers studying fin and blue whales in a 100,000-square-mile area of the Atlantic Ocean found that their entire research area was polluted by a single seismic survey. Sonar noise, and that from pinging and airguns, is intense but discrete and short-lived. Shipping noise is always there. Christopher Clark, a Cornell University professor and acoustic specialist, calls commercial shipping 'by far the most ubiquitous anthropogenic contributor to ocean noise'.

Sometimes whales can adapt to it, in the same way we raise voices in a nightclub or beside a noisy road. Some whales have shifted into higher frequencies when disturbed by noise. Sometimes they find ways round it or away from it: plenty of animals and fish have exhibited avoidance behaviour, fleeing the sound by swimming or diving. Beluga whales have taken evasive action against icebreakers 30 miles distant. Grey whales alter their migration routes by up to a mile.

None of this should surprise: who wouldn't flee unwanted, terrific sound? But dramatic change in behaviour is only part of the damage. Of increasing interest and worry to scientists is the cumulative impact of decades of constant low-level noise.

Roz Rolland is a right whale researcher at the New England Aquarium. She is a veterinarian by training, but arrived at whales 20 years ago and has not left. Like many right whale researchers, she spends time every year out on boats, and she has been doing this for years. She co-edited *The Urban Whale*, which is where I discovered her work with scat and dogs.

Rolland was looking at hormone levels in right whales and it was proving difficult. It is tricky enough to trap wild land-based mammals using helicopter chases, rocket netting or aesthetic darts. Whales are even worse. Their blubber is too thick for blood samples to be taken easily. Helicopter chases are neutralized by a simple fluking dive, head first and flukes last. Also, Rolland writes, 'there is no safe method for capturing a free-swimming large whale. For biologists accustomed to working on other animals, the sheer impossibility of capturing large whales, and the near-complete lack of information on their basic physiology, is astounding.'

Creative thinking was required. Animals excrete, whether on land or in water, and like the excreta of land-mammals, whale poop, or scat, is filled with bacteria, hormones and debris that can yield data about stress levels, food intake and toxic burden. Even better, right whale scat is pungent enough to be detected by human olfactory systems. It also floats, but only briefly. Initially, scat was harvested opportunistically, if someone smelled some, or if a whale defecated while being photographed. This made for a scanty research harvest, until Rolland thought of dogs.

Sniffer dogs sniff. If they can sniff on land, why not on water? She contacted Barbara Davenport in Washington State, who runs a sniffer dog training company. Davenport gets her dogs from city pounds or humane societies, because the worst pets often make the best sniffer dogs: they are rambunctious and lively and have a strong desire to play. These are good qualities for a reward-based training system. The first dog Davenport brought to meet Rolland was named Fargo, a three-year-old Rottweiler. At first he was trained on land to detect the scent of a right whale. Then they went to sea, along with a small platform that became known as the faecal flotation device. It was a piece of wood with a hole cut in it; a plastic jar with whale poop was inserted into the hole. The platform, the dog and the scientist went to sea, and the dog had to find the platform. Everybody was learning: the dog had to learn not to jump out of the boat when it tracked the scent. Rolland had to learn to read the dog's signals when it tracked the required scent: pricked ears, a moving tail, a different facial expression, quicker breathing.

Scat collection rates rose significantly, allowing Rolland to track stress hormones in the right whale population. It also enabled her to make one of the biggest breakthroughs in ocean noise research in decades. It was one of those delicious happenstance moments in science. An inadvertent illumination, a lucky fleeting thought. Rolland hadn't thought that whales might be damaged by noise, concentrating instead on other causes of stress, such as red tides, toxins and disease. Then in 2009, she attended a workshop organized by the US Office for Naval Research on the effect of underwater noise on ocean creatures. Rolland says that science is all about the question you are asking, and now she was asking a new question. She remembered that she had ten years of stress data, and she began to look back through it. Susan Parkes, an acoustic data specialist, mentioned how much quieter the ocean had been after 9/11. And Rolland remembered that of all her boat trips over all those years, some had been special.

On September 11, 2001, she was about to set out on a boat into the Bay of Fundy, as she did most years. The weather in those parts is unpredictable, but that week it was good: high pressure, very low winds. She would be foolish not to go out. But still, in the morning it was foggy, so the 6 a.m. departure time was postponed and then some more, and then someone on the dock said a plane had hit a Twin Tower. They rushed back to watch television and cried as the second plane hit. 'Then we sat around looking at each other and said, we can't just sit here and dissolve into a heap. We have to get on with our lives.' So they got on their boats and went out to sea. It was weird. There were no whale-watching boats or fishing vessels. There were no planes flying overhead. There were no container ships passing to and from the Cape Cod Canal or in and out of Boston. There was water and silence. 'It was very much like we were the only ones out there with the whales. It was a remarkable experience.'

For the whales, it was even more remarkable: they were swimming in a pre-industrial ocean. Rolland was on an ocean quieter than it had been for over a century. It stayed that way for most of the week. After the noise workshop, when she checked data for 11, 12 and 13 September, she was shocked. Usually, researching what noise does to right whales is extremely difficult. 'You're not able to take the noise away and then put it back and see if there is a response by the animal.' Even if you analyze hormones, the results can be inconclusive: stress hormone metabolites such as glucocorticoids could be produced for other reasons. But the message of the quiet ocean data was unmistakable. During the week that ships were stilled, underwater noise was lower by 6 decibels, and the levels of whales' glucocorticoids (stress-related faecal hormone metabolites) were lower too.

This story, though, is not what it seems. It is not a question of bad shipping and good environmentalists or innocent creatures and metal villains. Amy Knowlton, a colleague of Rolland at the New England Aquarium, has been studying the right whale since 1983.

On her first day, she saw a young male with its tail fluke severed. It mystified her. If right whales can hear each other, why can't they hear massive ships coming? Why don't they get out of the way? In the 1990s, Knowlton read an article about how sailboats can get sucked into the wake of big ships. She wondered if that could also be happening under water to whales, and began looking into hydrodynamics with the ocean engineering team at MIT. The team discovered that a ship's speed could be a factor in a whale's survival and that a whale emerging from depth could get sucked into the force around a propeller. Other theories were advanced elsewhere: that there is an area in front of a ship that is somehow soundless. It's called a 'bow-null' effect. Remedies were considered. If whales don't get out of the way in time, then maybe more time can be given to them by slowing or moving ships? Knowlton began to study marine policy: how the shipping industry operates, how policies are enacted, and what policies might help right whales.

By the mid-1990s there was more urgency. Every carcass they found seemed to be the result of a ship strike. A ship-strike committee was formed. Port authorities, industry people and whale people sat together. Ideas were put forward: can ships be slowed? Can whales be satellite tagged and ships warned in time so they avoid them? Maybe acoustic buoys in shipping channels were the answer, although experiments in using signals to deter whales from shipping channels had not been successful, as the whales headed straight for the signals. The best options were re-routing, changing shipping lanes, and imposing speed restrictions. All these may sound simple but they are not: they require the co-operation of a huge global industry of competing actors and changing international law. Even so, it was done. For a start, there was goodwill from the shipping industry. No-one wants to accidentally kill a whale. Knowlton once met a seafarer who had been on his bridge while passing through the Indian Ocean, when he spotted a whale. 'It was swimming along and coming towards the ship. He thought, I assume it will get out of my way. But it didn't, and he ran over it and killed it. It totally upset him.' The seafarer said that he understood now to actively avoid whales, because they don't hear him coming. He hadn't realized there were actions he could take.

Proposals to govern the actions ships take in coastal waters were submitted to the Fisheries Service of NOAA, where a 'tremendous advocate' named Lindy Johnson worked. Without Johnson, says Knowlton, it would have taken longer and probably never happened at all. But Johnson went to the IMO and somehow pushed the new rules through. Speed restrictions were put in place on a seasonal basis, once it was understood that a ship travelling at 17 knots would have a 90 per cent chance of killing a whale, but slowing the vessel to 10 knots gave the animal a 50–50 survival rate. And, incredibly and impressively, shipping lanes in the Bay of Fundy were moved. It was a matter of only miles, but the implications were wider than that: the Canadian Hydrographic Service had to change seven nautical charts at the cost of $30,000 per chart. It is too early for any serious assessment of the results, but Knowlton is sure of the difference at least anecdotally. 'When we're out in the Bay of Fundy now, we see ships on the horizon. Before, we'd see them bearing down on us where we were and where the whales were. The difference to our minds is dramatic.' She doesn't think ship strikes can be eliminated but she is sure they are being reduced.

As for the noise, pro-whale people have a strong weapon. A noisy propeller is an inefficient propeller. Inefficient propellers use more fuel, and now that fuel costs a fortune, the call to increase fuel efficiency has a receptive audience in shipping circles. But that is only for new ships. There is no chance of retrofitting the existing fleet of big, small and medium vessels that chug across oceans, trailing noise behind them. There is still no international regulation of noise in the ocean, and the IMO talks only of installing voluntary guidelines. Anyone can sign a voluntary guideline and voluntarily not follow it.

Without global regulations, acoustic pollution will grow because shipping is growing (by 26 per cent annually). Already, the acoustic habitat of the right whale – the range it needs to hear around – has been reduced to 10 per cent of what it was 100 years ago. Their chances of finding a mate and food, and probably of surviving, have all been decimated.

Efforts to deal with the atmospheric pollution of ships above the ocean surface are being accelerated. Stormy Mayo is not particularly optimistic about what happens beneath it. He is aware of the oddity of his position: he believes that the best thing for whales would be to leave them alone. 'But it turns out that we've decided we own the earth, we own their habitats.' He gave a talk once and remembers that he was feeling poetic, so he said this: 'These creatures live in an ocean that once was theirs and now it's walled by nets and crossed by ships. They once lived in a silent ocean except for the sounds of animals. They now live in an ocean whose noise impairs their very livelihood; that is perilous. They live in an ocean which arguably is changing in such profound ways that thousands of generations of them have never seen anything like it.' He thinks the future of ocean creatures and right whales is 'pretty tenuous', as much as Herman Melville did when he wondered whether 'Leviathan can endure so wide a chase and so remorseless a havoc'. The chase now is inadvertent, but the remorselessness remains, of noise pollution and other kinds, of a sonified, plasticated and damaged ocean.

Oil-blackened seamen are rescued, Second World War

10. RESCUE

The Bride in the Boat

Going back to the sinking of the *Britannia*, it must have
been horrific when shells were hitting the ship?
Yes, but somehow one seemed to be rather busy at the time.

—Ian McIntosh

It happened when *Kendal* was 15 days old. As the senior captain in
Maersk's container fleet, Captain Glenn often took ships out from
the yard. This time he was sailing this new K-class from the shipyard
in South Korea to Tanjung Pelapas in Malaysia. The weather was
poor, but as the captain wrote in the ship's log, the crew 'felt safe,
comfortable and proud on their new vessel, the weather having little
effect on such a large ship'. Cargo: containers. Wind: south-west
Force 6; sea/swell height: 3.5 metres, south-westerly direction.

On 7 August 2007, *Kendal*'s bridge team began to hear messages
from Singapore Port Operations Control Centre about MV *Pailin
Maritime*, a Thai general cargo ship carrying 24 men and 4700 logs,

that was in trouble. The ship was 30 years old and ill kept. Even as she set off from the Solomon Islands with her cargo, hoping to reach Ho Chi Minh City in Vietnam, her chief officer had worried about a frame in number two hold. It had already been repaired and patched, so before departure the chief had had a diver inspect the hull. Everything fine, sir. But the weather was bad, and *Pailin* pitched heavily, and the hull cracked exactly on the frame that had given the chief such concern. Captain Glenn, telling the story of *Pailin*, calls the ship 'this tired old girl'.

The tired old girl was listing heavily in the heavy seas. If she had been a motorbike with a rider, the rider's left knee would have been scraping the ground. That made it impossible to launch the port lifeboat, when it was almost under water. Then *Pailin* moved violently again so the starboard lifeboat was crushed and the crew could only jump into the water with lifejackets and life-raft pods. One crew member couldn't swim, wouldn't try, and went down with the ship. The rest 'took their chances in the warm seas' where some waves were four metres high. From the water they watched as the lights on *Pailin* flickered then failed. Fifteen minutes later, the ship had disappeared beneath the surface. They were left in darkness among furious seas. Shark territory.

Kendal was 170 miles from the last known location of *Pailin* when the first distress message had come through at 03:45. By 08:25 she was only 88 miles away and no-one else had responded. It is no small thing for great modern vessels – huge and time-pressured – to change course, and yet they do so frequently to help other ships in trouble. I read often of freighters and container ships that divert to rescue small ships or boats, of costly rescue exercises and efforts that seem at odds with a just-in-time stressed industry. The old code of honourable conduct at sea is surprisingly intact, though not always. In December 2009, British crab boat *Étoile des Ondes* was run down by the bulk carrier *Alam Pintar*, which did not stop. Several merchant vessels did not respond to distress signals, flares or messages from the French and British coastguards. It was, wrote Admiral Stephen Meyer, Chief Inspector of the UK's Marine Accident Investigation Branch, evidence of 'a dereliction of one of the most fundamental duties of the mariner, the moral and legal obligation to go to the aid of those in peril on the sea'. Even in wartime, 'civilised combatants went to great lengths to save the lives of sailors from enemy vessels they had sunk. Yet here we are, in the twenty-first century, finding ships failing to respond to Mayday messages.'

The International Convention for the Safety of Life at Sea (SOLAS) is plain, in its Regulation 33, Distress Situations: Obligations and Procedures. 'The master of a ship at sea which is in a position to provide assistance, on receiving information from any source that persons are in distress at sea, is bound to proceed with all speed to their assistance. This obligation to provide assistance applies regardless of the nationality or status of such persons or the circumstances in which they are found.' It is a comfort to find this old-fashioned notion of honour and duty in the middle of both dry legal documents and the wildness of the ocean. Of course the wildness is why the duty exists. All assistance is gratefully received from whatever source. Sailors used to call their highest-placed sails Trust-to-Gods, because who else could you rely on when you had to climb to their heights? (They were also known as Hope-in-Heavens.)

Four ships agreed by radio to attend to *Pailin's* distressed crew. They were *Al Laila*, *Cap Colville*, *Rio Imperial* and *Maersk Kendal*. By 11.30 a.m., *Kendal* was close enough to hail *Pailin*, but fruitlessly. At 12.08, she contacted *Kirmar*, a passing merchant ship. The language of the captain's log is spare but telling: '*Kirmar* was on scene but maintaining her passage.'

Kendal had already abandoned her passage, although there was a berth booked for her in port. Captain Glenn risked costing the company thousands of dollars by diverting and delaying. There was no question of doing otherwise. 'I think I was put on this planet for that.' What about the ships that did not respond, the ones whose passage was more important than anything else? Perhaps they didn't receive the messages. Perhaps the VHF was turned down, which was one excuse used by some of the ships that failed to assist *Étoile des Ondes*. Others, wrote Admiral Meyer, said they didn't see the distress flares, or they hadn't received the coastguard's alerts. This is the maritime equivalent of saying the traffic lights weren't working, and so improbable that the chief inspector, whose role is constrained by diplomacy, nonetheless adds an exclamation mark in brackets, the only indicator with which he is probably allowed to express his disbelief. Most alarmingly, 'some masters claimed not to understand they have a legal (and moral) duty to react'. Captain Glenn, in an account he later wrote of the *Pailin* incident, kept his dismay polite. 'The number of ships in the area that did not respond… was disappointing. Time-honoured traditions are slowly eroding.'

Kendal was further away than *Al Laila* or *Cap Colville*, but *Kendal* arrived and the other two did not. These were not seas empty of ships. *MV Liuhe* was six miles west of *Pailin's* last reported position but also continued on her passage. Singapore reported that a Vietnamese warship was in the vicinity and would arrive, along with a search-and-rescue craft. Instead, as Captain Glenn's log records, 'Neither vessel sighted during search and rescue operation so will not be mentioned further in this report.' *Rio Imperial*, a car-carrier, was on its way but 2.5 hours away.

In the hours that it took for *Kendal* to reach the scene, the captain prepared his crew, who had hardly any search-and-rescue experience besides the practice kind. They were as inexperienced as the equipment of their brand-new ship. None had been used beyond testing, including the rescue boat, a fast open craft. Even so, when the captain asked for crew to take the rescue boat out into stormy seas, three volunteered. Everyone was nervous. Even the captain was, he wrote, 'half-hoping we were not first to arrive, as then [the Master] may be responsible for the organisation of Search and Rescue overall and thus success or failure'.

Kendal arrived on scene at 12.30. Nineteen minutes later, an empty lifejacket was seen in the water. This was enough for the captain to set in motion his search plan: he knew from the currents, the winds and the drift rates that any survivors would probably have been carried north-east by now, but in case *Pailin*'s position had been wrongly reported, they also did a four-mile survey south-westerly. Nothing to see; so they went north. By this time *Rio Imperial* had arrived, and began to search north of *Kendal*'s search area, with the bridge officers communicating by radio.

What does the search part of search and rescue mean? It means looking, peering, staring at choppy seas, hoping to see something. It is tensing your eyes, screwing up skin, constantly straining. It is keeping the bridge windows wiped with the big windscreen wipers; it is binoculars for all in all directions. It is extremely difficult. Human eyes work best with things they can differentiate – a branch, a bollard. They are not built to look at endless water. When the German sail-training ship *Pamir* sank in 1957, 500 miles from the Azores islands, its survivors in a life raft watched in amazement as a ship failed to see them although it was only 300 feet away.

There was other work to be done. The captain and his first officer needed to calculate where survivors might be, by using charts, maths, physics and brains. This was what the captain was good at. (Henry the Navigator.) But it was the first mate who drew his attention to IAMSAR, the International Aeronautical and Maritime Search and Rescue Manual, which contained a series of tables showing the drift rates for life rafts. 'I'd forgotten about that. I knew what the wind had been doing and what the current was doing but I didn't know how far a boat would drift.' Now they did. They knew they were on the right path when wreckage floated past later in the day: bits of blue plastic, some ropes. The officers' calculations had predicted that survivors would be 29 to 36 miles away. 'Then,' the captain writes, 'after hours of just staring out to sea, it all began.'

At 17.20, many large logs were seen in the water. Five minutes later, a body went past, face down, his naked back exposed, his shirt rucked up to his neck. The sight unsettled the crew, but the man was obviously dead, so the captain ordered the ship to carry on, in search of the living. One and a half miles and five minutes later, the crew saw orange smoke, then a small rocket, though it was more of a damp squib. Imagine the hope behind that damp squib, the fierce and desperate hope: the sight of a ship, a ship. Later, *Pailin's* chief officer, one of the men in the water, told the captain that they had made out, only just, *Kendal's* funnel. Perhaps they had seen the white star or that sharp sky blue. They only realized that they had been noticed because of the smoke: the chief officer was a good enough seafarer to understand that it meant that *Kendal's* engines were going astern. The ship was braking. They had been seen.

By now light was dimming, but the captain decided to launch the rescue boat anyway. He did not do it lightly, but he did it quickly. His crew were reluctant because they were scared. The captain had no room for fear alongside his adrenalin. The sight of the dead body had upset everyone, but he was not scared because he knew what his ship could do, and he had faith in his crew. He is careful not to sound emotional, but the setting off of the boat is where his emotions emerge, because it meant the crew trusted him. 'You put them in harm's way and they trust you. They trusted me with their life, and I found that great.'

Everybody was alert. The chief engineer, even in his undersea, windowless engine room, understood that dusk was falling and sent up extra lights although no-one had asked him to. And the crew in the rescue boat headed towards the site of that orange smoke, careful to stay as long as possible in the lee of the ship, inside an area that the ship's mass turned into a shelter, because the captain was constantly positioning her to protect the rescue boat from wind. He doesn't say this, but that must have required great skill. He had promised the crew this, that he would always be between them and the sea. The conditions were dramatic. There were dark logs everywhere, the seas were blackening, and then suddenly there were two black heads in the black water among the black logs. The captain says 'they looked like two black tyres in the water', or two tiny tennis balls that were the heads of men grasping lifejackets as floats. In his log, the captain wrote, 'Bingo!' At 18.03, they were hauled into the rescue boat. The mood on the ship lifted. The nervous crew found the search and rescue exciting, almost fun, even though they had discovered that the all-in-one immersion suits they were wearing made the movement of fingers almost impossible. Luckily, they found, you can haul a man into a boat with mittens on.

The five men in the boat – three rescuers, two rescued – returned safely to *Kendal*. The Thai seafarers were 'alright, but only just'. One was Thanasan Kumsup, the 43-year-old chief officer of *Pailin*, which was a family concern: his brother was the captain, and another brother owned the one-boat shipping company in Thailand that operated the vessel. For all those hours in the water, he said, they had fended off furious logs. Their chests were deeply bruised by hours of blows and assaults. They had found themselves in the water with only the lifejackets, but during the hours they were in open sea, one smoke float, one rocket, three lifebuoys and three packets of survival food had floated past them, near enough to reach. Without them, Captain Glenn is sure they would have died. Once the swell died down, there would have been sharks. For anyone wrecked in this ocean, there are sharks. When USS *Indianapolis* was torpedoed by a Japanese submarine on a July night in 1945, 900 of its 1126 crew made it alive into the water. The shark attacks began at dawn. When rescue arrived four days later, 316 men were still alive. *Pailin's* crew had been 17 hours in the water and had travelled 35 miles by the time *Kendal* arrived.

Rio Imperial reported in by radio. She had seen a life raft three miles north-east of *Kendal*, so Captain Glenn proceeded north-east again, as the survivors had told them that two life rafts had survived the sinking. *Rio Imperial* retrieved 13 people from the life raft it had spotted. At 19.03, the look-outs on *Kendal*, still peering, still straining, saw something orange off their port bow one mile away. It was too dark to launch the rescue boat, so *Kendal* became a giant rescue ship instead, slowing by the raft and skilfully drifting to it. A squall began to blow, but the pilot ladder was lowered, four survivors climbed up it, and the raft was cut loose and allowed to drift away. The survivors were traumatized. They didn't speak much. *Kendal's* crew figured out from communicating with *Rio Imperial* that the captain and four others were dead. The survivors' moods, wrote the captain, ranged from 'visual depression, fear, relief, at the same time elation at being rescued'. He had never, he said, seen anyone so appreciative of a Maersk T-shirt.

But still, he says, sitting in his comfortable cabin on F-deck on *Kendal*, looking at a picture of the rescue crew, he is not at peace with *Pailin*. Nineteen saved and one lost but four never found. 'What still bothers me to this day is the thought that when we picked up those two small heads in the water, what if there were four more heads further off who could see us because we had our lights on. They could see our ship and they would see us leave. That still bothers me.'

For a moment, Captain Glenn was a hero. The Shipwrecked Mariners' Society presented him with a Lady Swaythling trophy for outstanding seamanship. He made headlines in papers in the north of England. Local skipper leads dramatic rescue. Tyneside captain leads rescue mission on the high seas. The *North West Evening Mail*, based in Cumbria, was inspired to publish an article apparently only because *Kendal* was named after a Cumbrian town. That the rescue made only small ripples is not surprising. You don't read much about Merchant Navy heroism any more, although it is common enough. The last time the Merchant Navy was thought heroic was 70 years ago, and its limelight was brief, like the sun breaking through clouds then gone again.

On the first floor of Liverpool's Merseyside Maritime Museum, there is a small section on the Merchant Navy. It is not crowded: most people are crammed into the *Titanic* area nearer the entrance. There, the crowds at the glass displays of disaster are three deep. But here among Merchant Navy history there is space formed by disinterest. I watch an old P&O recruitment video – 'Run away to Sea!' – for a while. A young boy comes and stands beside me for a few minutes, also watching, but glancing sideways at me now and then with puzzlement. He watches long enough to be told that if he runs away to sea to work with P&O his accommodation will be excellent and he will eat well, before he finds the courage to speak his mind. 'Isn't this about the *Titanic*?' Then he leaves, because it is not.

This is baffling. The *Titanic* attracts for its combination of glamour and tragedy. But so should the stories of the merchant seamen who fought in the Second World War, although for decades they were classed as neither veterans nor fighters, despite losing more men, proportionally, than any branch of the 'real' armed services, and despite enduring extreme danger and the constant chance of being torpedoed, of facing a death from drowning or burning by flaming oil, or countless days in an open lifeboat. Down the corridor from the *Titanic* crowds, I notice a newspaper cutting pinned to the wall. It is dated 1942, comes from the *Daily Mail*, and in headline and content is brief. 'Girl tended 51 men in boat of death. A 21-years-old English girl, a bride of a few months, played Florence Nightingale to

51 men and two women drifting in an open boat after their ship had been torpedoed in the South.'

This Florence Nightingale was Diana Jarman. Actually, she had been married for a few years, not months, and her husband was dead. So she was a 21-year-old widow, travelling as a passenger in 1942 on *City of Cairo*, a small liner heading from India to England, empire-backwards. The year 1942 was the deadliest of the war for ships at sea. Enemy battleships and U-boats had been active from four hours after war was declared on 3 September 1939, when *Athenia*, a passenger vessel, was torpedoed 200 miles from Ireland on her way west. Of her passengers – which included evacuating children, Jewish refugees and Americans heading home – 118 were killed. The attack was a mistake on two counts: the submarine captain thought he was targeting an auxiliary liner on military business, and it also contravened the Second London Naval Treaty of 1936, an international protocol signed by Germany which required attackers to give ships fair warning and only to sink civilian ships if passengers had been first delivered to safety. Even so, that was the beginning and so it went on. Warships, passenger ships, merchant ships: they were all targets. Merchant ships came off worst.

There was never any question that Britain would use its merchant seamen in war. How else do you stock an army? In 1939, Britain was the most important maritime power in the world. It had a third of the global deep-sea fleet and exported multi-million tons of iron, steel, chemicals, textiles and coal. Its 'merchant navy' consisted of 3000 deep-sea ships and 1000 coastal vessels. No-one was in merchant seafaring for the luxury of it: the master of a tramp steamer earned £24 a month and had to supply his own soap, uniform, sextant and charts. Even the best shipping companies, wrote historian Richard Woodman, like Alfred Holt's Blue Funnel line, 'thought that ten days of leave after six months' voyage without a weekend in port was enough to keep an officer happy'. Lady Astor, the first female MP, reported to Parliament in 1938 that 'a colleague who had taken a look at the conditions in which seamen lived had said he would not expect ferrets to live in such conditions'. (She also thought – apparently after her daughter had an affair with one – that seamen should wear yellow armbands to signify that they might carry venereal disease.)

Britain was also a politically and geographically isolated island. It had to be stocked by sea then as now. It had to export that coal and those chemicals to earn currency to buy imports. War does not change the economic necessity of trade, but adds to it: every war is fought on a foundation of supply, which is why logistics corps form the largest sector of most modern armies. The United States at war still sends more than 90 per cent of its supplies by sea. The tail of an army is long and it is afloat. Modern fighting methods have not changed this: television pictures during the Gulf Wars showed soldiers trooping down the belly of giant cargo planes, but their tanks and jeeps do not fly. Heavy weapons and material have to come by sealift, the same way they always did. Arms trade researchers can calculate illicit heavy weapons flows by monitoring ships and shipments.

When Mitt Romney chided President Obama for the small size of the US Navy during a presidential debate, the president responded with condescending humour. Military styles have changed, he said. We don't use longbows either, and we don't need a huge Navy when we have aircraft carriers. This was disingenuous: the United States needs ships as much as ever, but they are merchant ones needed to supply its military. Probably the only reason US ship owners fly the US flag is because laws require them to. The 1904 Military Cargo Preference Act requires 100 per cent of items owned, procured or used by military departments or defence agencies to be carried on US-flag vessels, while the 1996 Maritime Security Act provided financial incentives for ship owners to make their ships available in wartime or in a disaster. Even so, US commentators were shocked after the *Deepwater Horizon* oil spill in 2010: not only were most oil rigs off the US coast foreign-flagged, so also was most of the rescue and clean-up fleet.

Newly at war in early September 1939, Britain had enough merchant ships to do its shopping and selling: oil from the Gulf, the usual commodities from India. In the words of seaman Frank Laskier, who became Britain's most famous Merchant Navy star in the war years, 'they got the ship to Calcutta with munitions; and back to England with tea'. Across the Atlantic, from a still pacific United States, flowed precious timber, pit props to shore up blitzed houses, pig iron for all sorts of uses. America became Britain's corner shop. No sailor liked a cargo of pig iron, although it carried the blessing that a torpedoed ship loaded with iron will sink fast and clean, with no time to burn to death from ignited oil, or to be strafed by German guns. Nor were pit props popular: as the crew of *Pailin* discovered, timber does not float serenely but is launched at you by the force of the waves. The currents that a sinking ship created were even more murderous.

The ships were a mishmash of identities and interests. Some had been co-opted by the Royal Navy, but most were still privately owned, grouped together artificially in convoys as they were grouped together artificially, metaphorically, as something called 'the merchant navy'. King George V had been the first to sanction this phrase, after 15,000 merchant sailors died during the First World War carrying supplies. But by 1939, merchant seamen still had no standard uniform, no badge, no identifying features. When about 95 merchant ships were sunk during the first few months of the Second World War, their surviving sailors were required to pay their bus fare home, even if they were travelling there from a torpedoed ship; uniformed men were not. They had to endure scorn and spit for seeming to be non-combatants in their unofficial sailors' clothes.

In Canada, merchant seamen were called zombies. They were a national service that was not considered one. In *My Name is Frank*, a collection of his radio broadcasts, Frank Laskier tells of a sailor back from a seven-month trip at war. 'He's been dive-bombed, he's been shelled, he's been raided, he's been mined; he's done everything, and he's walking down the street with a deep-sea roll and his best civvies on, and an old lady comes along to him and pins a white feather on to him.'

Angry old ladies or Nazis: they were all confused about the status of these fighting civilians. For the first couple of years, enemy treatment of merchant seamen was inconsistent. Sometimes they shot at survivors in the water, sometimes they took them prisoner. Although merchant ships by now were sailing alongside Navy ships in convoys, until 1941 the pay of merchant seamen was stopped as soon as their ships were sunk. Widows received no compensation or pension. Exposure in a lifeboat, wrote the historian Richard Woodman, 'was an unpaid excursion'. And seamen continued to be disdained. Having survived being exploded into the sea when the SS *Ashby* was torpedoed, then several days in a lifeboat, a merchant seafarer named Bill Linskey took a train home to Newcastle. Then, 'soon I became aware of sideways glances from uniformed gigglers and realised how I must look to them. I was young, tanned, fit. Why wasn't I in uniform?... I looked at their complacent little faces and wondered how they thought the food arrived to fill their bellies, not to mention ammunition for their guns, petrol for the tanks and tinned food for their Mum's rations.'

After Germany invaded France, the U-boats became more lethal. They had French ports in which to be based, and could go further and stay out longer. Then someone at the Admiralty realized that seamen could be helpful propaganda. Finally the propagandists realized that it is hard to mobilize public opinion around something as amorphous as 'trade'. It is easier to stir people up about a battle, so there was a Battle of the Atlantic, and plucky merchant seamen fighting it mostly without weapons.

Winston Churchill called the Battle of the Atlantic decisive to the war effort. Now merchant seafarers became useful heroes too, loaded not just with cargo on their ships but with propaganda messages for a besieged island population. There were posters of housewives and businessmen thanking the Merchant Navy for bringing their dinner. Wartime Britons were urged to shop carefully – 'Let your shopping save our shipping' – and eat home-grown food, to ease the pressure on the merchant service.

Once the United States entered the war, Franklin Roosevelt followed rhetorical suit. In a 1941 letter to Admiral Emory S. Land, he wrote that 'if we are going to keep away from our shores the forces that have convulsed the Old World and now menace the New, the job will be done in large measure by the ships and sailors of the Merchant Marine and by the working men who build the ships and supply them. If they fail, the whole effort fails.' If only sensible practice had accompanied his rhetoric. Even by the spring of 1942, lax defences on the US east coast caused U-boat commander Peter Cremer to think them 'asleep, to put it mildly'. Behind them, Europe was blacked-out for war, but here the US coast was shining as if in peacetime, guiding friend and foe alike. Of course the watching U-boats took advantage of this helpfully illuminated submarine candy shop, and American and Allied merchant seamen were killed before even leaving territorial waters. On one evening alone, Cremer destroyed the *Amazone* and the tanker *Halsey* with hardly any effort. 'None of us had imagined it would be so easy,' he wrote, 'and it could not and would not continue.'

He was right, though not immediately. The lights stayed blazing for another three months. Then the United States began speed-building Liberty ships to add to the cargo-carrying fleet. But 1942 was the worst time to be at sea. Their attacks were so ferocious and so successful that Germans called this period 'The Happy Time'. Casualty statistics vary, but by the end of 1942 more than a thousand ships had been sunk, and 10,000 British merchant seamen had been killed. Survivors arrived at missions in the United States, Canada and Britain, often after days at sea in open boats. Staff at the Seamen's Church Institute in New York City distributed shoes, socks and underwear to shipwrecked crews from its Sloppes Chest, a name taken from the historical merchant navy term 'slops', clothing that seafarers wore when theirs wore out at sea. British arrivals were given a new suit through a deal with the British Consulate and a local department store. The institute didn't just cater to grown men: British child evacuees also passed through and were 'particularly delighted with the showers', having to be dissuaded from taking two or three before breakfast. The horror that the shipwrecked survivors had experienced was routine and the calmness of those submitted to it astonishing. In December 1941, four men arrived in New York after 13 days drifting in freezing seas off Iceland. They had suffered gangrene and exposure. Among the four, wrote Homer Strickler in the *New York Sun*, there was but one leg. Another journalist in the *New York Herald Tribune* told the story of the 'mad Russian', Waldemar Semenov, a US merchant mariner serving on SS *Alcoa Guide* when it was hit. While shells were crashing all about, 'Semenov went to his cabin to brush his teeth and put on his best clothes'. (He even took the time to choose between two neckties.) In the galley he stuffed his pockets with loaves of bread and from the library he picked out a book to while away the hours in a lifeboat. Then he borrowed $2 from a shipmate against the day he would again be set ashore. 'With his mind, body and finances accounted for, he announced himself ready to quit the ship.' Semenov survived long enough to donate his compass from that day to the National Museum of American History in 2005.

The pages of newspapers and *The Lookout*, the Seamen's Church Institute publication, are the only places to find the voices of these men. They were not talkers generally, and in wartime they knew that loose lips sink ships, as one of the many propaganda posters reminded them. But in the mission they could relax and talk. They could tell mission staff, as two American brothers from the Midwest did, about how their ship was torpedoed. 'The explosion shook them into the sea, they climbed onto a raft. It was blown high in the air by a second explosion, coming down and striking one of the brothers. He was knocked out but his brother was able to hold onto him until a rescue ship arrived. In typical American fashion, the one who had been hit by the raft said, "Well, I figured as it was my first voyage to sea, I was lucky to get the experience!"'

In 1942, the *New York Times* tried to educate its readers about the discrepancy between the merchant marines' slaughter and their status.

> Many come through three or four sinkings, yet do not hesitate when new ships are ready. No one turns in the street to admire their uniforms. They wear no uniform. No one steps up to the bar to buy them drinks. No moist-eyed old ladies turn to them in the subway to murmur, 'God bless you.' The cop on the beat, gentle with the tipsy soldier or the unsteady gob, is apt to put his nightstick to the breeches of a merchant sailor who has tippled heavily in the town's bar to celebrate his rescue from the sea.

After years of abuse from civilians and police alike, a silver Merchant Navy badge was finally given to British mariners, and a lapel pin to Americans. (Of course seafarers liked to turn the MN upside down and say it stood for 'Not Wanted'.)

I watch a British Pathé film called *Saved from the Sea*, about the rescue of yet another boat-load of torpedoed men. The war had some famous boat dramas, such as that of Poon Lim, a Chinese sailor who survived 133 days at sea. But this boat in *Saved from the Sea* is not famous. Just another sinking. 'A handful of survivors,' says the narrator, 'picked out of the sea after an experience which in peacetime would have made headlines in every newspaper in the world.' The camera shows men who are bearded, and thin and spent. They come onto the rescue ship and sink down rather than sit. They smoke. 'This is how men look after a month in an open boat,' the narrator continues. I see how they look as survivors, but how did they live while they were surviving?

Diana Jarman has left barely any trace and exists largely in the accounts of other survivors from *City of Cairo*, who remember her as a jolly blonde, as indefatigable, as a good egg who talked of liking tennis and living somewhere in Hertfordshire. She was an ordinary survivor of an extreme journey on an open boat.

Diana did not keep records of her 37 days in lifeboat number 1. Others did, including Jack Edmead, third steward and 'Ship's Writer', who, in his official survivor's report to the Admiralty, testified that *City of Cairo* carried 136 passengers, including nine officers of the Navy, Army and Merchant Navy, and 18 children. The crew numbered 197, including seven naval personnel and four military gunners. It was also carrying 10,000 tons of general stores.

Many passengers were women and children who were leaving India for personal reasons, for greater safety. It took four weeks to reach Cape Town, and they had travelled for another six days, departing on 31 October. The liner was no *Titanic* or *Athenia*, but scrappier and slower. It would not have been your first choice of transport, had you a choice. The route was dangerous, but not as dangerous as other routes further north. A U-boat wolf pack was known to be hanging around Cape Town, but *City of Cairo* was not powerless: she was armed with weapons that included one 12-pounder, two twin Marlins, two twin Hotchkiss guns and two

Oerlikons. There were four PAC rockets. She sailed alone because there were no convoys to join.

On 6 November at 8.30 p.m., the Indian stewards, dressed in native clothes, were clearing away food and tableware. The British Merchant Navy, despite King George V's blessing of it as such, was only half British. The other half consisted of Arabs and Somalis and lascars in the engine rooms, where they stoked the old coal-fired ships that were still being used, though they could only do seven knots at best. Chinese and Indians were stewards and sailors. The engine room men were the Black Gangs, named for the colour of coal, not of their skin, and they died in greater numbers than deck sailors. It was more difficult for them to escape the ship, to begin with, but also they were dressed more scantily to cope with the heat of the coal-fired engines, putting them at a disadvantage if they were suddenly ejected into the water or an open boat.

On *City of Cairo* the liqueurs had not yet been served when there was a terrific bang (said Joan Redl), or a sickening crack (said Dr Douglas Quantrill), or a heavy dull explosion (said Jack Edmead), or a BOOM! (said Marjorie Miller). The ship shuddered, glass broke, and then there was the silence of shock. I read survivors' accounts gathered on a website by Hugh Maclean, whose father Calum was a seaman gunner on *City of Cairo*, and they converge on one thing: there was no panic. People who had their lifebelts at their feet, as they were advised to do, took them and made their way to their lifeboat station. People who didn't have their lifebelts nearby headed for their cabins to fetch them. The ship carried nine lifeboats. Lifeboats, lifebelts, life rafts: as if naming an object with life gives it more power to save one.

Diana Jarman ended up in boat number 1 along with quarter-master Angus MacDonald. The boat was full up with lascars and women and children and male crew and passengers. When Mac-Donald said that some people needed to go overboard for a few minutes so they could better bail out the water, it was the women who immediately responded. They jumped into the water – even Lady Almond, who had three small children with her – and swam to a water tank floating nearby. While they were bailing, *City of Cairo* was sinking. 'There she goes,' said someone, and there she went, and then there was only quiet. 'There was no show of emotion,' wrote MacDonald. 'I expect the others, like myself, were wondering what would happen to us.'

The captain – a 46-year-old Liverpudlian named William Rogerson – had survived the sinking, perhaps because he made sure to keep fit while on board. Perhaps just because of good luck. It did not always happen. The captain often went down with his ship because he was delayed by duties on the bridge. The ship's confidential books had to be thrown overboard in the weighted bag provided for such a purpose. Radio operators also frequently died, as they stayed in their radio rooms sending out urgent messages and didn't make it out.

Although he was propelled far below the water, Captain Rogerson came to the surface alive. He called for all lifeboats to tie up together and to use their sea anchors, canvas contraptions that were trailed in the sea to slow the boat, to create some safety in numbers. There was colossal danger around them, in the form of an open ocean. But there was also the U-68, the submarine that had sunk them. It was likely to be around because U-boat captains often arrived after the violence, hunting for information and for senior officers to take as prisoners of war. Many captains spent uncomfortable and frightening weeks on U-boats. The commander of U-68, Karl-Friedrich Merten, asked for the captain, gave directions and distances for the nearest land – Brazil 2000 miles, Africa 1000 miles, St. Helena only 500 – then left. According to Ralph Barker in his book about *City of Cairo*, the U-boat did not leave before its captain said to the dazed passengers in number 6 boat, 'Good night, sorry for sinking you.'

Boat number 1 was open and wooden. It had nothing in common with *Kendal*'s enclosed orange capsules except that it also floated. It was little more than a jollyboat, a small wooden craft that is used for going from ship to shore, not for survival. Half the boat's drinking water had been lost in the confusion and bailing, but there were 30 gallons left, along with enough food to last for three months. That meant one tablespoonful of water – four ounces – for each person, morning and night. Also there was pemmican, a compressed meat and fat substance invented by Native Americans and popular with polar explorers and lifeboat equippers. There were some tablets of Horlicks, a malt extract. There was no fishing tackle: this was not thought vital until after the war. Nor were there barley sugar sweets, which were later understood to provide energy but also saliva. Countless lifeboat survivors found it impossible to masticate hard biscuits when their mouths had been dry for weeks.

Captain Rogerson advised a course of north by north-east, and all the boats set off. Diana Jarman was one of three women on board, and the youngest. There was not enough room for everyone to sit, so people sat and stood in shifts. The boat carried a medical doctor named Taskar, but his mind seemed to have been damaged in the sinking, so Diana took on most of the first aid. 'She could never do enough,' wrote MacDonald, 'either in attending to the sick and injured, boat work, or even actually handling the craft. She showed up some of the men in the boat, who seemed to lose heart in the beginning.'

What else were they losing? Hydration, obviously. Energy. Weight. *Kendal* may carry fancy closed lifeboats, but if her crew ended up in a life raft, they would be as exposed to as much physiological threat as Diana Jarman was in 1942. The open sea does not suit human physiology. We are not made for so much salt and air and wet. There are other things to consider: seasickness is inevitable once the protection of a high-sided ship is removed.

'A singular disadvantage of the sea,' wrote Stephen Crane in *Open Boat*, 'lies in the fact that after successfully surmounting one wave you discover that there is another behind it just as important and just as nervously anxious to do something effective in the way of swamping boats.' Sunstroke is another deadly threat. And all these privations are intensified by sleeplessness. Diana's boat was crowded. Legs had to stay in the same position for hours. Movement around the boat involved somehow stepping over 26 Indians who had congregated amidships. There was elbowing and kicking and little chance of rest. When Wilbert Widdicombe and Robert Tapscott spent 47 days in an open boat after SS *Anglo-Saxon* was sunk in August 1940, their diagnosis when they were rescued was pellagra, deranged nervous systems and insomnia.

Somehow a difficult night passed and before lunchtime on the first day in open sea, the first sharks appeared. They were not afraid and kept approaching the boat. At least the boat was more sturdy than other life-saving craft: when *Cingalese Prince* chief engineer R.H. Wilson was sunk in 1941 in the southern Atlantic Ocean, he spent 12 days on an open life raft. 'The whole time we were on the raft, day and night, we were constantly surrounded by sharks of different species… Very often they would come tearing towards the raft, then just before reaching it would turn over and scrub their belly on the side, no doubt to try to get rid of the parasites which grew on them.' But Diana's boat was making good speed, and the sharks were kept away. However, it was leaking. The chief officer in charge of boat number 1 decided then to set off for St. Helena without the others, in a race against time and leaks. It made sense, the captain agreed, and that was that.

I wonder about details. How do you go to the toilet in a lifeboat? The women rigged up some privacy with clothing and cloth, and after a while they didn't care. Nearly everyone was soon constipated anyway. In Bill Linskey's lifeboat – after his first torpedoing, for there were two more – 'a man had to hang his bum over the side to crap. The First Mate said, "It would be appreciated if all the shitting and peeing could go on well before we have our meagre meal." "And don't forget to wash your hands," someone shouted, "it can be quite dangerous."'

The first to die was Dr Taskar, whose mind had gone. After four days he was calling for beer, and then he was dead. It depressed everyone. The lascars were pleading for water: *Pani, sahib, pani.* MacDonald doesn't sound sympathetic to them in his account, and never gives them names. Jack Edmead dismisses them as lazy natives who did not do the work they could, so that Europeans had to do twice as much. Even in Richard Woodman's forensically researched account of the Battle of the Atlantic, these foreigners are usually blank 'Chinamen' or a mass of 'lascars'. They seem to die faster; they seem to fear that they are of a lower priority. When *Calchas* sank and its second officer jumped over the side of the lifeboat, 'this triggered fractious behaviour among the Chinese, "but after they had been threatened with an axe," reported Second Steward Curtis, "we managed to restore some kind of order [although] our position was none too secure".'

In the second week the deaths began properly. MacDonald remembers that Taskar died on day six; Edmead thinks it was day 10. Time slipped. Some Indians died, and they were pushed overboard, 'as the lascars never would help bury their dead'. Then it was the Europeans' turn. Curiously, the people who did not help others died first. Then it was death by domino: Miss Taggart and Mr Ball entwined together one morning, both dead. A few more lascars. A young engineer who tried to heed MacDonald's instructions to be more like Diana, always cheerful, but in the end 'dropped back and died'. The ship's stewardess, Annie Crouch, died in the bottom of the boat, with swollen legs and a mind swollen, too, by exposure. Then Tiny Watts, a large and good man; and Frank Stobbart, the ship's storekeeper. Some more lascars. A fireman – one of the black gang from the engine room, a coal-shoveller – jumped overboard, but he had forgotten to remove his lifejacket, so he floated helplessly until the sharks got him.

There was still food in the boat – under Board of Trade regulations a lifeboat was required only to carry dry biscuits – but with barely any water, it was impossible to chew. For this reason, anyone setting out to sea should take a button to suck on, to create saliva and sweep the food down. Norman Watts, a merchant seaman, sunk three times in two seas, described his lifeboat experience with scorn. What use was a shiny Merchant Navy badge when all they were given to survive was biscuits and brackish water in a foul tank? 'Even though the ship was new, the tanks hadn't been sterilized. It was good enough for seamen. Nobody gave a damn if seamen survived or not, really.'

By now most of the passengers were burned: the sun assaulted them every day, all day, and there was nowhere to hide from it. Everyone had sore throats. Everyone was desiccated. Most had salt-water boils and ulcers caused by chafing where salt crystals had collected on the joints. Everyone in the open at sea gets ulcers, because the circulation is poor from lack of nutrients and water and inactivity; muscle has wasted so there is less cushioning between the skin and bones; and the lack of protein makes healing difficult. But there was still bailing to be done, to keep the boat less wet, and it was heavy work even for someone with strength.

On the seventeenth night, there was sabotage: a young European man kept removing the plug, flooding the boat with water. He said, if we are all to die we may as well die together, but he was stopped and died the next day together with 'seven or eight lascars and a banker from Edinburgh'. On the jolly boat of the *Anglo-Saxon*, sunk by a German raider in 1940, the rudder detached on the thirteenth day, either by accident or by design. For Chief Officer

C.B. Denny, in charge of *Anglo-Saxon*'s survivors until then, it was enough. He was going overboard and asked if anyone would come with him, and Third Engineer Hawkes said yes. I don't know what is more extraordinary about this: that they carefully shook hands and jumped into the sea, where Hawkes' blond head could be seen above water for an uncomfortably long time after; or that they first had a short sleep. What can that sleep have been like? What did they dream? Wilbert Widdicombe, one of two *Anglo-Saxon* crew members who survived, took over the recording of the boat log, written on sailcloth. He didn't waste time with unnecessary words. 'Chief engineer and third mate go overboard. No water.'

No water but the sea. Everyone on boat number 1 was gargling with seawater by now. They were careful: everyone knew drinking seawater was deadly. In a lecture at the Royal College of Physicians in 1942, MacDonald Critchley, a physician who had studied survival at sea, said that 'seawater poisoning must be accounted, after cold, the commonest cause of death in shipwrecked sailors'. At first, it wouldn't seem so: seawater is liquid and it quenches. The relief would be immediate. But seawater has an average salt content of three per cent. This increases thirst dramatically, so that more seawater is drunk, and more, and salt levels go ever more haywire, until the body tries to regulate by urination, and you expel a litre of urine for every litre of seawater drunk, making matters worse. There are also complicated and intricate effects of seawater on cells, blood and tissue, but in essence, too much seawater can fry your brain. Then this happens, in the words of Critchley: 'The victim becomes silent and apathetic, with a peculiar fixed and glassy expression in the eyes. The condition of the lips, mouth, and tongue worsens, and a peculiarly offensive odour has been described in the breath. Within an hour or two, delirium sets in, quiet at first but later violent and unrestrained; consciousness is gradually lost; the colour of the face changes and froth appears at the corners of the lips. Death may take place quietly: more often it is a noisy termination, and not infrequently the victim goes over the side in his delirium and is lost.'

In some lifeboats, a powerful disincentive to drink seawater was developed. 'Whenever a seaman threatens to drink seawater,' a sailor explained to *The Lookout*, 'an officer knocks him out.'

Diana Jarman didn't drink seawater. She was too sensible. She was waiting for time to pass. Survivors have not recorded their methods for doing this. The excruciating slowness of the minutes must be best forgotten. MacDonald writes that by now 'a good few people sat all day with their heads on their chests doing and saying nothing'. This was dangerous: there was work to be done. The boat had to be steered. People had to keep watch for a ship, for anything. Sharks had to be batted off. By the third week, it still hadn't rained and the water had run out. They tried to eat a dogfish and drink its blood, but it was too disgusting to swallow. When Jack Oakie, Jack Litte and a Zanzibar fireman died, it took the others a whole day to find the strength to lift the three bodies into the ocean.

I wonder where they were by now. There are names on nautical charts: Orange Fan, the Angola Basic, the Discovery Seamounts, the Pernambuco Abyssal Plain. But to them it must have been an awful blank. Even Diana must have quietened, because she had the sickness that everyone had, which gave her a sore throat and yellow phlegm oozing from her mouth, probably from the constant dampness. Joe Green was next. He placed himself carefully, the night before he died, at the stern of the boat, so it would be easier to throw him off. Now they were three. Jack, Angus and Diana, lying in the bottom of the boat, drifting, 'thinking about water in all sorts of ways'. A stream. A hose spraying water around thoughtlessly. A simple glassful.

Diana sickened, but she could still talk about horses and tennis and how much she liked them, and that Jack and Angus should visit her in England when they were rescued. There was a rain shower and fresh water, and then, three days later, a German ship. Diana said it didn't matter that it was German, as long as it was a ship. They were taken aboard *Rakhotis* and treated well, but Diana's throat was too swollen and she couldn't swallow. For five days the men were kept in a cabin, and Diana stayed in the captain's quarters, fed by injections. The first night, MacDonald wet the bed, and for a year his bladder, strained by disuse, could not hold water for more than an hour. But the inflammation of Diana's throat persisted, and the ship's doctor decided to operate. Her hair had been washed and set, that lovely hair that got her the nickname Blondie, and she was thin but in good spirits. By seven o'clock that evening, she was dead. 'The doctor spoke,' writes MacDonald, 'and said in broken English that the operation was a success, but the girl's heart was not strong enough to stand the anaesthetic. I couldn't speak, and turned away broken-hearted.' The men went back to their bunks, these strong men who kept a boat afloat for 37 days with hardly any navigational equipment and watched their friends die: they cried in their bunks like babies, all night, for the loss of that young bride who was actually a widow, who had not only ministered to 51 people in a boat of death but steered its tiller, bailed its water, kept it going. She was buried at sea. It sounds like kindness to me: the enemy crew, lined up in uniform on deck, showing the greatest respect to an enemy girl, covering her coffin with a Union flag. They cried. Everyone had liked Diana. 'It was a gallant end,' wrote MacDonald, 'to a brave and noble girl.'

The end? Of course not. Even if your ship has just been torpedoed, you have to return home by sea, no matter how terrifying. The *Rakhotis* was shelled by an English ship on New Year's Day, and MacDonald was set to sea again in an open boat. Edmead was in another and reached Spain. MacDonald ended up on a U-boat, where the young captain took pity on his bladder – movement was restricted, as well as noise, on submarines, where either can betray you to listening enemy ships – and let him pee into bottles. On 4 January 1943, the U-boat reached St. Nazaire, and MacDonald went into Milag Nord as a prisoner until the end of the war. Then he went back to sea.

Such men as MacDonald and his American counterparts did their service, then were treated shoddily by peace. American merchant mariners weren't given veterans' status until 1988, although at least 5000 of them had died supplying and fuelling the war effort. Now, they are at least entitled to use veterans' hospitals and be buried in a national cemetery, although not to financial compensation for their service. Britons who sailed the Arctic convoys, in weather so cold that tears would freeze, were finally awarded medals in 2013.

The merchant seaman Frank Laskier had his leg blown off by a German torpedo. He did not swallow his anger but spat it out in his radio broadcasts and books, in which he addressed the enemy who had taken his leg and who had destroyed the passenger ship *Laconia* and 2000 of its passengers, so that he found drifting in the Atlantic one of *Laconia*'s open boats with 16 dead children in it. In one broadcast, Laskier addressed the captain of the *Von Scheer*, the German battleship that first torpedoed his ship then fired at the survivors in the water. 'You saw us, you watched our ship sink. And you machine-gunned us. But you didn't do the job properly. Because out of that ship's company ten men are alive, and those ten men know what you did. Three of us were wounded. Seven of us were not. Those seven are back at sea.'

Ashore

11. DISEMBARK

It's raining. Warm rain. Water on deck, oily and shiny. Flat grey sea. My mood is low and not shifted by running. I must be in pre-departure mourning. We are in the Malacca Straits now, which Chief Engineer Derek calls the M4 of shipping. I call them my final stretch, to be reluctantly travelled. The straits are 500 miles long, join the Indian and Pacific Oceans, and are surrounded by places of spice and treasure. They are also a captain's nightmare, because they are busy and narrow and overcrowded. They are less crowded than before, because there are fewer pirates now. This used to be the shipping channel most feared by seafarers, with reason. The pirates here were robbers rather than hijackers, but still brutal and often lethal. In the nineteenth century they drowned the young son of a captain while he watched, then cut off the captain's fingers joint by joint. In the twentieth century there were murders and beheadings. In the same way that Somali pirates have division of labour, the Indonesians were the foot soldiers – they are the poorest in the region – and

Malaysians and Chinese the managers. It is a terrible task to police these areas, with their thousands of islands, inlets and rivers, and thousands of coastal supporters and suppliers of piracy. Once I met a merchant seaman who had been on a ship here when a small boat approached. 'They said, "Fish? You want fish?"' No, thank you, said the crew, then the men showed their guns. They took everything they could then turned to leave. 'Then they signalled by light and all the palm trees lit up with signals back. All along the shore.' From 2004 the littoral governments of the straits – Malaysia, Singapore, Indonesia, Thailand – began mounting serious piracy patrols, using air, sea and intelligence. Attacks dropped from 75 in 2000 to 10 in 2005. By 2006, the Joint War Committee of Lloyd's had removed the Malacca Straits from its Hull, War, Strikes, Terrorism and Related Perils Listed Areas. Pirate experts desperate to solve the Somalia situation look at the Malacca Straits for answers, but there is no like to compare with like. There is nowhere as disintegrated as Somalia, spitting out its youngsters to the sea. Anyway, here in the straits there have been reports of attacks again, and a shift in pirate behaviour. Less robbery, more kidnapping and ransom along the Somali model. The latest judgement of war risks by Lloyd's finds some of Sumatra to be dangerous, but 'only the north eastern coast between 5° 40' N and 0° 48' N, excluding transit'.

This is the first time I've been allowed on deck for days. Further north in the Lakshadweep Sea the weather had been too bad for excursions. Beaufort wind scale 7, sea-state 6–7, sea description 'rough/very rough'. The captain sent me a message through the internal email: 'Flippers are out – Glenn'. *Kendal*'s stabilizing fins had emerged from the hull like wings, to make the ride smoother. But they were soon withdrawn, because they use too much fuel. Anyway, the ship never rolled or pitched much. We had it better than the small tanker that Julius watched from the bridge as it was tossed all ways and water covered the deck with each wave. 'Poor guys,' he said. 'They must be so seasick they're not even driving the ship.' *Kendal* was smoother, but my stomach was tuned to the waves still, and rolled enough for the captain to give me the medical definition for seasickness. 'It's when you ask for death.' At meal times seasickness was a welcome change of topic. By now most conversations were echoes. Now people competed with tales of hundred-foot waves and pitching through sea spray for weeks. The captain once saw seas so high that he thought he saw moonlight shining through a break in the clouds, but it was the crest of a wave.

Marius has done midwinter passages through the Pacific. He says that, given a choice between Pacific winter weather and pirates, he would choose pirates. Of course they joke. You must make a joke of everything at sea, wrote Richard Henry Dana in *Two Years Before the Mast*. 'If you were to fall from aloft and be caught in the belly of a sail, and thus saved from instant death, it would not do to look at all disturbed or to make a serious matter of it.' Behind the crosstalk and swaggering is a serious point. When crews are so small, there is rarely anyone to spare to stand in for someone crippled by nausea. A ship's cook once told me that in rough seas he was so sick he had one foot in the grave and one hanging on. He kept cooking.

By now the weather has subsided enough for me to go out. The captain accompanies me, in hard hat and jeans. He worries that he could lose his passenger and says, 'You are only as good as your last mistake.' We set off to the fo'c'sle, starboard route. The captain peers down the passageway. 'Sometimes you can see her flex. It's quite alarming to see.' On the fo'c'sle, which I have only just learned to pronounce to his satisfaction (long o like folk not short like fork), he introduces me to local clouds. Nimbus are different here. They are flatter-shaped than back home. He knows his clouds and enjoys them. 'We had to do meteorology as part of our training. I can plan when I'm going to hit fog from the temperature. I bet none of these foreign officers can.'

This is the first time in over a month that he has come on deck. I have questioned him often about his refusal to emerge. He says, 'But I go out on the bridge wings.' Or, 'The sea? It's cold and wet.' Sometimes he indulges me, following me out to the bridge wing to watch the water, just to watch. Then, he says, 'I love the sea and she loves me. We have this relationship. She's looked after me for 42 years.' It is a private relationship that is nobody's business.

He will retire soon after four decades, one rescue and no napkins, and I wonder how he will like it. He says that he can switch swiftly between his worlds, that sometimes he can be at home and someone will ask something straightforward about the ship and he'll have to think about it because he has his land head on. 'I definitely have two heads.' Once his land head won and he went ashore for six months. He had just married, his wife was pregnant and he wanted to be at home. That is the reason most men leave the sea: marriages stressed by so much absence last only with difficulty and need preservation. He got a job selling insurance and hated it. His charm meant he had no trouble getting the appointments but he couldn't get his head around selling an intangible thing like risk. All through those six months, he would drive to the coast to look out to the ocean. He watched the ships pass for comfort. Eventually, his doctor told him he needed to go back to sea.

There is time to go ashore in Port Klang, our port call in Malaysia. The captain could go too, but declines. He is too nervous about Singapore, which will be busy and dangerous because it always is. 'Maybe on the way back.' On the way back he will find another excuse. He went ashore recently at Laem Chabang and realized how much he used to enjoy it. Then he got back on board and forgot again. Port Klang is a small port attached to a small town with nothing to recommend it except its fish restaurants that sit on stilts over a lagoon, and its dentists. Both Dilbert and Archie need their teeth seeing to. Fleeting medical attention in port is normal for seafarers when there is none aboard beyond the second officer, who is responsible for first aid. The captain has done his share of assisting and ministering on his way up the ranks: the most memorable occasion involved a case of gonorrhoea and a pencil inserted into a penis. He has seen syphilis, non-specific urethritis, all sorts. HIV began to be a concern, so he talks to cadets when he can, rather laconically. 'If I were them, I'd give it a miss altogether.'

The ship's agent arrives at the gangway with diamond studs in his ears and flowers for me. It is a kind gesture but embarrassing: the crew on gangway watch find it hilarious. The agent offers to have me driven to Kuala Lumpur, an hour away. There is time. It would be no trouble. He proposes skyscrapers and shopping. But the thought of a city leaves me indifferent. I have only one day left on the ship and already I don't want to leave it. I go into Port Klang to change money and eat rice, but I hurry back. As we pass through the port gates I see the big blue ship in the docks and she looks like home. Briefly I think of changing my plans, of staying until Laem Chabang, and then coming all the way back too. Briefly my plans may be changed for me. All that zooming through pirate waters has left us with too much time, and now too little. The pointless port changes have also affected things: we arrived here at 14:00 to pick up the pilot as expected, and for no good reason he didn't turn up for hours. The captain tells me we may not stop in Singapore after all. The cargo can wait until the ship is on its way back, and I'll have to disembark into a launch boat as we steam past instead. But I have often watched the pilot boats zooming up to the ship like Starfighters approaching a Death Star. I have seen pilots climb up the rope ladders, up several sheer storeys of freeboard, and I know they sometimes get smashed against the side or miss their footing. To the captain, I translate all this anxiety as, 'But I'll have a laptop.' He actually says, 'Pish!' They do it all the time. There's nothing to it.

The drama lasts an hour or two and then the schedule changes again. Singapore it is.

At their narrowest point, the Malacca Straits are 1.7 miles wide. This is the oil highway from the Gulf to the East, and each year 60,000 ships must pass through that 1.7-mile chokepoint. The wheelhouse radars show a mass of dots, and each one is a ship. Alarms are already going off in the wheelhouse because the system overloads if there are more than 200 ships in a two-mile radius. There are more people than usual on the bridge, an air of concentration, and no time for tea or SkyFlakes. The captain is on the bridge constantly during these days, partly because Vinton has had the boxes stacked too high outside his cabin and blocked his ability to check from his day room for fools and delinquents driving other ships. But really he is pushed up the stairs by stress. Singapore always puts his stomach in knots. He exudes anxiety and I don't dare distract him with questions. Another reason for caution: we are near the spot where *Kendal* ran aground under the control of a previous captain who decided that going at 21 knots in the Malacca Straits was a good idea. It was as good an idea as driving at 100 miles an hour around a bowling green in a truck. Derek was on board at the time. He was in his engine room when it happened and remembers no thud or grinding, just a sudden removal of movement. Even so, he knew what that meant, but won't say what word came out of his mouth first. The damage cost millions and *Kendal* was in dry dock for months for repairs. The captain responsible was investigated and sacked, possibly because the bridge's black box – the Vessel Data Recorder – mysteriously didn't save its data as it was meant to. He is still skippering ships, for Germans. The captain's views on this are unprintable. His beautiful ship, crippled.

We wait for a gap in the sea traffic to allow us to cross into port. It is the captain's responsibility to decide when to cross. Overseers working for Singapore's Vessel Traffic Information Service office will tell him what is coming, but not when to go. He says aloud but to himself, 'If only we could get to those barges, we'll be all right.' He gets to the barges and we are all right and we safely berth again, as *Kendal* does dozens of times a month with no drama. We have sailed through an ocean infested by pirates; we have avoided ships, wooden boats, families of fishermen, fast ferries and reefs. We have transported what needs to be transported, travelled 9288 nautical miles through the wildest place on the planet, and done it safely and efficiently. All that is rewarded by a man coming to check our immigration status and another one selling SIM cards. I find the SIM card man in the mess room displaying his wares in a briefcase, and nearly buy one before I remember that his prices will be inflated for seafarers. More visitors begin to arrive up the gangway, the usual stream of port busybodies, and really by now I should have gone down it, but I dawdle. I don't want to leave the bridge and its windows, the boxes, the quiet nights at sea, the depth beneath. I don't want what Singapore has to offer: shops filled with choice and stuff, everything that we have been removed from on *Kendal*, while carrying it.

I find ways to put off departure. I show the crew a Malaysian ten-ringgit note that I got in Port Klang, because it has a picture of a container ship on it. Isn't it pleasing to see your work recognized on a banknote? They say, 'So what? We're only here for the money.' Vinton has found me a blue Maersk boiler suit and asks if I want work boots too. He has piles of boots that are of no use. Not even the Filipinos are size 6 but the office sent dozens of them. He doesn't know why.

Marius asks me, 'Will I be in your book?'

Maybe.

He thinks. 'Is it revenge for beating you at backgammon?'

*

Pinky is also paying off, along with her peppers, as are a handful of other crew. They may meet again, they may not. Friendship, say seafarers, ends at the gangway. Francis is staying, so I give him my Botlek-bought coffee-maker and packets of Rotterdam coffee. I leave a box of sea-themed books in the captain's cabin to be shipped back and for him to read, if he can be persuaded to read a book 'about facts'. Then down to the gangway, to sign out, to leave the sea. The cadets are leaning on the rail. There is no shore leave for them in this port, no need for parental advice from the captain. The Scottish lad, stuck with boring boxes for at least another two months, watches me go down the gangway, one hand for me, one for the ship. 'Take me with you?'

I asked the captain once whether *Kendal* was a happy ship. He said, 'Well, no-one's happy to be here.' Then he checked himself. I am a positive person, he says. Sunny by nature. But the last years have brought such dramatic changes, such cuts and slashes, such a diminishment, that he can't help the gloom. He knows he is training his replacements and recognizes that that is the way of things in a globalized world. 'I just wish they would be honest about it.' He wishes that he would be sent officers who knew their knots and how to use a sextant, whose levels of English, maritime or otherwise, were safer. They don't have to be British or American, they just have to be good. In 2012, the Philippines was almost blacklisted by the European Union for its poor quality of maritime training.

At a nautical seminar in Liverpool I met cadets back from sea phases who sounded shocked. Their sea phases had been served on ships where they didn't share a language with the crew. They had served under captains who had Soviet views on knowledge being power, and kept hold of theirs ferociously. The ship owners admitted that some cadets did their three years and never went back to sea. They talked constantly, as people talk in conferences and committee rooms, of the shortage of skilled sea people, of the worry of it. A parliamentary committee, in a report on the state of British shipping, wondered what would happen if Britain needed merchant ships to go to war again, as it did for the Falklands. It's all very well having foreign seafarers, they wrote, but what if they refuse to work for British military aims? During the Gulf War Japanese seafarers refused to crew supply ships. American politicians sometimes get excited about the same thing. But a truer measure of the value of the maritime industry is the fact that the Safe Port Act, an important maritime security bill, was only passed in 2006 when a provision about internet gambling was tacked onto it.

What would keep those two cadets at sea? An industry that learns to stop calling its most valuable assets a 'human element' and calls them humans instead. International conventions that can actually be enforced, and flag states that can be compelled into good behaviour. Oversight, governance, fair play. All the things expected on land that can dissolve 12 miles out, in open seas.

Disembarked, I wander around Singapore dispirited. It is half docks, this port city, but the dock area is high security and closely guarded. Singapore's port authority is always expecting terrorist attacks from Indonesia's Muslim terrorists, and even official visitors have to sign a non-disclosure agreement to visit. The cranes, though, are tall enough to tower over the highway and I look at them with wistful affection. I imagine them loading and unloading *Kendal*, swarming over her as she sits passively at the dock, having things done to her. The empty boxes will be exchanged for filled ones, sinking her further in the water with paint and Valium and chemicals and airbags. Thousands of moves, boxes taken and boxes put back, and at the end of it *Kendal* will look exactly the same.

Then, Julius and Marius will head for the fo'c'sle to haul in the ropes, the rat-guards too. They will switch on the machinery that hauls up the anchor chain, which will return to its casing reluctantly, spitting rust and dust, requiring all humans nearby to wear safety goggles but not face masks, adding to their respiratory infections and already damaged hearing. My cabin will have been cleaned by Francis and be empty, probably, and my note removed from the bridge. No more obligations on watch keepers to record dolphin sightings, no need for Pinky's portly replacement to learn that there are humans who don't eat meat, voluntarily. The pilot will signal verbally for departure, the captain will echo him, the engine room will spark to work, the wheel will turn. *Kendal* will set off with six thousand boxes, back to business.

During her return trip the captain emails. He wants to know whether my transition to land has gone well, whether he has safely delivered his supernumerary along with the cargo. Of course he didn't go ashore in Laem Chabang, not even with Derek's best efforts of persuasion. He has decided to read one of the sea books, and it has inspired indignation. He once gave me a few pages of his autobiography, full of the colour of his first three decades at sea, full of exotic ports, friendly maidens, unfriendly stevedores and reliable sextants. He concludes the autobiography by writing to an imaginary cadet, wondering if he will have as good an experience as he did. He thinks so, because:

> he will be in awe at the sight of his first vessel, looming so much larger before him than it was for me.
> He, a deck cadet, will be mesmerized by the technology on the bridge, more reminiscent of a jet aircraft cockpit.
> He, an engineer cadet, will be shocked at the jaw-dropping huge main engine, probably larger than his house.
> He may find that every day could be an adventure.
> He may not have so much time in port, but he will see the world, and he will get past the dockside areas of my day.

He will face the same high seas as I, and may even feel the
romance of the oceans.
He will behold sea-borne wild life such as dolphins, whales,
and lost souls of the Albatross, all in their natural state.
He will meet peoples of so many different cultures and creeds,
to become truly international in outlook.
He will meet Captains who will have time for him, not like in
my day, as they rarely spoke to lowly cadets.

It is a lovely, compelling picture of a life at sea. Who wouldn't sign
up if it was like that? A job that is vital. A career that will never
disappear, for we will always need ships, as the captain's mother
said. He must be feeling differently when he writes his email.
Perhaps he has his other head on. 'You can see how we are really
thought of,' he writes. 'Riff-raff that no-one really cares about, no
matter the lip service paid to our safety and welfare by the likes of
owners, flag state, IMO.' I picture him in his F-deck office, pinioned
at his computer by paperwork, kept from the ship-handling and
navigation that he loves, his job now to cut costs and speed at all
costs, his industry transformed, his fury rising as he steams towards
retirement. 'We are mere chattels, a human resource, dispensable
non-entities. We are the front line troops who dance forward into
the breach at point blank range to whatever tune is played. Whinge
over. I am right though.'

Acknowledgements

First, my thanks to Captain Glenn and the officers and crew of *Maersk Kendal*, who were kind and impeccable hosts for more than 9000 nautical miles. Kate Sanderson, publicist for Maersk Line at the time, arranged my trip, and Claire Sneddon, Kate's successor, answered follow-up questions. Thank you. June Thomas, then my editor at *Slate*, published a four-part series from my trip on *Kendal*. From the shipping industry, I have had many helpers and advisors, principally Alastair Evitt, Grant Hunter, Clay Maitland, Janet Porter, Gavin van Marle, Captain Kuba Szymanski. Michelle Wiese Bockman, Bloomberg's highly capable shipping correspondent, has been remarkably and consistently generous with her knowledge. Online, Glen Ford and David Rider, of OCEANUS-Live and Neptune Maritime Security respectively, have been illuminating and expansive with their insights into piracy, security and shipping in general. Captain Quentin Oates of EU-NAVFOR arranged my trip on *Vasco da Gama*, and the men and women of the Marinha

- ACKNOWLEDGEMENTS

Portugesa were kind enough to tolerate both me and my odd dietary requirements. (Apologies to the flight crew of Bacardi that I never bought them the crate of beer they requested.) Father Colum Kelly has welcomed me several times to Immingham, and I thank him for introducing me to the fascinating world of a port that I would otherwise have driven past without a backward look. The Mission to Seafarers has provided knowledge and archives and also trustingly lent me books; the Seamen's Church Institute of New York generously sent me a copy of their official history. I am grateful to Neil Bell for showing me his wonderful film about MV *Iceberg*, *The Pirates of Somalia: The Untold Story*, which will be distributed as a feature film next year. He also provided still images. Carlos Mustienes carried out interviews with Nicolàs Achard and then did impeccable translations: gracias, Carlos, and thank you to Nicolàs and Martin Atkinson for agreeing to talk about an abidingly painful time. Thank you to the International Transport Workers' Federation staff, including Roy Paul, Tom Holmer, Sam Dawson and others, who have patiently put up with my questions and interview requests for the last few years. I spent a fascinating day with the tug company McAllister in New York City, which never made it into the book. But my thanks nonetheless to Buckley McAllister and his father Brian, as well as to the tug crew who took me out to see New York City from a new and beautiful angle, from its working waters. (Especially memorable: the tug engineer with a hinge tattooed in the crook of his elbow. Why? 'Well have you ever seen one? No? That's why.'). Apologies to anyone who has helped me and here gone unthanked: it is not deliberate but still delinquent on my part.

These have been a difficult few years, and this was a difficult book to write. Not because of the subject matter, but because the research and writing were being done while my stepfather was suffering with Alzheimer's, and while my family were seeing him through a rapid deterioration into violence, sectioning and then death. Consequently

I am deeply grateful to my wonderful agents Erin Malone and Cathryn Summerhayes of William Morris Endeavor Entertainment, who throughout the hard times have been supportive, patient and never not kind. My editors, Philip Gwyn Jones of Portobello Books and Riva Hocherman of Henry Holt, have endured delays and more delays with forbearance and compassion. Thank you. I thank all my friends who have had to share the load. A team of readers found errors and vastly improved the manuscript: Michelle Wiese Bockman, Simon Winchester, Robert Sam Anson, Glen Ford, Sheila Wainwright, Molly Mackey, Ruth Metzstein and Tom Ridgway. My family Sheila Wainwright, Simon George, Nicholas, Julie, James and Alice Wainwright, Allison Bramall and Patrice and Amelia Green: thank you. John Michael Wainwright, 1938–2011 and Emma Louise Page, 1970–2013: rest in peace.

Notes

All references to tons/tonnes reflect the original source data.

Epigraph

vii   Maurice Oliver, quoted in Tony Parker, *Lighthouse*, London: Eland, 2006, p.118

Introduction

2   *Decayed and bankrupt master butchers*   There were also sailors of the kind described in 1968 by anthropologist Jesse Lemisch: 'His bowed legs bracing before him as if the very Broadway beneath his feet might begin to pitch and roll. In his dress he is in the words of a superior "very nasty and negligent", his black stockings ragged, his long, baggy trousers tarred to make them waterproof. Bred in that "very shambles of language", the merchant-marine, he is foul-mouthed, his talk alien and suspect.' Lemisch quoted in David James Stewart, '"Rocks and storms I'll fear no more": Anglo-American maritime memorialization, 1700–1940', DPhil dissertation, Texas A&M University, May 2004. Decayed and bankrupt master butchers: Henry Mayhew, Letter III, *Morning Chronicle*, 26 October 1849.

3   *Trade carried by sea has grown fourfold*   International Maritime Organization, *International Shipping, Carrier of World Trade*, background paper, 2005.

- NOTES

- *360 commercial ports* American Association of Port Authorities, US Public Port Facts, http://www.aapa-ports.org
- *More than 100,000 ships* United Nations Conference on Trade and Development (UNCTAD), *Review of Maritime Transport 2011*, p.36.
- *746 million bananas* Maersk Line company facts and information, http://www.maerskline.com
4 *The UK shipped in half of its gas* Gas supplies, though, are changeable. In the last three months of 2012, LNG imports, mostly from Qatar, were only 18 per cent of all supplies, and Norwegian imports by pipeline had risen. Even so, the UK is widely expected to be mostly reliant on gas imports by 2016. UK Government Department of Energy and Climate Change, *December 2012 Energy Trends*, p.95.
- *Two-thirds of its oil* 'Paradox in US seaborne crude oil imports', *Lloyd's List Intelligence*, 16 August 2012.
- *38 million metric tons of crude oil* Michelle Wiese Bockman, 'Oil tanker surplus seen by Clarkson persisting for a third year', *Bloomberg Businessweek*, 30 January 2013.
- *Sea blindness* 'Ministers accused of "sea blindness" by Britain's most senior Royal Navy figure', Jasper Gerard, *Telegraph*, 12 June 2009.
5 *Dipped their jibs* Funeral of Sir Winston Churchill, BBC Archive, http://www.bbc.co.uk/archive/churchill/11026.shtml
6 *Denmark's largest company*   Martin Adeney, Maersk McKinney Møller obituary, *Guardian*, 22 April 2012. http://www.guardian.co.uk/world/2012/apr/22/maersk-mckinney-moller-obituary
- *He allowed his driver to carry his briefcase up* Robert Wright, 'Møller on course to step back from helm', *Financial Times*, 6 June 2008.
- *Order of the Elephant* Maersk Media Center, http://www.mmm.maersk.com/en/Practicalities/Media-Center
6 *Reuters*   AP Møller-Maersk A/S, Profile, http://www.reuters.com/finance/stocks/companyProfile?symbol=MAERSKa.CO
7 *Revenues in 2011 amounted to $60.2 billion* Maersk press release, 27 February 2012. Microsoft's 2011 revenues were $69.943 billion, http://www.microsoft.com/investor/reports/ar11/financial_highlights/index.html
- *An ice-hockey arena* The expected 20-strong fleet will also be able to carry 3.64 billion iPads, enough for half the world's population; and one ship's worth of containers, stacked end to end vertically, would break through the

earth's stratosphere. Allianz Global Corporate & Specialty, *Safety and Shipping 19122012*, p.48.

– *12,800 MP3 players* Some other items carried by SS *Santa* included 2000 martini glasses, 4000 pairs of women's knickers, 3000 poker tables and 19,500 pairs of men's and boys' socks. Tim Spanton and Charles Rae, 'One hull of a Christmas', *Sun*, 3 August 2007.

– *A better public image* 'The economic impact of the UK Maritime Services Sector', *Oxford Economics*, December 2012, p.23.

8 *Over the last decade, there were 63* International Chamber of Shipping, *Annual Review 2012*, p.17.

– *Nothing inherently wrong* Further, 'Pejorative terms such as "flags of convenience" have more to do with industrial relations issues of the 1980s than the situation which pertains to 2012', International Chamber of Shipping, op. cit., p.45.

– *Managed anarchy* 'Brassed off', *Economist*, 16 May 2002.

– *142,462 working seafarers* The Merchant Navy Welfare Board, *Almonising Working Group Report*, April 2005, II.

– *1268 ships* 'Comparison of US and foreign-flag operating costs', US Department of Transportation, Maritime Administration, September 2011, p.7.

– *British seafarers number around 24,000* There was a 10 per cent decrease in the number of UK seafarers between 2011 and 2012, due to a drop in ratings and uncertified officers. Eight per cent of officers are women. Seafarer Statistics 2012, Department for Transport, January 2013.

– *Fewer than 100 ocean-going US-flagged ships* According to the US Maritime Administration, there are 92 foreign-going US ships and 98 operating under the Jones Act. Properly called the Merchant Marine Act of 1920, but named for Senator Wesley Jones, the Jones Act's main aim was to protect US shipping and ensure that the United States had enough US-flagged ships to call on in an emergency. To protect US interests, it bans foreign-flagged ships from carrying freight between US ports. It is not popular and is expensive. A 1999 study by the US International Trade Commission found that ending it would save more than $1.3 billion a year. But there are nearly 40,000 ships with some American ownership, just not American flags. US Department of Transportation, Maritime Administration, US Water Transportation Statistical Snapshot, February 2011. $1.3 billion a year, *Bloomberg Businessweek*, editorial, 'How the Jones Act blocks natural disaster relief', 1 January 2013.

- NOTES

- *US fleet has declined by 82 per cent since 1951* 'Comparison of US and foreign-flag operating costs', US Department of Transportation, Maritime Administration, September 2011, p.26.
9 *A legal order for the seas and oceans* United Nations Convention on the Law of the Sea (UNCLOS), Preamble, p.25.
10 *Consensual but rough* Baroness Jane Campbell has called for an inquiry into Akhona's death on the grounds that *Safmarine Kariba* was a UK-flagged ship. As she said in the House of Lords in 2011, 'For women, living and working on board ship requires great dedication, tolerance and self-belief. Often they will be the only female on board, with a group of men used to a male only environment. At sea it is impossible to walk away, to change one's surroundings, or one's ship-mates.' Julian Bray, 'Safmarine death probe call', *Tradewinds*, sourced January 2013 from http://safewaters.wordpress.com/2011/03/07/maritime-safmarine-death-probe-call/
- *An internal inquiry by Safmarine also concluded suicide* Adam Corbett, 'Latest probe casts doubt over death', *Tradewinds*, 7 July 2011.
11 *What happens at sea, stays at sea* Mzilikazi wa Afrika, 'SA teen's horror on the high seas', *Sunday Times*, 18 July 2010.
- *Internet access at sea* The research was done by questionnaire; 1533 questionnaires were returned. Thirty-nine per cent of respondents were from the Philippines, 32 per cent were Chinese, 15 per cent were Indian, 12 per cent were UK nationals and 3 per cent were of other nationality. N. Ellis, H. Sampson, I. Acejo, L. Tang, N. Turgo and Z. Zhao, *Accommodation on Contemporary Cargo Ships*, Lloyd's Register Educational Trust Research Unit/Seafarers' International Research Centre (SIRC), Cardiff University, December 2012, p.3.
- *Astonishing abuses* 'Out of Sight, Out of Mind: Seafarers, Fishers, and Human Rights', International Transport Workers' Federation, June 2006, p.5.
- *The £20 million they recovered in 2010* Personal communication with ITF.
12 *Lincoln of the Sea* Furuseth, when threatened with jail, also said, in a thick Norwegian accent, 'I put my inyunction in my pocket and to go yail.' Leah Robinson Rousmaniere, *Anchored within the Vail: A Pictorial History of the Seamen's Church Institute*, The Seamen's Church Institute of New York and New Jersey, 1995, p.27.
- *Better in UK prisons* Erol Kahveci, 'Port-based welfare for seafarers', Seafarers' International Research Centre, Cardiff University, p.51.
- *544 seafarers are being held hostage* – ICC International Maritime Bureau,

'Piracy and armed robbery against ships, report for the period 1 January–30 June 2010', p.20.

– *1500 journalists* Cesar Illiano and Terry Wade, 'Chilean miners rescued after 69 days underground', *Reuters*, 13 October 2010.

Chapter 1: Embarkation

17 *Being in a ship is being in a jail* Johnson, wrote James Boswell, was trying to get his servant Francis Barber, who had gone to sea, back to shore. Barber's master 'kindly interested himself in procuring his release from a state of life of which Johnson always expressed the utmost abhorrence'. He said, 'No man will be a sailor who has contrivance enough to get himself into a jail; for being in a ship is being in a jail, with the chance of being drowned.' And at another time, 'A man in a jail has more room, better food, and commonly better company.' Life of Johnson, 1759, Project Gutenberg, http://www.gutenberg.org/files/1564/1564-h/1564-h.htm

18 *Scottish filleters* The fish is caught, frozen, unfrozen for filleting, then refrozen for the return journey. 'The joke that "a fish travels more dead than alive"', said an official from the Scottish Fishermen's Federation, 'has become a reality.' Mike Merritt and Rob Edwards, 'The madness of filleting Scottish fish in China', *Sunday Herald*, 23 August 2009.

21 *Three young men were found in the sea* Rupert Saunders, Jason Downer and James Meaby were all experienced sailors. They were wearing lifejackets when they were found. James Meaby was 40 miles from the others, and probably survived for up to a dozen hours in the water. Nothing was ever found of *Ouzo*. 'Report on the investigation of the loss of the sailing yacht *Ouzo* and her three crew, South of the Isle of Wight, during the night of 20/21 August 2006', Accident Investigation Branch, Report No 7/2007, April 2007.

22 *A quarter of a million of them are at sea* The International Labour Organization puts the global total of seafarers at 1.2 million. The Commission on Filipinos Overseas calculates that there are 369,104 'seabased workers'. Stock Estimate of Filipinos Overseas, December 2011.

24 *40,000 seafarers a year* – 'Review of Maritime Transport 2011', UNCTAD, p.159.

– *£4.3 billion in remittances* 'President Aquino conducts historic trilateral meeting with EU leaders at ASEM9', Department of Foreign Affairs press release, 6 November 2012.

- NOTES

24 *Minimum seafarer wage* International Chamber of Shipping, op. cit., p.30.
– *SS Warrior* Marc Levinson, *The Box: How the Shipping Container Made the World Smaller and the World Economy Bigger*, Princeton: Princeton University Press, 2006, p.33.

Chapter 2: Aboard

35 *A mess of coal-dust* Joseph Conrad, *The Mirror of the Sea*, London: Folio Society, 2005, p.64.
36 *Laid some blame on the ferry watch officer's photochromic lenses* Marine Accident Investigation Board, 'Report on the investigation into the loss of the sailing yacht Ouzo and her three crew south of the Isle of Wight during the night of 20/21 August 2006', p.22.
37 *With a more or less serene brow* Conrad, op. cit., p.30.
41 *18 million containers* Confusion reigns about how many containers exist, as different bodies use different calculations. There are various figures and estimates for how many containers exist or are moving around the planet. UNCTAD calculates that as of January 2011, the global number of TEUs travelling worldwide was 29 million. The United Nations Office on Drugs and Crime (UNODC), meanwhile, uses a figure provided by the Bureau International des Containers (BIC), which estimates 2025 million actual containers (as not every container is a TEU). As for container movements, UNODC uses the figure of 500 million, an up-to-date figure based on a calculation made by the World Customs Organization. On the online search engine Yahoo, the most popular answer to the question 'how many containers are there?' is 'a lot'. Personal correspondence with UNODC; UNCTAD, op. cit., p.39.
– *Keith Tantlinger* 'In 1958, the *New York Times* described the new technology this way: "A trailer is loaded, for example, in Springfield, Mo. It travels by road to New York or San Francisco, sealed, virtually damage-proof and theft-proof. By ship it goes to France or to Japan, eliminating warehousing, stacking and sorting. Each ship takes on her cargo with a few hundred lifts, compared to 5,000 individual lifts by the old method."' Margalit Fox, 'Keith Tantlinger, builder of cargo container, dies at 92', *New York Times*, 6 September 2011.
– *Dockers came twenty-ninth* Levinson, op. cit., p.26.
42 *A can of beer* The nature of shipping means that prices can fluctuate wildly. 'Economies of scale made steel', *Economist*, 12 November 2011.

43   *Between 2 and 10 per cent* The United Nations Office on Drugs and Crime uses the lower figure. 'Executive director lauds container control programme in tackling the smuggling of drugs and cultural artefacts', UNODC press release, 11 May 2011.

–   *17 million containers a year* The US Army Corps of Engineers calculated an inbound total of 17,083,057 TEUs in 2011. Nearly 12 million more foreign-going TEUs left US ports. US Army Corps of Engineers, Waterborne Commerce Statistics Center, http://www.ndc.iwr.usace.army.mil/wcsc/by_ porttons11.html. The Government Accountability Office, however, calculates that 'about 10.7 million' ocean-borne containers arrived in US ports in 2011. Stephen L. Caldwell, Director of Homeland Security and Justice, United States Government Accountability Office, Testimony before the Subcommittee on Maritime Security, Committee on Homeland Security, House of Representatives, 7 February 2012.

44   *More than the GDP of 150 countries* Hugh Griffiths and Michael Jenks, 'Maritime transport and destabilizing commodity flows', Stockholm International Peace Research Institute Policy Paper 32, January 2012, p.1.

–   *Some had paid £30,000* The women working in the brothels were citizens of China, Korea, Thailand, Vietnam, Malaysia, Singapore, Hong Kong, Japan, Taiwan and Laos. A 21-month investigation discovered that the criminals 'attempted to avoid law enforcement scrutiny by using code words when talking on the phone. They referred to the women as ethnic foods, makes of cars or as ships.' United States Attorney's Office, Western District of Washington, press release, 23 February 2007.

–   *The international counter narcotics effort* United States Government Accountability Office, *Drug Control: Cooperation with Many Major Drug Transit Countries Has Improved, but Better Performance Reporting and Sustainability Plans are Needed*, July 2008, p.5.

–   *Six times more likely* Griffiths and Jenks, op. cit., p.23.

–   *Carried by boat and exploded in a port* Letter from Albert Einstein to F.D. Roosevelt, 2 August 1939, accessed February 2013 from the President Roosevelt Presidential Library and Museum, http://www.fdrlibrary.marist. edu/archives/pdfs/docsworldwar.pdf

45   *Hitting the US economy with every available means* Toby Harnden, 'US casts doubt on bin Laden's latest message', *Daily Telegraph*, 28 December 2001.

–   *Poor man's missiles* Stephen Cohen, 'Boom Boxes: Containers and terrorism', in *Protecting the Nation's Seaports*, edited by Jon D. Haveman and Howard J. Shatz. San Francisco: Public Policy Institute of California, 2006, p.116.

- *Shipping uranium is legal* Howard Kurtz, 'ABC says it shipped uranium as safety test', *Boston Globe*, 12 September 2003.

- *Pyongyang Death Jam* *Lloyd's List*, 11 February 2011.

46 *Belfast, overland* 'Pyongyang death jam', *Lloyd's List*, 11 February 2011.

- *You can't swing a dead cat* Quoted in Michael Richardson, 'A Time Bomb for Global Trade: Maritime-related terrorism in an age of weapons of mass destruction', Institute of South East Asian Studies, 25 February 2004, p.10.

- *They had done nothing wrong* Griffiths and Jenks, op. cit., p.8.

- *A layered security strategy* Caldwell, op. cit.

47 *Non-intrusive inspection equipment* 'Supply Chain Security', General Accounting Office, January 2008, p.2.

- *Qasim, a port in Pakistan* Caldwell, op. cit., p.16.

48 *One Hong Kong terminal* Caldwell, op. cit., p.16.

- *Sniffer bees* In fact, research into honeybees (*Apis melifera*) has shown that their odour detection is as good as that of dogs. 'It is quite remarkable', writes Ivan Hoo, chief executive officer of Inscentinel, 'to know that our single automatic training unit can produce 500 trained sniffer bees in just five hours; training a single sniffer dog takes up to six months.' The bees would be inserted in special 'bee-holders', trained to detect explosives, then used in a handheld detector. The company is still looking for funding. Ivan Hoo, 'Using sniffer bees for bulk screening of cargo', *Port Technology International*, May 2012, pp.146–147.

- *Could cost world trade €17 billion* 'Secure Trade and 100% Scanning of Containers', European Commission Staff Working Paper, February 2010, p.5.

- *2014, and counting* Caldwell, op. cit., p.2.

49 *Those stokers are at it again* Theodora Fitzgibbon's book compiles examples of nautical cookery that include hamburgers, invented, she claims, by Jewish emigrants travelling on ships. 'Jewish emigrants were able to bring large quantities of their own kosher dried beef with them which they scraped off, or chopped finely and made into little cakes, sometimes with chopped onion or even soaked bread to make it go further. When they settled in the United States they continued to make Hamburg steaks as the patties were then called, and as the popularity of these meat cakes spread, they became

known as "hamburgers".' *A Taste of the Sea in Food and Pictures*, Vancouver: David & Charles, 1977, p.13.

— *A third sort of persons* John Flavel, *Navigation Spiritualized. Or, a new compass for Seamen Consisting of 32 points Of pleasant observations, Profitable applications And Serious reflections, All concluded with so many Spiritual Poems*, Newburyport: Edmund M. Blunt, 1770, accessed February 2013 via openlibrary.org, http://archive.org/stream/navigationspirit00flav#page/n5/mode/2up, p.34.

50 *The time it takes to say eight words* Personal interview with Father Colum Kelly, Immingham Seafarers' Centre, and Marine Accident Investigation Bureau, 'Report on the investigation of work undertaken in a dangerous enclosed/confined space and the consequent attempted rescue on board ERRV *Viking Islay* resulting in the loss of three lives at the Amethyst gas field, 25 miles off the East Yorkshire coast, UK', 23 September 2007.

51 *Two miles away... straight down* Richard Woodman, *The Real Cruel Sea: The Merchant Navy in the Battle of the Atlantic, 1939–1943*, London: John Murray, 2004, p.562.

Chapter 3: Harbour

54 *The flies were murderous* Frank Laskier, *Log Book*, London: George Allen & Unwin, 1942, pp.32–33.

55 *A sex-starved sailor* Dunton's technique of offering printed advice in the *Athenian Gazette* was later copied by Daniel Defoe, who set up the *Review* in 1704 and employed himself as its 'agony uncle'. Lucy Mangan, 'A brief history of agony aunts', *Guardian*, 13 November 2009.

57 *Rather a heavy sea on, sir, and a headwind* Dickens unsurprisingly suffered great nausea. 'I lay there, all the day long, quite coolly and contentedly; with no sense of weariness, with no desire to get up, or get better, or take the air.' The nausea overtook him so comprehensively that 'if Neptune himself had walked in, with a toasted shark on his trident, I should have looked upon the event as one of the very commonest everyday occurrences.' Charles Dickens, *On Travel*, edited by Pete Orford, London: Hesperus Press, 2009, pp.18–19.

59 *Simon, ship's cat on HMS Amethyst* Simon's initial career wasn't promising. His siblings were taken on ships as rat-catchers, but his black colour made him unlucky to sailors, so he was stuck scrounging in the docks for two years. But he charmed Captain Griffiths of HMS *Amethyst*, and once on board always accompanied the captain on his evening patrols through the ship. When the

ship was attacked on the Yangtze River, 25 crew members were killed and Simon was hit by shrapnel. He slowly recovered, and gained his rank of Able Seamen Simon for killing a huge rat, named Mao Tse-Tung by the crew. Val Lewis, *Ships' Cats in War and Peace*, Shepperton: Nauticalia, 2001, pp.21–39.

– *Chief Petty Officer (K9C), Dog* United States Coast Guard, Frequently Asked Questions, http://www.uscg.mil/history/faqs/Sinbad.asp

61 *More than half had been denied shore leave* 'Out of Sight, Out of Mind', International Transport Workers' Federation, p.33.

– *AMOSUP* Ibid.

– *Some sort of microcosm* Tony Lane, 'Study looks at mixed nationality crews', *The Sea*, March–April 2001, p.4.

– *Zero Recruitment in Europe* 'Piracy as a business', *Lloyd's List*, 1 December 2009.

62 *Falsifying papers* Select Committee on Transport, Eighth Report, July 2006, p.68.

63 *Sixty per cent of shipping accidents are due to human error* The International Union of Maritime Insurance (IUMI) reported that in the 15-year period up to 2008, 60 per cent of accidents involving the serious or total loss of vessels over 500 gross tonnes were due to human error. That works out at two serious incidents a day. Maritime and Coastguard Agency, *The Human Element: a guide to human behaviour in the shipping industry*, April 2010, p.v.

– *Exxon Valdez* Maritime and Coastguard Agency, op. cit., p.47.

– *I shot the cook* Seamen's Church Institute of New York, *The Lookout*, vol. 33, no. 5, May 1942.

67 *SL-7 ships* – Levinson, op. cit., pp.229–230.

69 *Scatter the painted ashes* Burial at sea is permitted in the United States under the Ocean Dumping Act. According to the US Environmental Protection Agency's frequently asked questions on ocean burials, the requirements for whole-body burials are 'all plastic and fabric materials be removed from the casket before burial at sea. EPA recommends that a minimum of six 3-inch holes be drilled into the casket to facilitate rapid flooding and venting of air. To further aid in rapid sinking, EPA recommends that additional weight be added to the casket based upon a four to one ratio of the body weight. For example, a whole body that weighs 150 pounds would need an additional 600 pounds to offset the buoyancy of both the body and the casket. Finally, the casket should be wrapped with stainless steel chain along both axes. EPA

does not recommend the use of shipping straps due to the rapid deterioration of such materials in the marine environment.'

– *West Point sewage treatment plant* Curtis Ebbesmeyer and Eric Scigliano, *Flotsametrics and the Floating World: How One Man's Obsession with Runaway Sneakers and Rubber Ducks Revolutionized Ocean Science*, New York: Harper Collins, 2009, pp.183–185.

70 *Secret weapon of the Filipinos* Gunnar Lamvik, 'The Filipino Seafarer: A Life between Sacrifice and Shopping', Doctoral thesis submitted to Norwegian University of Science and Technology, 2002.

Chapter 4: Open Sea

73 *Two thousand seafarers die at sea* All death rates for seafarers, given the complicated, disparate nature of the industry, are estimates. ITF uses the 2000 figure. The IMO puts the annual fatality rate at 1000 a year, of which 100 were 'lives lost in the fishing sector, 400 in domestic operations, and around 500 in other categories, including international shipping'. However, maritime safety expert Detlef Nielsen, in an investigation into how casualty statistics are gathered, concluded that there was severe under-reporting, by up to nine times. IMO, 'Lives lost at sea halved and piracy eradicated should be targets, says Sekimizu', press release, 8 January 2013. Detlef Nielsen, 'Safety and working conditions in international merchant shipping', PowerPoint presentation, http://www.cepal.org/usi/perfil/iame_papers/proceedings/nielsen.ppt

– *The following year it was four times worse* Maritime and Coastguard Agency, op. cit., p.v

– *More than two ships are lost a week* 106 vessels were recorded as losses in the 12 months up to 25 November 2012, or nine per month on average. Busy shipping lanes around South China, Indochina, Indonesia and the Philippines contributed twice as many losses as any other region. Allianz Global Corporate & Specialty, *Safety and Shipping Review 2013*, p.3.

76 *Six thousand sheep were stranded at sea* RSPCA, 'Livestock deaths just the tip of the iceberg', media release, 21 December, 2009.

– *Loony lefties* While writing about the deaths of men and beasts, the author continued that animal rights activists 'live by the three B's: beans, brown rice, and bullshit'. *Meat Trade News Daily*, 20 December 2009.

79 *Shocked, trapped, he began to recite his prayers* Ahmad Harb interview, accessed

December 2012 via http://www.youtube.com/watch?v=cfZ7hm7amJo

81 *They had to cut it off him* Owen Milloy video, entitled 'Captain John Milloy: Rest in Peace Dad', accessed January 2013 via http://www.youtube.com/watch?v=yagysu7tmF4&noredirect=1

– *Falling into a lifeboat* Tom Kington, 'Costa Concordia captain claims he tripped and fell into a lifeboat', *Guardian*, 18 January 2012.

81 *If some people want to stay, they can stay* After the *Oceanos* sank it was discovered that it was the third ship owned by Epirotiki Lines to have sunk in three years. Avranas was found negligent by a Greek board of inquiry but never jailed, and later worked on a Greek ferry. *New York Times*, 'Headliners: Career overboard?', 11 August 1991.

82 *I'm not a rank, I'm a guitarist* Moss Hills, 'My story of the sinking', accessed February 2013 via http://www.oceanossinking.com/mystoryofthesinking.htm

83 *Ethiopian Airlines flight 409* BBC News, 'Ethiopian Airlines jet crashes into sea off Beirut', 25 January 2010.

84 *68 per cent of ships* UNCTAD, op. cit., p.xv.

85 *Flagging out an American ship can save millions* US Department of Transportation Maritime Administration, *Comparison of US and Foreign-Flag Operating Costs*, September 2011, pp.1, 6.

– *A genuine link* Article 94 of the Convention, on nationality of ships, requires that 'every State shall fix the conditions for the grant of its nationality to ships, for the registration of ships in its territory, and for the right to fly its flag. Ships have the nationality of the State whose flag they are entitled to fly. There must exist a genuine link between the State and the ship.'

– *Brings their profoundly impoverished country millions of dollars a year* The embassy of Liberia in London offers a figure of $18 million for the revenues provided by the Liberian International Ship and Corporate Register (LISCR) to the government of Liberia, but that dates from 2000. Cables captured by Wikileaks talk of gross revenues to LISCR in 2007 as $38 million, with the revenues then disbursed to the Liberian government of $13 million, or six per cent of the country's GDP. The latest figures on LISCR's website put the number of ships flying the Liberian flag at 3750. http://www.liscr.com, cable reference 09MONROVIA70 accessed via http://www.cablegatesearch.net/cable.php?id=09MONROVIA70, cable dated 21 January 2009.

– *Sovereign Ventures* In another cable captured by Wikileaks, a local maritime official describes Sovereign Ventures as 'pretty cunning', and mentions an all-expenses-paid trip to Singapore made by the transport minister of Tuvalu, a small Pacific island nation also approached by Sovereign Ventures. Sovereign Ventures has no obvious web presence, but the mailing addresses for both Kiribati and Tuvalu – in the same building on Anson Road in Singapore – are strangely similar. Cable 07SUVA169 accessed via http://www.cablegatesearch.net/cable.php?id=07SUVA169&q=cook-islands

86   *A pet dog trained to carry registry documents* Brad Berman's paper 'Does the UNCTAD Convention on the Registration of Ships need amending?' is available on the ITF website at http://www.itfglobal.org/seafarers/icons-site/images/120_BERMAN.pdf.

–   *Funding rebels in neighbouring Sierra Leone* According to an investigation by Global Witness, a group that investigates resource exploitation, after Charles Taylor came to power in Liberia in 1997, he launched a court action against IRI, the company that had run Liberia's shipping registry for 40 years. The new company, the Liberian International Ship and Corporate Register, was linked to Taylor's lawyers. When IRI then sued the government of Liberia for breach of contract, its lawyers claimed that Taylor was pocketing a third of the shipping revenues. Not only that: one container, which Taylor claimed contained presents for his wife, contained armaments, according to a witness present at its unloading. A UN expert panel on Sierra Leone condemned the Taylor government for 'the improper use of its maritime registry'. When I searched the website of LISCR for 'Charles Taylor', I found no results. Global Witness/ITF, *Taylor-made: The pivotal role of Liberia's forests and flag of convenience in regional conflict*, September 2001.

–   *Cat's cradles* 'Brassed Off: How the war on terrorism could change the shape of shipping', *The Economist*, 16 May 2002.

87   *Russian doll of ownership* Cour d'Appel de Paris, pôle 4 chambre 11E, n° RG 08/02278, arrêt rendu le 30 mars 2010.

–   *The shrug in Savarese's voice* Tom Mangold, *From Our Own Correspondent*, http://news.bbc.co.uk/hi/english/static/audio_video/programmes/correspondent/transcripts/883110.txt

–   *Anonymity of ownership* 'Ownership and Control of Ships', Organisation for Economic Co-operation and Development (OECD), Directorate for Science, Technology and Industry, March 2003, Appendix B, p.23.

88   *A cloaking device* The OECD report is reproduced in a report of the Secretary-

General, Oceans and the Law of the Sea, Consultative Group on Flag State Implementation, 5 March 2004.

– *€1500 for moral damage* Cour d'Appel de Paris, op. cit., p.173 (Lambion), p.461 (Courmier).

– *Lloyd's Register* Terry Macalister, 'Lloyd's Register and the art of staying afloat in troubled waters', *Guardian*, 5 June 2012.

89 *Only 58 per cent of ships lost at sea* Michael Richardson, 'Crimes Under Flags of Convenience', *Yale Global Online*, 19 May 2003, http://yaleglobal.yale.edu/content/crimes-under-flags-convenience

– *The top four registries according to tonnage lost* Personal communication with ITF.

92 *Delinquent* 'Brassed off', *Economist*, 16 May 2002.

Chapter 5: Sea and Suez

95 *Three million ships or bits of ships* UNESCO, http://www.unesco.org/new/en/culture/themes/underwater-cultural-heritage/the-underwater-heritage/wrecks/

– *SS Storaa* R (oao Rosemary Fogg and Valerie Ledgard) v Secretary of State for Defence & John Short, Case No: CO/132/2005, High Court of Justice, London. Transcript accessed February 2013 via http://www.richardbuxton.co.uk/v3.0/node/196#_jmp0_

96 *Are we not human beings?* Tom Kington, 'Priest appeals for justice for African migrants "left to die" on boat', *Guardian*, 7 September 2011.

– *Human beings adrift at sea are not toxic cargo* Office of the High Commissioner for Human Rights, press release, 15 September 2006.

98 *11 grams of CO2 per ton per mile* Natural Resources Defense Council, 'Clean by Design: Transportation', http://www.nrdc.org/international/cleanbydesign/transportation.asp

– *A relatively small contributor to atmospheric emissions* International Maritime Organization, *International Shipping Facts and Figures – Information Resources on Trade, Safety, Security, Environment*, March 2012.

– *Narcissus* 'She resembled an enormous and aquatic black beetle, surprised by the light, overwhelmed by the sunshine, trying to escape with ineffectual effort into the distant gloom of the land. She left a lingering smudge of smoke on the sky, and two vanishing trails of foam on the water. On the place where she had stopped a round black patch of soot remained, undulating on the swell – an unclean mark of the creature's rest.' Joseph Conrad, *Narcissus*, Chapter Two, Project Gutenberg e-book, accessed February 2012 via http:// www.gutenberg.org/files/17731/17731-h/17731-h.htm

99 *Emitting as much as 760 million cars* John Vidal, 'Health risks of shipping pollution have been "underestimated"', *Guardian*, 9 April 2009.

– *By 2008, there were more than 400* Robert D. Diaz and Rutger Rosenberg, 'Spreading Dead Zones and Consequences for Marine Ecosystems', *Science*, vol. 321, no. 5891, 15 August 2008, pp.926–929; 146 dead zones in 2003, United Nations Environment Programme, GEO Year Book, 2003.

– *The admonishing binders of eco rules* Even when seafarers report environmental crimes, they can be detained for months as material witnesses. Most cases in the United States involve a 'magic pipe', an illegal hose discharging oily water overboard in contravention of MARPOL laws which require oil to be separated and incinerated. Under a 1987 whistle-blowing law, seafarers who report crimes can earn a fortune. In 2012, Salvador Lopez, a crew member on Malta-flagged *Aquarosa*, was awarded $462,500 by a US court for reporting that *Aquarosa* had discharged oily water and sludge into Baltimore waters using a magic pipe. Candus Thompson, 'Judge awards whistle-blower $462,500 in high-seas pollution case', *Baltimore Sun*, 18 April 2012.

101 *They sent us in a floating coffin… to drown* 'Tanker skipper blames Spain at oil disaster trial', *The Peninsula*, 14 November 2012.

– *Northward-thrusting men of Novgorod* Peter Kemp (ed.), *The Oxford Companion to Ships and the Sea*, Oxford: Oxford University Press, 1988, p.604.

102 *60,000 cardiopulmonary and lung cancer deaths annually* James J. Corbett, James J. Winebrake, Erin H. Green, Prasad Kasibhatla, Veronika Eyring and Axel Lauer, 'Mortality from Ship Emissions: A global assessment', *Environmental Science and Technology*, vol. 4, no. 24, 2007, pp.8512–8518.

– *Annual mortalities would increase by 40 per cent by 2012* In my correspondence with James Corbett, he wrote that given the shipping recession and efforts to instill the use of cleaner fuels, this may not have come to pass, but he had not reviewed the current global data.

– *Low sulphur diesel for cars is supposed to contain 10 ppm* J.J. Winebrake, J.J. Corbett, E.H. Green, A. Lauer and V. Eyring, 'Mitigating the Health Impacts of Pollution from Oceangoing Shipping: An assessment of low-sulfur fuel mandates', *Environmental Science & Technology*, vol. 43, no. 13, 2009, p.4776.

103 *The lack of urgency* In 2011 the IMO did pass strong measures to cut sulphur

content in fuel, both in ECAs and in general. Bunkers will have to cut sulphur content from 3.5 to 0.5 per cent by 2020, as long as low-sulphur fuel supplies allow it. If they don't, the deadline will be 2024. House of Commons Environmental Audit Committee, *Reducing CO2 and Other Emissions from Shipping*, Fourth Report of Session 2008–2009, printed 12 May 2009, p.3.

105 *No skid marks on the ocean* Amy Ellis-Nutt, 'The Wreck of the Lady Mary', *The Star-Ledger*, 21–24 November 2010, http://www.nj.com/news/index. ssf/2010/11/the_wreck_of_the_lady_mary_cha_1.html

106 *Known among ship drivers as the 'Filipino Monkey'* Andrew Scutro and David Brown, 'Filpino Monkey behind threats?', *Navy Times*, 11 January 2008.

108 *From the ranks of peasantry* http://www.suezcanal.gov.eg

112 *2000 containers are lost every year* EU weblog, 'EU must act on containers lost at sea', 14 February 2013.

– *Fifteen 40-foot boxes that in 2004 fell from the Med Taipei* Monterey Bay Aquarium Research Institute news release, 'MBARI teams with Monterey Bay National Marine Sanctuary to study effects of shipping containers lost at sea', 7 March 2011.

113 *There was nothing living down there* Maggie Koerth-Baker, 'Under the Sea: Life on a lost shipping container', *BoingBoing.net*, 7 July 2011, accessed February 2013 via http://boingboing.net/2011/07/07/under-the-sea-life-o.html

114 *Greek marbles* Office of the Commissioner for Federal Judicial Affairs Canada, citation Ford Aquitaine Industries SAS v. Canmar Pride (The) (F.C.), 2005 FC 431, [2005] 4 F.C.R. 441, 31 March 2005. Docket:T-1291-03.

Chapter 6: High Risk Area

120 *A membership of nations that is described as fluid* Congressional Research Service, *Piracy off the Horn of* Africa, 27 April 2011, p.25.

121 *Routes of 70 per cent of global oil traffic* The Indian Ocean includes two major oil 'chokepoints', in the Strait of Hormuz and the Suez Canal. Robert D. Kaplan, 'Center Stage for the 21st Century: Power plays in the Indian Ocean', *Foreign Affairs*, March/April 2009.

125 *544 seafarers* ICC International Maritime Bureau, *Piracy and Armed Robbery Against Ships, Report for the Period 1 January–30 June 2010*, p.20.

– *Forty-two thousand merchant vessels* Nick Hopkins, 'Outgunned Somali pirates can hardly believe their luck', *Guardian*, 8 May 2012.

126 *Three times the size of a full stop* House of Commons Foreign Affairs

Committee, *Piracy off the Coast of Somalia*, Tenth Report of Session 2010–12, 20 December 2011, Ev. 13

– *Firing AK47s at a warship* Ibid., Ev. 57.

128 *Trying to choke them out or to death* Oceans Beyond Piracy, *The Human Cost of Somali Piracy*, June 2011, p.15.

129 *Saviours of the sea* Jay Bahadur, *Deadly Waters: Inside the Hidden World of Somalia's Pirates*, London: Profile Books, 2011, p.15.

– *Violence against maritime navigation* Congressional Research Service, op. cit., p.19.

130 *Augustine* Marcus Rediker, *Villains of All Nations: Atlantic Pirates in the Golden Age*, Boston, MA: Beacon Press, 2004, p.174.

– *Hunted down his captors, and crucified them* Plutarch does not specify that the talents were silver, but as a Greek writing for a Greek readership, where talents generally were silver, perhaps he didn't need to. Plutarch, *The Parallel Lives*, vol. VII, p.443, http://penelope.uchicago.edu/thayer/e/roman/texts/plutarch/lives/caesar*.html

– *Colonel Frederick Philipse* Michael Scott Moore, 'We Were Pirates Once, and Young: An American way to understand Somali pirates', *The New Republic*, 22 October 2011.

131 *'The Throats of them that took us'* Rediker, op. cit., p.168.

– *The violation of Somali waters* President of Puntland press release, 22 October 2011.

132 *The coastguard turned pirate in about a day* Robert Young Pelton, 'Somali pirates' rich returns', *Bloomberg Businessweek*, 12 May 2011.

– *Attacks have been against fishing vessels* Ibid.

– *By guess and by God* House of Commons Foreign Affairs Committee, op. cit., Ev. 17.

134 *Assaulted by deckchairs* Matthias Gebauer and Dietmar Hipp, 'Passengers fought pirates with tables and deck chairs', *Spiegel Online*, 28 April 2009.

136 *In a monkey house* Parker, op. cit., p.13.

139 *Which way is it to Somalia?* US embassy cable captured by Wikileaks, accessed via http://www.cablegatesearch.net, cable reference 09PORTLOUISE146

– *Combat trauma, explosive and intelligence-gathering* Captain Alexander Martin, US Marine Corps, 'Pirates Beware: Force recon has your number', published on US Naval Institute website, http://www.usni.org, 24 July 2010.

142 *USS Nicholas* 'US sentences Somali pirates to life', *Al Jazeera*, 15 March 2011.

- NOTES

- *Abduwali Abdiqadir Muse* Tom Hays, 'Somali pirate sentenced in NYC to over 33 years in prison', NBC, 16 February 2011.
- *There was a stampede* Justin Penrose, 'Prison officers swap Isle of Wight for the Seychelles... to guard Somali pirates', *Daily Mirror*, 12 February 2012.
- *Model prisoners* US embassy cable via Wikileaks, accessed at http://www.cablegatesearch.net/cable.php?id=10PORTLOUIS44&q=high-seas-affairs

Chapter 7: No Man's Land

149 *None of these is piracy* Hugh Williamson, 'Piracy at Sea: The Humanitarian Impact', presentation given at International Conference on Piracy at Sea, 16–18 October 2011, Malmo, Sweden.
150 *Yo-Ho-Toe* David Willetts, 'Yo-ho-toe: Navy nab pirate with 24 digits', *Sun*, 6 February, 2012.
- *A thin Somali in a yellow jumpsuit* Indian Ocean with Simon Reeve, Kenya and the Horn of Africa, BBC, released 22 April 2012.
- *Profit-maximizing entrepreneurs* 'The Economics of Piracy: pirate ransoms and livelihoods off the coast of Somalia', *Geopolicity*, May 2011, p.ii.
- *$300,000 to kit out a pirate attack* Pelton, op. cit.
151 *100 most important people in shipping* '4. Garaad Mohammed, Pirate, Somalia Inc.', *Lloyd's List*, 14 December 2010, http://www.lloydslist.com/ll/incoming/article351642.ece
- *Hostages killed in 2011* 'A Moment for Victims of Piracy At Sea', OceanusLive.org, 1 January 2012, http://www.oceanuslive.org/Main/ViewNews.aspx?uid=00000389
- *Violent assaults in South Africa* Oceans Beyond Piracy, *The Human Cost of Somali Piracy*, 6 June 2011, p.4.
152 *Amputated the hand of its captain* Somalia Report, 'Pirates Copy Al-Shabab's Amputation Tactic', 24 January 2012.
153 *Detestable activity* House of Commons Transport Committee, *Eighth Report*, printed 26 June 2006, http://www.publications.parliament.uk/pa/cm200506/cmselect/cmtran/1026/102604.htm#_jmp0_
157 *'sneak through'* Nancy Knudsen, 'Released hostage sailors' regrets – first interview', Sail-World.com, 28 October 2011, http://www.sail-world.com/Asia/Released-hostage-sailors-regrets---first-interview/90054

– *A gleeful article* 'Somali pirate offers to release Danish family in return of hand of daughter', *Daily Mail*, 28 March 2011.

158 *'It's like sailing out of Falmouth'* Decca Aitkenhead, 'Paul and Rachel Chandler: How we survived being kidnapped by Somali pirates', *Guardian*, 30 October 2011.

– *0.26 per cent risk of being attacked* George Kiourktsoglu, 'Somali Piracy vs Flag of Attacked Vessel', University of Greenwich, 2010, supplied by author. Available from http://uk.linkedin.com/pub/george-kiourktsoglou/13/bb6/a7

– *Fifty die each month* House of Commons Foreign Affairs Committee, *Tenth Report of Session 2010–2012*, Ev 18.

159 *The average period of capture was 250 days* Stephen Askins, a maritime lawyer at the London firm Ince & Co, has kept a rolling average of detention times for years; 250 days was among the highest averages. Figure of 250 days, House of Commons Foreign Affairs Committee, op. cit., Ev.7. Tanker figures provided by Stephen Askins.

164 *STOP signs* Somalia Report, *Into the Heart of the Pirate Lair*, 13 May 2011.

165 *Being a pirate town did not pay* Anja Shortland, 'Treasure Mapped: Using satellite imagery to track the developmental effects of Somali piracy', Chatham House Africa Programme paper, January 2012.

166 *Chinese sailors, rail-thin* Robert Young Pelton, op. cit.

167 *Budiga was the Devil* Chirag's crewmate Sandeep Dangwal, who was also trussed and tortured, called Budiga 'the nastiest pirate devil ever'. Colin Freeman, 'Somali pirates raise ransom stakes', *Telegraph*, 4 May 2011.

169 *A floating piece of space* Allan Sekula, *Fish Story*, Düsseldorf: Richter Verlag, 1995, p.116.

171 *Rival pirate gangs fought over a $5 million ransom* James Kraska, 'Freakonomics of Maritime Piracy', *Brown Journal of World Affairs*, vol. XVI, no. II, Spring/Summer 2010, p.114.

173 *$8 for every day of abuse* The translator involved in the Marida Marguerite hijacking, Mohammed Saaili Shibin, also known as Khalif Ahmed Shibin or just Shibin, was convicted in a US court in April 2012 for his part in the hijacking of the US yacht *Quest* in which four Americans were killed. He was also indicted for being the negotiator for the pirates holding *Marida Marguerite*. The Virginia court sentenced him 'to 10 concurrent life sentences for piracy, two consecutive life sentences for the use of a rocket-propelled grenade/automatic weapons during crimes of violence, 10 years consecutive

on six counts charging discharge of a firearm during a crime of violence, and two 20-year sentences for the remaining counts of discharge of a firearm during a crime of violence'. He also had to pay $5,408,000 in restitution. FBI Norfolk Division, press release, 13 August 2012.

– *Reduce premiums if armed guards are on board* Michelle Wiese Bockman, 'Armed Guards Can Help Cut Insurance Costs for Shipping Companies', *Bloomberg*, 11 May 2012, accessed from http://www.bloomberg.com/news/2012-05-11/armed-guards-can-help-cut-insurance-costs-for-shipping-companies.html

174 *Mistaking them for pirates* Some 2.3 million fishermen work in the Indian Ocean and many carry weapons. Italy has objected to India's prosecution on the grounds that the fishermen were killed in international waters and because the marines are active-duty personnel. 'Such a view', P.S. Gopinathan, a Kerala High Court judge, wrote in a 29 May judgment allowing the case to go forward, 'will not merely be a bad precedent, but a grossly unjust one.' Alan Katz, 'Fighting Pirates Goes Awry with the Killings of Fishermen', *Bloomberg*, 17 September 2012, accessed from http://www.bloomberg.com/news/2012-09-16/fighting-piracy-goes-awry-with-killings-of-fishermen.html

Chapter 8: Sanctuary

178 *Balikbayan* Lamvik, op. cit., p.128.

179 *A series of discontinuous encounters* E. Kahveci, T. Lane and H. Sampson, 'Transnational Seafarer Communities', SIRC: Cardiff University, March 2002, p.9.

180 *A priest for every ship* A Commander RN, 'Religion on Board Ship', *The Churchman*, vol 19, no. 7, April 1905, p.355.

– *The destitute seamen of East London* Royal Museums Greenwich, Port Cities, http://www.portcities.org.uk/london/index-2.html

– *Does your mother know you're out?* L.A.G. Strong, *Flying Angel: The Story of the Mission to Seamen*, London: Methuen, 1956.

– *Flogging was only banned in 1850* US Navy, Navy Department Library, http://www.history.navy.mil/library/online/flogging.htm

181 *Marlin spikes, hand spikes* Greg Marquis, 'Review of *Brutality on Trial: "Hellfire" Pedersen, "Fighting" Hansen and the Seamen's Act of 1915*, by E. Kay Gibson', *Law and Politics Book Review*, vol. 17, no. 1, January 2007, pp.1–4.

182 *Ecclesiastical maritime architecture* Leah Robinson Rousmaniere, *Anchored*

within the Vail: A pictorial history of the Seamen's Church Institute, Seamen's Church Institute of New York and New Jersey, 1995.

183 *Goodnight, boys* 'Port of Missing Men', *The Lookout*, vol. 25, no. 5, May 1934.

– *Effective friendliness* Royal Museums Greenwich, Port Cities, op. cit.

– *Ng Sing Flying Angel*, Missions to Seamen newsletter, London, 1965.

184 *36 per cent said two hours* – E. Kahveci, 'Port Based Welfare for Seafarers', SIRC: Cardiff University, 2007.

– *Graham Cardwell* '"Reggie Perrin" father escapes punishment', BBC News, 8 June 1999.

187 *Only 14,021 attendances at its church services* Seamen's Church Institute of New York, *The Lookout*, vol. 7, July 1942.

– *Port of London Mission in 1965 fared even worse Flying Angel*, Port of London branch of Mission to Seafarers newsletter, 1965.

190 *A pair of those long socks called sea-stockings* Hansard, vol. 128, 3 August 1943, p.955.

191 *They can share my emptiness* Kahveci, op. cit., p.22.

– *The chaplain asked me how I slept here* Ibid., p.25.

192 *To keep their security gates more tightly* Arsham Mazaheri, 'How the ISPS Code Affects Port and Port Activities', University College of Borås School of Engineering MSc thesis, 2008.

196 *The money taken from them under duress* 'Philipp crew "robbed" by crewing agent in Manila', ITF media release, 25 October 2011.

– *Not because Vietnamese like eating dogs* Yevgenia Borisova, 'Abandoned crew starves in city port', *St. Petersburg Press*, 1995.

Chapter 9: Animals Beneath

202 *Shed tears* Conrad, op. cit., p.79.

203 *The blubber victim* Bob Welch, 'It's still whale of a tale to tell for blubber victim', *Eugene Register Guard*, 14 January 2008. For a video of the explosion and other background, http: www.theexplodingwhale.com

204 *A tanker brought a whale into Baltimore* D.W. Laist, A.R. Knowlton, J.G. Mead, A.S. Collet and M. Podesta, 'Collisions Between Ships and Whales', *Marine Mammal Science*, vol. 17, no. 1, 2006, pp.35–75.

– *A whale draped over its bow, long dead* 'Container vessel carries whale', Port of Rotterdam Authority, press release, 6 June 2012.

205 *53 varieties of whalebone items* Mr Sevey also listed busks, back supporters

and forearm bones. List of items accessed December 2012 via http://www. scran.ac.uk/packs/exhibitions/learning_materials/webs/40/articles.htm

209 *75 per cent of right whales have been or are entangled* Scott D. Kraus and Rosalind M. Rolland, (eds.), *The Urban Whale: North Atlantic Right Whales at the Crossroads*, Cambridge, MA: Harvard University Press, 2007, p.382.

210 *Enormous Carnivores, Microscopic Food* Ibid., p.140.

212 *A whale sailed through the middle of London* Euan Ferguson, 'After a day of struggles, the London whale dies a lonely death', *Observer*, 22 January 2006.

– *67 right whale carcasses* Kraus and Rolland, op. cit., p.410.

216 *A foghorn-like signal* Michael Jasny, 'Sounding the Depths: The rising toll of sonar, shipping, and industrial ocean noise on marine mammals', Natural Resources Defense Council (NRDC), November 2005, p.3.

– *800 species of fish use hearing* 'In 1962,' Slabbekoorn writes, 'Rachel Carson wrote about a "silent spring" in the context of the detrimental impact of the use of pesticides on singing birds. Here we call attention to a "noisy spring", and the possible detrimental impact of increasing levels of anthropogenic noise on fishes.' H. Slabbekoorn et al., 'A Noisy Spring: The impact of globally rising underwater sound levels on fish', *Trends in Ecology and Evolution*, vol. 25, no. 7, July 2010, pp.419–427.

217 *The constant creation of tiny bubbles* R. Leaper and M.R. Renilson, 'A review of methods for reducing underwater noise pollution from large commercial vessels', *Transactions RINA*, vol. 154, part A2, *International Journal Maritime Engineering*, Apr–Jun 2012.

– *Increasing by 3 decibels every decade* Andrew J. Wright and Lauren Highfill (eds.), 'Considerations of the Effects of Noise on Marine Mammals and Other Animals', *International Journal of Comparative Psychology*, vol. 20, no. 23, 2007, p.127.

– *Noise from commercial shipping had doubled* A.J. Wright (ed.), Report of the International Workshop on Shipping Noise and Marine Mammals, *Okeanos* – Foundation for the Sea, Hamburg, Germany, 21–24 April 2008, background paper: 'An Ocean Full of Noise'.

218 *Polluted by a single seismic survey* NRDC, op. cit., p.29.

– *Ubiquitous anthropogenic contributor* Kraus and Rolland, op. cit., p.326.

219 *The near-complete lack of information* Kraus and Rolland, op. cit., pp.235–236.

221 *The week that ships were stilled* Rosalind M. Rolland et al., 'Evidence that ship

noise increases stress in right whales', *Proceedings of the Royal Society B*, vol. 279, 2012, pp.2363–2368.

Chapter 10: Rescue

227 *One seemed to be rather busy at the time* Vice Admiral Ian Stewart McIntosh, oral interview, Imperial War Museum, recorded 15 April 1991, catalogue number 11950.

229 *A dereliction of one of the most fundamental duties* Marine Accident and Investigation Board, Safety Digest, 2010, p.7.

231 *The search part of search and rescue* Frank Laskier writes of convoy duty, 'We wore our eyelids out, looking for submarines; we did watch and watch and watch and watch.' Frank Laskier, *My Name is Frank: A Merchant Seaman Talks*, London: Allen & Unwin, 1941, p.48.

— *The German sail-training ship Pamir* Of a crew of 86, only six survived. In one lifeboat, two died from exposure in the first 24 hours, and two others drank seawater, went mad and jumped overboard. Frank Golden and Michael Tipton, *Essentials of Sea Survival*, Champaign, IL: Human Kinetics, 2002, p.189.

233 *USS Indianapolis* The ship had delivered the world's first operational atom bomb to the island of Tinian on 26 July 1945. She was hit by two torpedoes fired by a Japanese submarine, and sank in 12 minutes. It was the worst disaster in US naval history. Survivors' stories are gathered on http://www.ussindianapolis.org

235 *Kendal was named after a Cumbrian town* 'Kendal's ship in dramatic rescue', *North West Evening Mail*, 16 August 2007.

236 *Enough to keep an officer happy* Richard Woodman, op. cit., p.43.

237 *Venereal disease* Ibid., p.44.

— *More than 90 per cent of its supplies by sea* This is as true today as in 1941, when Winston Churchill wrote that '[t]he whole power of the United States, to manifest itself, depends on the power to move ships and aircraft across the sea. Their mighty power is restricted; it is restricted by the very oceans which have protected them; the oceans which were their shield, have now become both threatening and a bar, a prison house through which they must struggle to bring armies, fleets, and air forces to bear upon the common problems we have to face'. Pierre Bélanger and Alexander Scott Arroyo, 'Logistics Islands: The global supply archipelago and the topologics of defense', National Defense University, *Prism*, vol. 3, no. 4, p.57.

• NOTES

-   *Sealift* The last time the UK military conscripted merchant ships was in the 1982 Falklands conflict, where more than 50 merchant vessels became STUFT, or Ships Taken Up From Trade. The most famous were the passenger lines *Canberra* and *QEII*, converted into troop carriers, but there were also tugs, ferries and fishing trawlers.

238 *Deepwater Horizon* Offshore oil rigs are treated as ocean-going ships in legal terms. Deepwater was flagged to the Marshall Islands, along with 34 other rigs owned by Transocean. Andrew Clark, 'BP oil registration raised in Congress over safety concerns', *Guardian*, 30 May 2010. Tom Hamburger and Kim Geiger, 'Foreign flagging of offshore rigs skirts US safety rules', *Los Angeles Times*, 14 June 2010.

-   *They got the ship to Calcutta with munitions* Frank Laskier, *Log Book*, p.56.

-   *About 95 merchant ships were sunk* Terry Hughes and John Costello, *The Battle of the Atlantic*, New York: Dial Press, 1977, quoted in American Merchant Marine at War, accessed February 2013 at http://www.usmm.org/battleatlantic.html

239 *In Canada, merchant seamen were called zombies* Woodman, op. cit., p.62.

-   *A white feather* Laskier, *My Name is Frank*, p.28.

-   *Tinned food for their Mum's rations* Bill Linskey, *No Longer Required: My War in the Merchant Marine*, London: Pisces Press, 1999, p.111.

240 *If they fail, the whole effort fails* President Franklin D. Roosevelt, letter to Admiral Emory S. Land, 22 May 1941.

-   *U-boat commander Peter Cremer* Peter Cremer, *U333: The Story of a U-boat Ace*, London: Triad Grafton, 1986, p.75.

241 *Particularly delighted with the showers* Robinson Rousmaniere, op. cit., pp.74–75.

-   *There was but one leg* Seven legs were amputated in Iceland to stem gangrene. Homer Strickler, *New York Sun*, 2 December, 1941, quoted in *The Lookout*, vol. 33, no. 1, 1942.

-   *The 'mad Russian'* *The Lookout*, 'Sea Heroes', vol. 33, no. 6, June 1942.

-   *To donate his compass* Owen Edwards, 'A compass saves the crew', *Smithsonian*, September 2009.

242 *Lucky to get the experience* *The Lookout*, vol. 33, no. 5, May 1942.

-   *Gentle with the tipsy soldier or the unsteady gob* Editorial, *New York Times*, 22 June 1942.

243 *Jack Edmead* His account to the Admiralty, ADM199/2143, is reproduced

on http://www.sscityofcairo.co.uk, along with accounts from survivors Dr Douglas Quantrill, Gladys Usher, Angus MacDonald, Joan Redl, Marjorie and Donald Miller, Eileen Sims, Dulcie Kendall and Robert Faulds.

245 *Good night, sorry for sinking you* Ralph Barker, *Goodnight, Sorry for Sinking You: The Story of the SS City of Cairo*, London: Collins, 1984, p.72.

247 *In the way of swamping boats* Stephen Crane, 'The Open Boat: A tale Intended to be after the Fact. Being the experience of four men sunk from the steamer Commodore', *Scribner's Magazine 21*, May 1894, p.728.

– *Pellagra, deranged nervous systems* Woodman, op. cit., p.169.

– *Cingalese Prince* Ibid., p.376.

248 *Don't forget to wash your hands* Linskey, op. cit., p.98.

– *Threatened with an axe* Woodman, op. cit., p.300.

249 *Nobody gave a damn if seamen survived* Norman Watts, oral interview, Imperial War Museum sound archive.

250 *Chief engineer and third mate go overboard* Woodman, op. cit., p.167.

– *MacDonald Critchley* William H. Allen, 'Thirst. Can shipwrecked men survive if they drink seawater?', *Natural History*, December 1956.

251 *An officer knocks him out* The Lookout, vol. 33, no. 3, March 1942.

253 *Weren't given veterans' status until 1988* 'Wartime Merchant Seamen to Get Veterans' Status', *New York Times*, 21 January 1988.

– *At least 5000 of them had died* Casualty statistics vary because of the disparate nature of the merchant wartime fleet.

– *who sailed the Arctic convoys* Three thousand men died in the Arctic convoys. Winston Churchill called the convoy route 'the worst journey in the world'. The first medals, a newly created award named the Arctic Star, were handed out by Prime Minister David Cameron in March 2013, 70 years after the convoys ended. BBC news, 'Convoy veterans given first Arctic Star medals'. March 19, 2013, http://www.bbc.co.uk/news/uk-england-hampshire-21845753

– *Those seven are back at sea* Laskier, My Name is Frank, p.65.

Chapter 11: Disembark

255 *Then cut off the captain's fingers joint by joint* Peter Gwin, 'Dark Passage', *National Geographic*, October 2007.

256 *The latest judgement of war risks* Lloyd's Market Association Joint War Committee, 'Hull War, Piracy, Terrorism and Related Perils Listed Areas', JWLA/

020, 28 March 2012, accessed February 2013 from http://www.lmalloyds.com/Web/market_places/marine/JWC/Joint_War.aspx

257 *It would not do to look at all disturbed* Richard Henry Dana, *Two Years Before the Mast*, Project Gutenberg e-book, accessed January 2013 from http://www.gutenberg.org/cache/epub/4277/pg4277.html

260 *60,000 ships must pass through that 1.7-mile chokepoint* US Energy Information Administration, 'World Oil Transit Chokepoints', 22 August 2012.

262 *The Philippines was almost blacklisted* Philip C. Tubeza, 'EU may ban PH seamen over training deficiencies', *Philippine Daily Inquirer*, 8 March 2012.

263 *It's all very well having foreign seafarers* House of Commons Select Committee on Environment, Transport and Regional Affairs, *Twelfth Report*, 26 May 1999.

– *A provision about internet gambling* The Unlawful Internet Gambling Enforcement Act appears as Title VIII in the Security and Accountability of Every Port Act of 2006. Accessed from http://www.gpo.gov/fdsys/pkg/PLAW-109publ347/html/PLAW-109publ347.htm

Further Reading

Auden, W.H., *The Enchafèd Flood or the Romantic Iconography of the Sea*, London: Faber & Faber, 1951.

Baboulene, David, *Jumping Ships: The Global Misadventures of a Cargo Ship Apprentice*, Chichester: Summersdale, 2009.

Bahadur, Jay, *Deadly Waters: Inside the Hidden World of Somalias' Pirates*, London: Profile Books, 2011.

Barker, Ralph, *Goodnight, Sorry for Sinking You: The Story of the SS City of Cairo*, Glasgow: William Collins & Sons, 1984.

Buckley, Christopher, *Steaming to Bamboola*, London: Flamingo, 1983.

Bullen, Frank Thomas, *The Men of the Merchant Service, Being the Polity of the Mercantile Marine for 'Longshore Readers*, London: John Murray, 1900.

Crane, Stephen, *The Open Boat*, e-book, Electronic Text Centre, University of Virginia Library, 1995.

Cremer, Peter, *U333: The Story of a U-boat Ace*, London: Triad Grafton, 1986.

de Botton, Alain, *The Pleasures and Sorrows of Work*, London: Hamish Hamilton, 2009.

Dickens, Charles, *On Travel* (ed. Pete Orford), London: Hesperus Press, 2009.

Ebbesmeyer, Curtis and Scigliano, Eric, *Flotsametrics and the Floating World: How*

- FURTHER READING

One Man's Obsession with Runaway Sneakers and Rubber Ducks Revolutionized Ocean Science, New York: HarperCollins, 2009.

Ekin, Des, *The Stolen Village: Baltimore and the Barbary Pirates*, Dublin: O'Brien Press, 2008.

Evans, Bob, *A Dog Collar in the Docks*, Birkenhead: Countyvise, 2002.

Evans, Bob, *Mersey Mariners*, Birkenhead: Countyvise, 2002.

Fitzgibbon, Theodora, *A Taste of the Sea in Food and Pictures*, Vancouver: David & Charles, 1977.

George, Bill (the Bosun), *On the Bridge: A Story of King Billy and the Derby Grange*, self-published, no date.

Golden, Frank and Tipton, Michael, *Essentials of Sea Survival*, Champaign, IL: Human Kinetics, 2002.

Hanson, Neil, *The Custom of the Sea: The Shocking True Tale of Shipwreck and Cannibalism on the High Seas*, London: Corgi Books, 1999.

Hardberger, Max, *Seized: A Sea Captain's Adventures Battling Pirates & Recovering Stolen Ships in the World's Most Troubled Waters*, London: Nicholas Brealey Publishing, 2010.

Heaton Vorse, Mary, *Time and the Town: A Provincetown Chronicle*, New Brunswick, NJ: Rutgers University Press, 1991.

Hohn, Donovan, *Moby-Duck: The True Story of 28,800 Bath Toys Lost at Sea and of the Beachcombers, Oceanographers, Environmentalists and Fools, Including the Author, Who Went in Search of Them*, New York: Farrar, Straus, Giroux, 1990.

Johnson, Captain Charles, *A General History of the Robberies and Murders of the Most Notorious Pirates*, London: Conway Maritime Press, 1998.

Kemp, Peter (ed), *The Oxford Companion to Ships and the Sea*, Oxford: Oxford University Press, 1988.

Koeppel, Dan, *Banana: The Fate of the Fruit that Changed the World*, London: Plume, 2009.

Kraus, Scott D. and Rolland, Rosalind M., *The Urban Whale: North Atlantic Right Whales at the Crossroads*, Cambridge, MA: Harvard University Press, 2007.

Langewiesche, William, *The Outlaw Sea: Chaos and Crime on the World's Oceans*, London: Granta, 2005.

Laskier, Frank, *Log Book*, London: George Allen & Unwin, 1942.

Laskier, Frank, *My Name is Frank: A Merchant Seaman Talks*, London: Allen & Unwin, 1941.

Levinson, Marc, *The Box: How the Shipping Container Made the World Smaller and* the World Economy Bigger, Princeton, NJ: Princeton University Press, 2006.

Lewis, Val, Ship's Cats in War and Peace, Shepperton: Nauticalia, 2001.

Linskey, Bill, No Longer Required: My War in the Merchant Marine, London: Pisces Press, 1999.

Macdonald, Kenneth, Three Dark Days, Isle of Lewis: Acair, 1999.

Melville, Herman, Moby Dick: or, the White Whale, Kindle edition.

Parker, Matthew, Hell's Gorge: The Battle to Build the Panama Canal, London: Arrow Books, 2008.

Parker, Tony, Lighthouse, London: Eland, 2006.

Phillips, Richard, A Captain's Duty: Somali Pirates, Navy SEALs, and Dangerous Days at Sea, New York: Hyperion, 2010.

Raban, Jonathan, The Oxford Book of the Sea, Oxford: Oxford University Press, 1992.

Rediker, Marcus, Villains of All Nations: Atlantic Pirates in the Golden Age, Boston, MA: Beacon Press, 2004.

Roberts, Calum, Ocean of Life: How our Seas are Changing, London: Allen Lane, 2012.

Roland, Alex., Bolster, W. Jeffrey and Keyssar, Alexander, The Way of the Ship: America's Maritime History Revisioned 1600–2000, Hoboken, NJ: John Wiley & Sons, 2008.

Rousmaniere, Leah Robinson, Anchored within the Vail: A Pictorial History of the Seamen's Church Institute, New York: The Seamen's Church Institute of New York and New Jersey, 1995.

Sekula, Allan, Fish Story, Düsseldorf: Richter Verlag, 1995.

Sekulich, Daniel, Ocean Titans: Journeys in Search of the Soul of a Ship, Guildford CT: Lyons Press, 2007.

Sekulich, Daniel, Terror on the Seas: True Tales of Modern-Day Pirates, New York: Thomas Dunne Books, 2009.

Sharpsteen, Bill, The Docks, Berkeley: University of California Press, 2011.

Smith, Angela (ed.), Gender and Warfare in the Twentieth Century: Textual representations, Manchester: Manchester University Press, 2004.

Stopford, Martin, Maritime Economics (3rd ed.), London: Routledge, 2009.

Strong, L.A.G., Flying Angel: The Story of the Mission to Seamen, London: Methuen, 1956.

The Missions to Seamen, Convoy X.K.234 Arrives: The War-time Story of the 'Flying Angel', London: The Missions to Seamen, 1947.

- **FURTHER READING**

Trotter, Henry, *Sugar Girls and Seamen: A Journey into the World of Dockside Prostitution in South Africa*, Athens, OH: Ohio University Press, 2011.

Winchester, Simon, *The Atlantic: A Vast Ocean of a Million Stories*, London: HarperPress, 2010.

Woodman, Richard, *The Real Cruel Sea: The Merchant Navy in the Battle of the Atlantic, 1939–1943*, London: John Murray, 2004.

INDEX

• INDEX